Theories of Anxiety

Theories of Anxiety

WILLIAM F. FISCHER
Duquesne University

HARPER & ROW, PUBLISHERS
NEW YORK, EVANSTON, AND LONDON

Designed by Michel Craig
Set in Electra and Garamont no. 248
Composed, printed and bound by Vail-Ballou Press, Inc.
HARPER AND ROW, PUBLISHERS

Miscellaneous quotations in Chapters 1 and 3 are from *The standard edition of the complete psychological works of Sigmund Freud*, revised and edited by James Strachey. Permission to quote was granted by Sigmund Freud Copyrights, Ltd., The Institute of Psycho-Analysis, and The Hogarth Press, Ltd.

Miscellaneous quotations in Chapter 7 are from *Metamorphosis* by Ernest G. Schachtel, © 1959, by Basic Books, Inc., Publishers, New York.

Miscellaneous quotations in Chapter 8 are from *The organism: a holistic approach to biology derived from pathological data in man*. Reprinted by permission of the Beacon Press, copyright 1939 by the American Book Company, © 1963 by Kurt Goldstein.

Theories of Anxiety

LIBRARY OF CONGRESS CATALOG CARD NUMBER: 71-103914

For
Connie
and
Mike

Many persons nowadays seem to think that any conclusion must be very scientific if the arguments in favor of it are all derived from twitching frogs' legs—especially if the frogs are decapitated—and that, on the other hand, any doctrine chiefly vouched for by the feelings of human beings—with their heads on their shoulders—must be benighted and superstitious.

Ralph Barton Perry
The Thought and Character of William James

Contents

Introduction   ix
Acknowledgments   xiii

1. The Orthodox Freudian Approach   1
2. Neo-Freudian Approaches: Harry Stack Sullivan   19
3. The Ego-Psychological Approach: Edith Jacobson   36
4. The Physiological Approaches   50
5. The Learning-Theory Approach   60
6. The Existential Approach   82
7. The Approach of Ernest Schachtel   98
8. The Approach of Kurt Goldstein   107
9. The Experience of Anxiety   119
10. Integration: One   137
11. Integration: Two   161

Index   169

Introduction

The serious student of human behavior already knows that the concept of anxiety assumes a central position in most of our theories of behavior and/or personality. However, this very same student must also realize that—despite the prevailing consensus as to significance—there is little agreement among theoreticians as to the nature of the phenomenon. This is certainly a curious state of affairs. How is it possible that different theorists could concur as to the importance of anxiety when they cannot agree as to its constitutive aspects? One would imagine that given this concurrent presence, as well as an absence of unanimity of viewpoints, the psychological literature would be filled with works comparing and contrasting the various theoretical approaches. Presumably, such diverse, open, and nondisparaging discussions of both the theories and their guiding assumptions would facilitate the sought for integration and consensus. Surprisingly, however, such comparative works do not exist. Instead, there is a continuous proliferation of primarily correlational research; operationally defined indices of anxiety are related to almost every other conceivable variable. Supposedly scientific psychologists act as if a theoretical consensus can be achieved only in the wake of a mountain of disconnected, essentially unrelated research. When papers or books do discuss the multiplicity of theories, they invariably present only a few. Further, there is the distinct suggestion that truth resides in only one of these systems and that the others are hardly worth mentioning. We want to say that it seems a little early for some psychologists to be so convinced about and satisfied with their theoretical efforts.

In writing this book, the author's primary goal was to include and set forth a representative sampling of various theoretical approaches to the phenomenon of anxiety. Hence, while the varieties of Freudian, physiological, and learning-theory formulations are adequately depicted, the reader is also given the opportunity to acquaint himself with the thought of existential, organismic, and independent thinkers. Thus the first eight chapters of this volume present the formulations of Freud, Sullivan, Jacobson, Schachter and other physiologically oriented theoreticians, Dollard and Miller, Eysenck, Kierkegaard, Heidegger, Schachtel, and Goldstein.

As the conception of anxiety that each of these theorists espoused is woven into the general fabric of his thinking, it was necessary to present a preliminary discussion of the major constructs, overall purposes, and domains of each system. Finally, in order to facilitate dialogue and integration—rather than disparagement, argument, and segregation—every theory is described as impartially as possible.

A second purpose of this volume is to explore the reasons for the simultaneous presence and absence of unanimity noted. That is to say, we wanted to understand how it was possible for various theoreticians to agree as to the significance of anxiety, but be so completely at odds when describing its constitutive aspects. We realized that in order to do this, it would be necessary to illuminate the guiding, a priori, metaphysical commitments of the respective thinkers. In other words, if the various theoreticians in question began with agreement as to the significance of the phenomenon, then this must have meant that they were sharing some common ground or realm of experience. Subsequent differences emerged, therefore, only because the respective thinkers felt constrained to formalize their originally common experiences in terms of differing assumptions as to the ultimate nature of reality. In writing this text, we wanted to thematize the original common experiences, the theorists' varying metaphysical commitments, and the transformations of the experiences that these commitments induced. Thus, as an introduction to each theoretician's system, we discuss what we term his basic frame of reference. In this context, we have included a brief résumé and analysis of each theorist's specific metaphysical commitments. As the thoughtful reader may already realize, this usually amounted to some particular variation of the overall perspective of natural science.

A third, rather tentative, aim of this work is to make an initial attempt at integration. Obviously, none of the theories has a monopoly on the truth and probably each articulates its own truths—at least insofar as its metaphysical commitments have allowed them to emerge. Thus we were not about to throw away as insignificant any of the approaches discussed. However, the first problem we faced in attempting an integration was to find some basic ground, open to all of the theories; otherwise, dialogue and discussion would be impossible.

In the pursuit of this universal medium, we realized that the original, common experiences referred to earlier would provide what we were after. That is to say, we grasped what appears to us to be a fundamental truth about science building and theorizing: all theories, whether hypothetico-deductive or informal, are nothing more than particular versions of the theorist's own experience. Further, this experience has now been coded, guided, and molded by specific, a priori, metaphysical commitments as to the nature of reality. Thus, we were faced with the concrete task of rediscovering the experiential phenomena that subsequent formalization had obscured. We believed that the best way to retrieve this original experiential ground was through a phenomenological analysis of anxiety experience. In other words, rather than try immediately to go back through each theory, we sought to experience for ourselves, by way of reflection, the theorists' original common ground.

After analyzing and reflecting upon a number of articulate, descriptive protocols, we realized that the term "anxiety" is, in fact, an abstraction. As such, it simultaneously refers to and subsumes distinctly different experiential phenomena: anxious experiencing and the experience of myself-or the other-being-anxious.

With regard to the first of these, that is, anxious experiencing, we found that it is a structural phenomenon constituted by both an identity and a world pole, and integrated through motive-action-ability sequences. To be more specific, anxious experiencing revealed itself to be that which occurs when the achievement of some milestone, integral to the individual's actualization of a to-be-realized identity as well as a lived-for-and-toward world, emerges as possibly superior to his already-apprehended and lived evaluation of his ability. With regard to the experience of the other-being-anxious, we were able to delineate the bodily, the impersonal, and the essentially distant, worldless character of the person observed.

Thus when we went back to our already-presented-and-discussed theories, we discovered that we were able to relate each of them to one or both of these original and primary experiential phenomena. That is to say, every theoretical formulation presented in the first part of this book was found to be a particular formalization of either anxious experiencing and/or the experience of the other-being-anxious. For example, the three forms of anxiety described in orthodox Freudian theory, i.e., reality anxiety, moral anxiety, and neurotic anxiety, were grasped as attempts by the analyst to account for his varying experience of the other-being-anxious. However, this accounting for is accomplished by empathically imputing a particular instance of anxious experiencing to the other and then describing his anxious behavior in terms of allegedly utilized defense mechanisms.

As we re-examined each system in the light of our phenomenological analysis, we found ourselves able to retranslate the often esoteric jargon and to uncover the theorist's original experience. Further, we were occasionally able to point to the manner in which this primary experience was transformed in the process of being formalized.

In the final chapter, we attempted to synthesize anxious experiencing and my experience of my body when I am anxious. Our goal here is to reunify that which was already a unity before any analysis. The reader may judge for himself the merits of our effort.

Acknowledgments

Writing a book, especially a text, is always a collaborative affair, even if only one name appears as author. Therefore, I should like to express my indebtedness to the following people for their unfailing assistance, enthusiasm, and ingenuity: Mark McConville, Emily Mann, Richard Alapack, James Knox, and Jane Merrill.

I should also like to acknowledge the courtesy of the following publishers for permitting the inclusion of excerpts published by them: Basic Books, Inc., Beacon Press, The Hogarth Press, Ltd., International Universities Press, The Institute of Psycho-Analysis, The Journal Press, Robert R. Knapp, The McGraw-Hill Book Company, W. W. Norton and Company, Sigmund Freud Copyrights, Ltd., Tavistock Publications, Ltd., and Stanford University Press.

W. F. F.

Theories of Anxiety

I

The Orthodox Freudian Approach

Anyone familiar with the immense and continually expanding body of clinical literature has already realized that the present author could have exclusively devoted himself to a presentation of psychoanalytic theories of anxiety. Such a book would not only have traced the historical intricacies of Freud's thought on this subject, but would have also elaborated upon the neo-Freudian and ego-psychological modifications thereof. In brief, there would have been separate chapters for each of the following: Freud, Jung, Adler, Rank, Horney, Fromm, Sullivan, Hartmann, Rapaport, White, and Jacobson. Even with this, it would not have been exhaustive.

In this work there is neither the space nor the inclination for the enterprise just outlined. As our original purpose was to cover an even wider sampling of psychological perspectives, it has been necessary to restrict our focus to Freud, one of the neo-Freudians, and a contemporary ego-psychologist. Thus in this chapter we shall present and discuss the theories of the founder of psychoanalysis; in the next, the formulations of Harry Stack Sullivan; and in the third, the revisions of Edith Jacobson.

As stated in the Introduction, our first task with each of the theoretical perspectives presented in this book will be to comprehend the goals, presuppositions, and strategies that constitute the approach and frame(s) of reference of the theorist in question. In the case of Freud, this is no mean task; the later constructions formulated by the founder of psychoanalysis emerged from at least six different—yet interrelated—points of view: the economic, the dynamic, the structural, the genetic, the phylogenetic, and the adaptive. Further, they were often couched in a metaphorical idiom that enabled the reader to identify with either Freud the natural scientist or with Freud the interpreter of human experience. Nonetheless, some clarification is both necessary and possible.

As an effort at overall characterization, we shall claim that although Freud began his investigations for principally pragmatic reasons (the explanation and treatment of neuroses), he gradually moved toward an archeology of the human being and even a metaphysics of living and nonliving. Our use of the term archeology is not in the least capricious because the founder of psychoanalysis himself, in his discussion of "Constructions in Analysis" (1937), described one of the roles of the analyst as, in fact, archeological. Freud wrote:

His [the analyst's] work of construction, or, if it is preferred, of reconstruction, resembles to a great extent an archeologist's excavation of some dwelling place that has been destroyed and buried or of some ancient edifice. The two processes are in fact identical, except that the analyst works under better conditions and has more material at his command to assist him, since what he is dealing with is not something destroyed but something that is still alive (1964, Vol. XXIII, p. 259).

In order to understand more fully the meaning of the preceding characterization, it is necessary concretely to delimit the sense in which the Freudian enterprise was an archeology. Every archeological excavation is a search, but as such, it is not just a casual process of observing. It is an active seeking which is guided beforehand by some preconception of that which is sought. Further, it is always limited by the tools that are available to the excavator. Finally, it is assumed that although the object of the search is currently hidden, it can be uncovered.

In the case of Freudian psychoanalysis, that which was sought can be described as the wellspring or source from which the human mode of living emerged. It was conceived to be the original and continuing vitality from which and because of which man appears as the creature he is. The preconceptions guiding this search were interrelated products of Freud's commitment to Darwinian thought as well as the overall perspective of natural science. In other words, the founder of psychoanalysis had already taken for granted man's fundamentally animal heritage, both phylogenetically and ontogenetically. Further, he assumed that human reality, in *all* its aspects, was ultimately reducible to physical, biologically given, causally graspable determinants. Thus the source of human living was, on a priori grounds, understood to be the animal, the instinctual, the *id*. The veneer or facade (the ego), which both covered and yet derived from this wellspring, was also conceptualized in terms and constructs of natural science. That this was, in fact, the strategy may be clearly seen from the following excerpt, taken from "An Outline of Psychoanalysis" (1938):

The starting point [for psychoanalysis] . . . is provided by a fact without parallel, which defies all explanation or description—the fact of consciousness. Nevertheless, if anyone speaks of consciousness, we know immediately from our own most personal experience what is meant by it.

Freud adds a footnote at this point:

One extreme line of thought, exemplified in the American doctrine of behaviorism, thinks it possible to construct a pyschology which disregards this fundamental fact.) . . . It is generally agreed, however, that these conscious processes do not form unbroken sequences which are complete in themselves; there would thus be no alternative left to assuming that there are physical or somatic processes which are concomitant with the psychical ones and which we should necessarily have to recognize as more complete than the psychical sequences. . . . If so, it of course becomes plausible to lay the stress in psychology on these somatic processes, to see in them the true essence of what is psychical and to look for some other assessment of conscious processes. . . . Psychoanalysis is obliged to assert . . . the supposedly somatic concomitant phenomena as being what is truly psychical. . . . Whereas the psychology of consciousness never went beyond the broken sequences which were obviously dependent upon something else [the unconscious, instinctual, animal sources], the other view [psychoanalysis] enabled psychology to take its place as a natural science like any other (1964, Vol. XXIII, pp. 157–158).

Thus man was conceived to be an object of nature, an animal among animals, in principle no different from others and certainly not the higher mammals. To paraphrase Ludwig Binswanger (1963), this conception of man as *Homo natura* was the great idea that marked Freud as an innovating genius, a revolutionary. Long before the psychoanalytic upheaval there were discussions about "the unconscious"; the interpretation of dreams had been an art even in Biblical times; speculations as to the nature of some irreducible forces, allegedly operative in human beings, occurred in the days prior to Socrates. But with Freud came the unheard of idea that the human being, in his totality and not just his body, was a natural object. He could be studied by the scientist by using the very same procedures and constructs that had been successfully applied to other objects. He was totally governed by laws. His thoughts, feelings, and aspirations, as well as his actions, could be causally and quantitatively analyzed, codified, and reduced to fundamental biological principles. The apparent spontaneity of consciousness was misleading. Hypothesized forces were at work and could be inferred from the gaps that have just been noted in the sequences of awareness. It all made sense if one could only grasp the underlying key, the unconscious, biologically given, instinctual meanings.

So much for the source and ultimate reality of man. But how shall we understand and conceptualize the facade, the ego, behind which the insatiable animal always lurks? Freud's answer to this question is clear. The ego is both a product of and a mediator for the compromises that the human animal makes with a repressive society in the service of survival. The ego is born of conflict and pain. It survives and develops primarily for the purpose of keeping peace, while, at the same time, sustaining the animal, its lifelong wellspring. The factors that condition the development of the ego are sufficient to explain its present form as a facade. Thus the goal of the psychoanalytic archeology is not only to arrive at the foundation of human being—it has, in fact, presupposed this—it is also to trace, genetically, the natural history of the human facade. This natural history is called psychosexual development.

From the preceding characterization and discussion, it should be evident that we consider the Freudian enterprise to be consistent with the overall orientation of natural science. As there are many psychologist–scientists who have derogated and continue to criticize Freud for his lack of precision, for his speculations about and concern with human experience, and for his frequently metaphorical language, it might be appropriate, at this point, to further justify our judgment.

If one is a serious investigator of human life and yet aspires to be accepted by one's colleagues as a scientist, there immediately appear insurmountable problems. At first glance, at least, there is no question but that human experiencing—acts of consciousness—constitute an extremely significant function in the mediation of behavior. Certainly, it is difficult to dismiss the perceptions, thoughts, feelings, and imaginations of people as "merely subjective," as having no significant role in the determination of their behavior. Yet, as Freud himself acknowledged in the excerpt quoted earlier, this is, in fact, the starting point of most scientific psychology. With the exception of the experiences of the scientist himself (Stevens, 1939; Bergmann and Spence, 1944)—and even there with some qualifications—human experience is to be distrusted at best; in general, to be dismissed as not amenable to scientific formulation. Thus, while he insisted that man, in his totality, could be studied by science, Freud was faced with the problem of naturalizing that which had heretofore been conceived of as unnatural—namely, human consciousness. And this he theoretically accomplished through the following processes of reasoning.

1. Given the assumption that consciousness should be a logical and lawful realm, it is no longer possible to understand this domain of human being as self-sufficient (Descartes), or as having within itself its own foundation. As Freud states:

the data of consciousness have a very large number of gaps in them; both in healthy and in sick people psychical acts often occur which can be explained only by presupposing other acts, of which, nevertheless, consciousness affords no evidence. . . . Our most personal daily experience acquaints us with ideas that come into our head we do not know from where. . . . All these conscious acts remain disconnected and unintelligible if we insist upon claiming that every mental act that occurs within us must also be necessarily experienced by us through consciousness (1957, Vol. XIV, pp. 166–167).

2. In order to explain these gaps, deficiencies, and inconsistencies, it is necessary and legitimate to postulate the existence of a second, more comprehensive realm of mental functioning: the unconscious. In so doing:

A gain in meaning is a perfectly justifiable ground for going beyond the limits of direct experience. When, in addition, it turns out that the assumption of there being an unconscious enables us to construct a successful procedure by which we can exert an effective influence upon the course of conscious processes, this success will have given us incontrovertible proof of the existence of what we have assumed (1957, Vol. XIV, p. 167).

Thus the ground and meaning of consciousness, and hence human experience, is to be located in the unconscious, an assumed realm whose existence is to be confirmed by its fruitful utility.

3. But what is the stuff of the unconscious? What are its constitutive elements? Freud's answer is clear and concise: the instincts, or more precisely, their representations and derivatives. And what are they? They are the biological, quantitative, corporeal givens of human nature. They are the essence, the ultimate reality of human beings. Further, as should be obvious by now, they are legitimate constructs of natural science. Thus that which had been labeled as merely subjective, as unamenable to the formulations of science, can in fact, be grounded in constructs that are completely acceptable to the scientific community.

Fortified with these assumptions and constructions, Freud proceeded to describe, examine, and explain most significant human phenomena, as well as their interrelations. As was stated earlier, he ultimately tried to comprehend each of these events from an economic, a dynamic, a structural, a genetic, a phylogenetic, and an adaptive point of view. The general nature of these perspectives may be succinctly summarized in the following manner.

The Economic.   Within this purview, the mind or mental apparatus is grasped as a closed energy system. Quanta of excitation arise from one part, the id, and are borrowed, transformed, defended against, displaced, or otherwise altered by the other two parts, the ego and the superego. At any given time or in any particular situation, the functioning of the mental apparatus as a whole can be described in terms of the distribution of excitation within its various parts.

The Dynamic.   This point of view is concerned with the vicissitudes of any given instinctual impulse. The formulations that emerge here are, in essence, descriptions of the course of hypothetical motives, beginning with their primitive instinctual meanings and terminating with their disguised, transformed overt manifestations.

The Structural.   From this perspective, Freud was able to locate any given phenomenon within or between sections of the mental apparatus. Thus, as we shall see, the ego is said to be the seat of anxiety. The id is the reservoir of instinctual urges, while the superego is that portion involved with idealized personifications of self as well as with one's own personal "Ten Commandments."

The Genetic.   In this, as well as the phylogenetic and adaptive points of view, Freud evidences the seriousness with which he took Darwin's thought. He also affirms the natural scientific assumption of a deterministic universe. Essentially, the genetic point of view suggests that any phenomenon that occurs in the present has its roots and historical ties in the past and can, in fact, be explained by reference to that past. Thus the prototype of all subsequent anxiety is to be found in the anxiety experienced during the process of birth.

The Phylogenetic.   As Darwin had already demonstrated man's fundamentally animal heritage and brotherhood, all human phenomena must have their counterparts in the rest of the animal world. To put it somewhat emphatically: there is nothing new with man.

The Adaptive.   Because, as Darwin stated, only that which facilitates existence survives, all aspects of human life must have, at least originally, some adaptive value and purpose. Nothing appears by chance and everything that the organism manifests must, in some way, be an effort at self-preservation.

We are now ready to trace and make explicit the evolution of Freud's thinking about anxiety. Originally, the founder of psychoanalysis directed himself to this phenomenon because of his concern with people suffering from psychopathology. As he himself states:

I have no need to introduce anxiety itself to you. Every one of us has experienced that sensation, or, to speak more correctly, that affective state at some time or other. . . . But I think the question has never been seriously enough raised of why neurotics in particular suffer from anxiety so much more and so much more strongly than other people (1963, Vol. XVI, pp. 392–393).

Thus Freud's inquiry into and analysis of anxiety was, at least initially, motivated by his interest in explaining and eventually treating the symptoms of people suffering from neurosis. Further, he anticipated that, as a result of his analysis, he would be able to comprehend many of the essential features of human functioning, pathological and otherwise. He asserts:

the problem of anxiety is a nodal point at which the most various and important questions converge, a riddle whose solution would be bound to throw a flood of light upon our whole mental existence (1963, Vol. XVI, p. 393).

As has been suggested above, anxiety, for Freud, was an everyday phenomenon; there was nothing strange about it; it needed no introduction. The difficulty emerged when he tried to understand why certain people seemed to be more vulnerable to it and why they suffered it more intensely. One of the first questions that he raised in the face of this difficulty was with regard to the univocality of anxiety. In other words, Freud asked if the anxiety endured by normal people was qualitatively the same as the anxiety endured by neurotics? Did they differ only in frequency and severity? The answer he gave was an emphatic "No!" The anxiety of everyday life with which we are all familiar and which requires no introduction was, for Freud, "realistic" anxiety. It referred to certain objects in the real external world and was essentially synonymous with what is usually meant by the term *fear*. The founder of psychoanalysis writes:

Realistic anxiety strikes us as something very rational and intelligible. We may say of it that it is a reaction to the perception of an external danger, that is, of an injury which is expected and foreseen. It is connected with the flight reflex and it may be regarded as a manifestation of the self-preservative instinct (1963, Vol. XVI, pp. 393–394).

Neurotic anxiety, on the other hand, whether free-floating or phobic— that is, whether it is referable to no particular object or state of affairs, or whether it is referred to an object that appears quite harmless to another observer—seems quite irrational. It has more in common with the phenomena of infancy and childhood than with those of adult life.

Following his examination of different forms of anxiety in various populations (infants, children, adults, normals, and neurotics), Freud concluded:

Infantile anxiety has very little to do with realistic anxiety [fear] . . . but, on the other hand, is closely related to the neurotic anxiety of adults. Like the latter, it is derived from unemployed libido [the energy of the sexual instincts], and it replaces the missing love-object by an external object or situation (1963, Vol. XVI, p. 408).

So too with the phobic:

The same thing happens with them [phobics] as with children's anxiety: unemployable libido is being constantly transformed into apparently realistic anxiety and thus a tiny external danger is introduced to represent the claims of the libido (1963, Vol. XVI, pp. 408–409).

Summing up Freud's initial conception of nonrealistic anxiety, we may say that it is a consequence and direct manifestation of unemployed libido. In other words, when the sexual instincts are not allowed to express themselves directly, their energy is diverted and converted into anxiety. How is this possible? Under what conditions can libido become blocked, or dammed up, eventually expressing itself as anxiety?

Freud states that when an idea or wish that is embodied in some instinctual impulse is too threatening to the preservation of the ego, the latter must defend itself against its expression. The primary means of accomplishing this is through repression: "Repression corresponds to an attempt at flight by the ego from libido which is felt as a danger" (1963, Vol. XVI, p. 410). But the repression can only block off or inhibit the expression of the idea component of the impulse. It cannot deter the affective energy associated with that idea. Thus there is a splitting of the idea from its affective energy element. The latter must be discharged and this is done through its automatic conversion into anxiety. For Freud, at this point in his thinking, anxiety was the fate of libidinal energy that encountered repression.

Let us now inquire as to Freud's later and final conception of anxiety. Our point of departure will be "The Problem of Anxiety," originally published as "Inhibitions, Symptoms and Anxiety" in 1926. After discussing the phenomena of inhibition and symptom formation, Freud attempted a definitional analysis of anxiety. He reasoned as follows:

Anxiety, then, is in the first place, something that is felt. We call it an affective state, although we are also ignorant of what an affect is. As a feeling, anxiety has a very marked character of unpleasure [however] . . . not every unpleasure can be called anxiety, for there are other feelings such as tension, pain or mourning, which have the character of unpleasure. Thus, anxiety must have other distinctive features besides this quality of unpleasure. . . . Besides having this special feature which is so difficult to isolate, we notice that anxiety is accompanied by fairly definite physical sensations, which can be referred to particular organs of the body. As we are not concerned here with the physiology of anxiety, we shall content ourselves with mentioning a few representatives of these sensations. The clearest and most frequent ones are those connected with the respiratory organs and with the heart. They provide evidence that motor innervations—that is, processes of discharge—play a part in the general phenomenon of anxiety. Analysis of anxiety states, therefore, reveals the existence of (1) a specific character of unpleasure, (2) acts of discharge, and (3) perceptions of these acts (1959, Vol. XX, pp. 132–133).

Bringing these three aspects together and insisting that the efferent or discharge phenomena differentiate anxiety from other unpleasurable states, Freud writes, "Anxiety, then, is a special state of unpleasure with acts of discharge along particular paths" (1959, Vol. XX, pp. 133).

Having answered the question of what constitutes anxiety, Freud then attempted to specify the causes and phases of anxiety's development. Further, he described its meaning from each of his six perspectives.

There are two developmentally determined stages of anxiety in orthodox psychoanalytic theory. The first is usually termed *primary anxiety*, while the later one is generally referred to as *subsequent anxiety*. Consistent with the genetic and economic points of view, primary anxiety—the essence of which is the "traumatic state," and the prime example of which is the birth process—is conceived to be the model for all subsequent anxiety. According to Fenichel, "States in which the organism is flooded by amounts of excitation beyond its capacity to master are called traumatic states" (1945, p. 42). Further, "This flooding with excitation without an adequate defense apparatus is, according to Freud, a model for all later anxiety" (1945, p. 34). Finally, in Freud's own words: "anxiety is modeled upon the process of birth" (1959, Vol. XX, p. 134).

It might be useful at this point to digress for a moment and specify the relations that exist between Freud's and Rank's view of birth. The latter also posits a birth *trauma* as being the prototype of all anxiety, but Freud expands upon this singular account, adding to it the notions of economic upheaval and helplessness. Rank maintains that the circumstances of birth are deeply imprinted upon the psyche of the infant. Further, he claims that they often appear symbolically in the dreams and free associations of patients undergoing analysis. Certain individuals, he asserts, are always attempting to reconstruct the allegedly blissful conditions of intrauterine existence. For example, the stuporous phase of catatonic schizophrenia is held to be a vivid instance of just such an effort. The act of birth, according to Rank, marks a radical upheaval for both the psychic and physical points of view. It produces a psychic shock of great consequence, a *trauma* to which the individual is never reconciled.

As noted earlier, Freud believed that the process of birth is the first experience attended by anxiety. As such, it is the model for all later manifestations of this affect. In contrast to Rank, however, Freud does not wish to claim that the birth process leaves an indelible imprint upon the psyche of the infant. He writes, ". . . we certainly may not presuppose that the foetus has any kind of knowledge that it is in danger of annihilation; the foetus can only sense 'a wholesale disturbance in the economy of its narcissistic libido.' " (1960, p. 754). The difference between these two theories lies in the contrast of the term trauma as opposed to process.

To return to our discussion of Freud's conception of primary anxiety, it is extremely important to keep in mind the following four constitutive factors: (1) the flooding and overwhelming of the mental apparatus with excitation; (2) the passivity and helplessness of the organism; (3) the existence of separation fears that correspond to the actual physical separation of the fetus from the mother; and (4) the automatic quality of the organism's affective experiencing. Of these, the passive character of the anxiety experience is, perhaps, the most pertinent to the distinction between primary and subsequent anxiety. To quote Fenichel again, ". . . primary anxiety is created by external and internal stimuli, still unmastered, and insofar as it is experienced as a conscious painful feeling, it is experienced passively, as something that occurs to the ego and has to be endured" (1945, p. 42). With regard to the qualities of helplessness, separation and automaticity, Freud writes:

As an automatic phenomenon and as a rescuing signal, anxiety is seen to be a product of the infant's mental helplessness which is a natural counterpart of its biological helplessness. The striking coincidence by which the anxiety of the new-born baby and the anxiety of the infant in arms are both conditioned by separation from the mother does not need to be explained on psychological lines. It can be accounted for biologically; for, just as the mother originally satisfied all the needs of the foetus through the apparatus of her own body, so now, after its birth, she continues to do so, though partly by other means (1959, Vol. XX, p. 138).

Thus, in terms of the six perspectives outlined above, we may say that *economically* speaking, primary anxiety refers to the flooding of the mental apparatus with unmastered and unmasterable quantities of excitation. *Dynamically,* the motives that overwhelm the psyche during primary anxiety are biologically given responses to a sense of danger (separation from the mother) and are demands for a return of that mother as a source of need satisfaction. From a *genetic* point of view, primary anxiety has its model in the birth process and, eventually, it will constitute the basis of all subsequent anxiety. *Structurally,* primary anxiety is experienced by the whole mental apparatus during birth and by the primitive, relatively undeveloped ego, during infancy. In both cases, the affect is passively endured with most of the energies involved being discharged automatically via the vegetative nervous system. With regard to the *phylogenetic* perspective, Freud writes, "Anxiety is a reaction which, in all probability, is common to every organism, certainly every organism of a higher order" (1959, Vol. XX, p. 134). Finally, from the *adaptive* perspective, primary anxiety is seen as an appropriate response to danger (loss of the mother) in that:

the discharge [of anxiety] being directed into the respiratory and vocal muscular apparatus, calls its mother to it, just as it activated the lungs of the new-born baby to get rid of the internal stimuli (1959, Vol. XX, p. 137).

Elsewhere, we find:

The innervation involved in the original anxiety state probably had a meaning and purpose, in just the same way as the muscular movements which accompany a first hysterical attack. . . . Thus, at birth, it is probably that the innervation, in being directed to the respiratory organs, is preparing the way for the activity of the lungs, and, in accelerating the heart-beat, is helping to keep the blood free from toxic substances (1959, Vol. XX, p. 134).

The gradual shift from primary to subsequent anxiety is correlated with the maturation of the mental apparatus—that is, its differentiation into ego, superego, and id processes. This maturation and differentiation of function, especially that of the ego, means that the organism has acquired some ability to defend itself from internal and external danger. It should be noted that the dangers alluded to here are primarily those of overstimulation, while the defenses acquired are essentially techniques of avoiding or inhibiting such stimulation. It is also true that with increasing ego development, the individual demonstrates a heightened sensitivity to the so-called external world. Even more significantly, the possibility of anticipating both the obstructions to and the fulfillment of need-satisfaction has emerged. As Fenichel points out: ". . . if every need could be immediately taken care of, a conception of reality would never develop" (1945, p. 34)—nor, may we add, would anxiety.

Because the ego plays such a vital role in the occurence of and the coping with subsequent anxiety, we shall devote some time to an elaboration of its development. We should also keep in mind our initial characterization of the ego as a facade. It is the veneer that constitutes both a basis for and an expression of the specifically human form of living. By referring to this component of the total mental apparatus with the German word "ich," Freud implied that the sense of "I," the sense of being a separate human entity, emerged secondarily from an impersonal animal ground. The German word that has been translated as "id" was "es"—a pronoun usually understood to mean "it". Thus the foundation and continuing source of the human mode of being, the wellspring of the ego, is conceived to be an impersonal, instinctually constituted, animal array of possibilities. As has been stated before, the ego appears and becomes differentiated under the influence of a restrictive, frustrating external world. It arises in response to the id's instinctual demands, as well as the counterdemands that reality, in the form of society, makes upon the mental apparatus.

Ontogenetically speaking, the origins of both the ego and a sense of reality (the external world) are but two aspects of one developmental process. Integral to this phenomenon is the emerging primitive perception of oneself as being bodily. At first, there is only the glimmering awareness of tension that has the quality of being "with" and "inside" something. Later, after repeated experience of need, presence of some object, and then need-satisfaction, there emerges the vaguely apprehended realization that an independent, "outside" object exists to still this tension. Finally, through further experiences of tension, pain, and satisfaction, the infant comes to grasp the notion that his body is simultaneously an inside and an outside something. With the concurrent occurrence of outer tactile and inner sensory data, the infant's body becomes both part of the external world and yet something apart from other objects. On this basis, the differentiation of self (my body) from nonself (other objects) is made possible. In other words, the sense of "I" is originally and throughout most of life grounded in one's sense of being bodily. Psychoanalytically speaking, the sum of the mental representations of the body and its organs, the so-called body image, constitutes this idea of "I" for the infant and is of basic importance for the further formation of the ego. Needless to say, the body image does not always coincide with the "objective" body.

According to Fenichel, the primitive ego's first realization of the external world occurs in the service of the latter's abolition. That is to say, nonself objects of the external world come to be recognized only insofar as their procurement leads to need-satisfaction, quiescence, and a reunification of the ego with the id instincts. It is at this point that a conflict of basic importance to human life arises. From this point forward the mental apparatus will manifest an ambivalence between its striving for complete relaxation and tension reduction on the one hand, and its longing for objects—its stimulus hunger—on the other. The former characteristic, a direct expression of the constancy principle and a form of homeostatic behavior, is, necessarily for Freud, the more primordial process. The ultimate and lifelong goal of all living is peace through unification: death as an individual entity. Objects of the external world, therefore, originally acquire their importance only because they are recognized as means to the goal of quiescence, inertia, and eventual nonexistence of the individual as such.

As long as stimuli from the external world or the body continue to flood the mental apparatus, they are experienced passively. However, the erection of a perceptual and defense apparatus, the primitive ego, brings about a change in orientation, a movement from passive to active experiencing. Perceptions of external objects as well as internal bodily states (tensions) may be regarded as the first attempt at mastering both the underlying animal and the external world. They constitute the basis of the early perceptual and memory systems, as well as the origins of a more differentiated consciousness. As these increasingly independent functions develop, the mental apparatus is in a position to defend itself against the influx of overwhelming stimulation. This is primarily accomplished by "closing off" the perceptual system, a procedure that, according to Fenichel, is the prototype of all subsequent defense mechanisms mobilized against both internal pains and external frustrations.

A clear grasp of the functioning of the ego is essential to a comprehension of subsequent anxiety because, structurally speaking, the ego is the locale of the anxiety experience. By virtue of its relation to the perceptual system, the ego gives mental processes an order in time in the sense of world or clock time. Further, it submits these processes to reality testing—that is, it determines whether they are suitable at this time and in this situation. Finally, by interposing the process of thought between impulse and action, the ego secures a postponement of motive discharge and controls motility.

All experiences of life that originate from without enrich the ego. The id, however, stands in relation to the ego as a second external world. While it must, in a sense, also be mastered, continual compromise is necessary. No matter how alien the id's demands may appear, they can never be totally repressed, for to do so would constitute a radical separation of the ego from its ultimate source of vitality. The primary means through which the ego accomplishes its aims vis-à-vis the id may be described as follows: first, it withdraws libidinal energy from the id impulses—i.e., it desexualizes them. Then it transforms the object-cathexes of these impulses—the libidinal energy invested in desired psychic objects—into its own structures. By this maneuver, the ego both sustains and differentiates its possibilities for further mediational functioning.

There are two paths by which the primitive, instinctual content of the id can penetrate into the ego. One is directly and the other leads by way of the ego-ideal, a substructure of the superego that is constituted by reaction formations, tendencies diametrically opposed to the instinctual demands of the id. In other words, personal ideals of a social-familial origin assist the ego in mastering, or at least controlling, the asocial animal impulses. As a result, there is a movement in ego growth and development—from simple perception of and compliance with instinctual demands to compromise with and, occasionally, to control of them.

In general, however, the ego owes service to and must maintain peace among "three harsh masters." Consequently, it is forever menaced by three dangers: from frustration and attacks by the external world; from unrealistic, animal instinctual demands of the id; and from severe chastisement by the superego. As anxiety is the ego's basic expression of retreat from danger, three different forms of this affect correspond to the previously noted three sources of peril. These forms are reality anxiety (a reaction to threat from the external world), moral anxiety (a reaction to threat from the superego), and neurotic anxiety (a reaction to threat from the id impulses).

Reality anxiety, which is essentially synonymous with fear, is a painful emotional experience based upon perception of a dangerous condition in the external world. This means that either some required object is absent, or that some present object threatens the continued existence and functioning of the organism as a whole. Speculating upon the ultimate sources of reality anxiety, Freud wonders whether they are innate in the sense that man inherits a tendency to become afraid in the presence of certain environmental conditions. On the other hand, he notes that certain reality anxieties are obviously acquired through simple learning processes in the course of life. To give an example of this ambiguity, fear of darkness could be inborn because past generations of men were constantly being endangered during the night when they had no means of making light. Individually speaking, however, fear of darkness could be acquired because one is more likely to have fear-arousing experiences at night. Finally, Freud suggests that it might even be the case that both heredity and experience are, in an interactive sense, co-producers of certain fears. Nonetheless, the founder of psychoanalysis, consistent with his genetic perspective, concludes that reality anxiety is related to and derived from early experiences of helplessness. Any situation of later life that threatens to reduce the ego to a state of infantile helplessness will arouse an anxiety signal.

Moral anxiety, which is usually experienced by the ego as guilt or shame, develops through the perception of danger coming from the superego, particularly that portion known as conscience. As an internalized agent of parental

authority, the conscience threatens to punish the ego for either doing or thinking something that transgresses upon the perfectionistic aims of the ego-ideal.
The original fear from which moral anxiety is derived is an objective one—
namely, fear of the punitive parents. Subsequently, however, after the inter-
nalization of parental standards and the development of the superego, the
source of moral anxiety is intrapsychic, within the mental apparatus itself.
However, unlike reality anxiety, moral anxiety cannot be averted through
flight.

Neurotic anxiety is caused by the perception of danger from the id instincts. In a sense, it is the fear of what would happen should the defenses
(counter-cathexes) of the ego fail to prevent instinctual demands from dis-
charging themselves in impulsive action. Basically, the defenses of the ego are
deployed in order to hold down anxiety-arousing, animal, asocial impulses. If
such a binding of the to-be-warded-off instinctual energies fails, then these energies themselves would produce anxiety of a primary infantile variety.

In its efforts to protect itself against instinctual dangers, the ego occasionally resorts to maladaptive defensive maneuvers. As a result, neurosis and neurotic symptomatology occur. Psychoanalysis, as a remedial process, seeks to
bring this (these) unknown repressed instinctual danger(s) into consciousness
and thereby transform neurotic anxiety into reality anxiety.

Freud states that neurotic anxiety can be displayed in three forms: free-
floating anxiety, phobic anxiety, and the panic or near-panic state of an anxiety
attack. The first of these varieties, free-floating anxiety, is characterized by a
general apprehensiveness that displays a readiness to attach itself for the time
being to any new possibility that might arise. People who experience this form
of anxiety are markedly pessimistic, fearful, and are classified by Freud as suffering from anxiety neurosis.

The common element that characterizes all phobic anxiety is an intense
fear of some object or state of affairs. Further, the intensity of this reaction
seems all out of proportion to the danger inherent in the situation as viewed
by an "outside observer." Many phobias are demonstrably acquired later in life
while some, such as fears of darkness, thunder, and animals, seem to have ex-
isted from earliest infancy.

The third form of neurotic anxiety, that of the panic or anxiety state, evidences no apparent connection between the reaction itself and the danger
dreaded. It either accompanies symptoms or manifests itself independently,
whether as an attack or as a condition that persists for some time. In any case,
there is never any visible justification, in the sense of an external danger that
an observer may note, for the anxiety. Acting out frequently appears with the
panic reaction and is said to be an example of discharge behavior that aims to
rid the person of excessively painful neurotic anxiety by doing that which the
id demands, in spite of ego and superego prohibitions.

Neurotic anxiety is based upon reality anxiety to the extent that the person associates the instinctual demand in question with some external danger. This is the manner in which man, according to Freud, learns to fear his instincts. As long as libidinal discharges do not lead to pain or punishment, one has nothing to fear from instinctual object-cathexes. However, when impulsive behavior gets a person into trouble, he learns how dangerous his instincts—the animal within him—can be.

The healthy, effectively functioning ego learns to cope with the possibility of anxiety. Instead of waiting for it to come and then passively enduring it, the ego uses its ability to anticipate danger and take appropriate steps to defend itself against it. This ability consists of being able to recognize very slight feelings of apprehension as the signal for something that will become more dangerous unless it is stopped. The judging ego declares that the situation, which is not yet traumatic, might become so. Such a judgment sets up a state of affairs similar to, but much less intense than, that of the traumatic state previously described. Although this, too, is experienced by the ego as anxiety, it is far different from the original, passively endured, distressful state. Instead of an overwhelming attack, a more or less moderate fear is experienced. This is utilized by the ego as a signal to prepare for what might come; such preparations involve mobilization of suitable defense mechanisms and actions. In this way the ego acquires control over the affect of anxiety.

A rather articulate, though highly technical model of anxiety, as well as other affects, has been systematically elaborated by Rapaport (1960). We shall attempt to paraphrase and schematize his conceptions, as they constitute an excellent summary of the phenomenon of subsequent anxiety. Let us imagine the following events occurring in the mental apparatus, on the one hand, and in the external world on the other. Suppose that some instinctual impulse or its derivative, originating in the id, has reached threshold intensity—that is, the ego has just become aware of its presence. At this point, there occurs what Rapaport calls "structuralized delay"; the ego must perform the following functions before any action can occur:

1. It must determine whether a suitable instinct-satisfying object is present in the environment.
2. It must, as it were, consult with the superego to determine whether action directed toward attainment of this object is morally permissible.
3. It must also consult with itself—that is, determine if it has other interests that might conflict with or be incompatible with its openly securing the present object.
4. If the object is present in the environment, the ego must decide if it can be procured safely.

As we shall see, reality anxiety, moral anxiety, neurotic anxiety, or instinctual gratification could eventuate—depending upon the answers to these four issues. If a suitable instinct-satisfying-object is not present and cannot be procured, or if it is present but its attainment involves danger of attack from the environment, then reality anxiety emerges. If a suitable instinct-satisfying-object is present and can be safely procured, but the superego deems such action and possession as immoral, then it "communicates" this to the ego in the form of guilt or shame (moral anxiety). If a suitable instinct-satisfying-object is present and can be safely procured, but such action and/or possession conflicts with other ego interests, then neurotic anxiety occurs. Finally, if and only if a suitable instinct-satisfying-object is present and can be safely procured without danger from without or conflict within, will the possibility of instinctual gratification without anxiety exist.

Comments

As was suggested in the introductory part of this chapter, one encounters considerable difficulty in an attempt to summarize and evaluate Freud's contribution to a specific subject area. This is so because a literal reading of his works drastically violates the frequently metaphorical, suggestive character of his language. Obviously, the unbelievably stimulating power of this man's revolutionary thought has not come from his readers' "letter-of-the-law" acceptance of the words. On the other hand, if one reads these writings as merely speculative, as armchair reflections, then one loses Freud's equally obvious concern with the perspective, principles, and logic of natural science. While it would be ideal if we could combine these viewpoints, there seems to be no ready method for accomplishing this. In a certain sense, the reader is forced to put his money down and take his choice. Nonetheless, as one of our most basic goals is to be as unbiased as possible, we shall present two equally valid and probably complementary interpretations of Freud's contribution.

A rather literal reading of Freud, which would be consistent with his Darwinian orientation and natural scientific inclinations, reveals a conception of anxiety couched in terms of energy distributions—the economic point of view. The mental apparatus, itself an energy system, strives to maintain a certain optimal level of excitation within its boundaries. In other words, it is regulated by the principle of homeostasis. To achieve its goals (it appears that one cannot help speaking in teleological terms), it must cope with and master quantities of energy that emerge from one of its component parts, the id reservoir, or from the external world. When it cannot do this adequately, when excesses of energy are automatically discharged via particular bodily pathways, anxiety is experienced. In essence, anxiety is the experiential or felt aspect of a more fundamental breakdown in the energy-distributing mechanisms of the mental apparatus. As has been stated above, this breakdown may have a number of causes: the inadequate development of the primary energy distributor (the ego) or a conflict between various energy subsystems (the ego versus the id, the ego and the id versus the superego, the ego and the superego versus the id, or the ego and the id versus the external world). Depending upon the particular cause of the anxiety, different types are experienced (realistic, moral, neurotic, as well as primary and subsequent). From the energy point of view, however, we gain little insight into the experience of anxiety; we avoid, as the constitutive assumptions of natural science say we must, the inner experiential world of the individual. Nevertheless, we are provided with a thoroughly comprehensive, causal explanation of the phenomenon.

A reading of Freud that recognizes and accepts as valid the metaphorical character of his language provides a much richer description of the human experience of anxiety. It also suggests an alternative ontological interpretation of Freudian metapsychological constructs. Such a reading implies that the phenomena of human life, including anxiety, can only be grasped when one considers the ego, the superego, the id, and the external world as constituting four interrelated frames of reference. To speak of these constructs as frames of reference is to suggest that they are fundamentally different yet mutually interdependent meaning matrices. For example, the ego is that system of logically consistent, verbally mediated meanings that somehow strives to reflect that array of meanings experienced as the external world, while, at the same time, sustaining its own organization in the face of demands for modification and change made by the id and the superego, respectively. The id, on the other hand, would be an illogically, inconsistently organized array of meanings continually demanding expression (integration into the ego) and always reflecting the impersonal, bodily condition of the individual. Anxiety, within this perspective, would always involve a conflict between the ego and one of the other meaning matrices. It would be experienced as meaninglessness, an inability of the ego to synthesize and sustain consistent meaningfulness. Successful coping with anxiety-arousing conditions would mean that the ego has been able to sustain its already existing organization or that it has reconstituted a new logical synthesis, primarily by consolidating its boundaries and connections, thereby preventing inconsistent meanings from entering into and disrupting its matrix. In other words, the ego would sustain itself through repression or some other defensive tactic. Ineffective or neurotic coping with anxiety might mean that the ego has not found a way to sustain its organization, or, that it has had to split its organization, creating isolated systems of alien meaning that would be expressed in the form of symptoms. In any event, as the ego is "the actual seat of anxiety," and because it is the function of this system to maintain accurate relations with the organization of external world meanings (i.e., effectively to mirror), anxiety, a breakdown in ego functioning, would always mean a disruption in the individual's realistic relations with the world.

REFERENCES

Bergmann, G., and Spence, K. W. The logic of psychophysical measurement. *Psychological Review*, 1944, 51, 1–24.

Binswanger, L. *Being-in-the-world*. (Trans. by Jacob Needleman). New York: Basic Books, 1963.

Fenichel, O. *The psychoanalytic theory of neurosis*. New York: Norton, 1945.

Freud, S. The unconscious (quoted text written in 1915). In the *Standard edition of the complete psychological works of Sigmund Freud*. (Trans. by James Strachey). London: The Hogarth Press, 1957, vol. XIV, pp. 159–215 (New York: Basic Books).

Freud, S. Introductory lectures on psychoanalysis (quoted text written in 1917). In the *Standard edition of the complete psychological works of Sigmund Freud*. (Trans. by James Strachey). London: Hogarth, 1963, vol. XVI, pp. 243–496.

Freud, S. Inhibitions, symptoms and anxiety (quoted text written in 1926). In the *Standard edition of the complete psychological works of Sigmund Freud*. (Trans. by James Strachey). London: Hogarth, 1959, vol. XX, pp. 77–175.

Freud, S. Constructions in analysis (quoted text written in 1937). In the *Standard edition of the complete psychological works of Sigmund Freud*. (Trans. by James Strachey). London: Hogarth, 1964, vol. XXIII, pp. 255–269 (New York: Basic Books).

Freud, S. An outline of psychoanalysis (quoted text written in 1938). In the *Standard edition of the complete psychological works of Sigmund Freud*. (Trans. by James Strachey). London: Hogarth, 1964, vol. XXIII, pp. 141–207 (New York: W. W. Norton).

Hinsie, L. E., & Campbell, R. J. *Psychiatric dictionary*. New York: Oxford, 1960.

Rapaport, D. The structure of psychoanalytic theory: A systematizing attempt. Psychological Issues, 1960, Vol. II, No. 2, Monograph 6.

Stevens, S. S. Psychology and the science of science. *Psychological Bulletin*, 1939, 36, 221–263.

2
Neo-Freudian Approaches: Harry Stack Sullivan

In their introduction to the social psychological, neo-Freudian theories of personality, Hall and Lindzey (1957) state:

the psychoanalytic theories of personality formulated by Freud and Jung were nurtured by the same positivistic climate that shaped the course of nineteenth century physics and biology. Man was regarded primarily as a complex energy system which maintains itself by means of transactions with the external world. The ultimate purposes of these transactions are individual survival, propagation of the species, and an ongoing evolutionary development. The various psychological processes that constitute the personality serve these ends (1957, p. 114).

While these claims are certainly consistent with the comments made in the previous chapter, I believe that they are insufficient—especially when one tries to understand that against which the neo-Freudians revolted. Not only were Freudian theories tending toward positivism, mechanism, and biologism (particularly of the Darwinian variety) but also, and perhaps more profoundly, they were constructed within a Cartesian conception of the human condition. The Freudian man is filled with drives, instincts, and complexes, while his environment is always understood to be the critical external world. Thus the relationships of man to society and man to culture are continually pervaded with a sense of repression and/or alienation. At best, the environment merely acts as a kind of release mechanism, a restricted, demanding arena in which the organism with its drives and complexes struggles for expression and gratification. There is no dialogue, only war. Further, culture itself is conceived to be nothing more than a product of this struggle; it is the unhappy by-product of communal existence and personal limitation. If man could be himself, that is, if he could be natural man, then there would be no culture. If man could directly gratify his instincts and drives, there would be no art, no music, no society.

With the development of astounding improvements in international transportation and communication, with the shrinking of the world, the possibility of understanding and comparing life in different societies emerged. As a result, there occurred a proliferation of anthropological and cross-cultural studies. Researchers observed and participated in the everyday life of communities all over the world, from Alaska to Samoa. The criteria through which social scientists grasped and evaluated development within a given culture were no longer confined to those manifest on the western, European-American scene. One of the major consequences of this revolution was that society—and more particularly, the relationship of man to society—was no longer conceivable in terms of the Freudian framework. True, there may be elements of war and struggle in this relationship, but it also involves dialogue. Social and cultural institutions both create and are created by man. Further, they do not merely repress his growth and self-expression, they also facilitate and channel it. Man is no longer conceivable except in terms of his continuing dialogue with society; they are co-defining and co-evolving, not simply independent, basically antagonistic forces.

Thus the theories of psychological development that occurred in the context of these changes had, in some sense, to alter the Freudian model of man versus society. Psychologists and psychiatrists working and speculating under the influence of these new sources of information were impelled selectively to accept as well as reject some of the conceptions proposed by the founder of psychoanalysis. While the degree to which Freudian conceptions were affirmed and/or abandoned varied from theorist to theorist, the overall result was the neo-Freudian perspective. As Wyss (1966) states:

the crucial difference between the Neo-Freudian and Freudian schools lies in the degree of importance which they attach to environmental influences for the development of neurosis. Both schools concede that constitutional—hereditary—factors exercise an influence. In the Neo-Freudian view, however, it is above all the environment which lays in infancy the seeds of subsequent neurosis. . . . The Freudians on the other hand tend to think . . . that the environment merely acts as a release mechanism for the complexes but that it is the complexes which actually produce the neurosis (1966, p. 517).

While the degrees to which the neo-Freudians have accepted the basic Freudian conceptions vary from theorist to theorist, one may still point to general areas of affirmation and/or rejection. For example, both Freudians and neo-Freudians share the view that:

1. The personality or psyche operates according to the principle of homeostasis. Thus the principles of pleasure and displeasure are understood as functions of tension level.

2. Personality or psychic processes are explained in terms of causal laws, especially in accordance with the formula: that which occurs earlier is the cause of that which shows itself later.
3. A distinction is made between conscious and unconscious processes of the personality. While the conceptualizations of these two sets of processes differ from that offered by the founder of psychoanalysis, the meanings are essentially similar. Further, the basic idea of repression or defense against unconscious processes is maintained.
4. Parental influences are conceived to be of prime importance for the development of personality.
5. Inner conflicts and defenses against them constitute the essential ingredients of personality dynamics. As a result, the behavior that emerges at any level of development is always understood to be a compromise—usually ambivalent.
6. All motivation, whether conceived in terms of drive, impulse, integrating tendency, or whatever, is grasped from the observer perspective. Further, it is ultimately grounded in natural science thinking: i.e., forces, tensions, etc.

It is also possible, however, to point to that which was not accepted by the neo-Freudians. We may assert that, as a group, these thinkers rejected:

1. The primordiality of libido and the privileged position of sexual motivation.
2. The priority of the biological over the environmental.
3. The reification of structural concepts such as ego, id, superego, and "the unconscious."
4. The paramount importance of dreams, especially in the therapy process.

In selecting one theorist to represent the neo-Freudian perspective, we have been guided by two concerns: the degree to which the full impact of the cross-cultural and anthropological studies have been utilized in the formulations produced, and the relative sufficiency or completeness of the theory. On both counts, the published lectures and papers of Harry Stack Sullivan seem to meet our concerns adequately.

Prior to our exposition of Sullivan's thought, it might be helpful to know something about the man. Helen S. Perry (1961), in her Introduction to *Schizophrenia as a Human Process*, writes:

One of the most significant differences between Freud's and Sullivan's approach to mental illness is implicit in their differences in cultural background. Freud came from a middle-class Viennese, Jewish background; Sullivan came from a Catholic, Irish-American family. Freud had the orientation of a typical middle-class neurotic of his day and time. Sullivan had the first hand information of the peculiarly isolating experiences of a young Irish Catholic boy, son of an immigrant father, growing up in a farming area where all the other families were Protestant and mostly old Yankee. Freud's thinking reflects a talmudic background, scholarly, thoughtful, and deep; Sullivan's thinking is almost Joycean in its intricate processes, rich and varied, occasionally almost poetic, but difficult and complex. . . . It is academic to set their thinking in opposition. . . . Sullivan began his work with the findings of Freud; although he moved far away from Freud's thinking in many areas, he never saw himself as being in opposition to Freud (1961, pp. xi–xii).

Harry Stack Sullivan was born in 1892 and died in 1949. His intellectual and professional careers were largely centered in Baltimore and New York City. At the former's Sheppard and Enoch Pratt Hospital, he conducted, lectured about, and to some extent wrote of his work with schizophrenic patients. After he moved to New York City in 1931, he began to treat and investigate obsessional processes in private patients. With the outbreak of World War II, he served as an advisor to the Selective Service System, meanwhile continuing his investigative efforts and lecturing, this time at Chestnut Lodge. Finally, with the end of the war, Sullivan worked with the United Nations, striving to achieve his lifelong goal: the fusion of psychiatry and social science as a means to world understanding and peace.

Whereas a reading of Freud introduces one to the potential impact of such thinkers as Descartes, Nietzsche, Darwin, Helmholtz, and Brücke, a study of Sullivan's thought—though it must begin with his relation to Freud —reveals the influence of almost every twentieth-century discipline concerned with the problems of human life. To mention but a few, there are the philosophers, George Herbert Meade, Charles Evans Cooley, and Alfred North Whitehead; the investigators of language, Alfred Korzybski and Edward Sapir; the cultural anthropologists, Ruth Benedict, Bronislaw Malinowski, Margaret Mead, and Hortense Powdermaker; the psychiatrists, Sigmund Freud, William Alanson White, and Adolph Meyer; and the psychologists, Gordon Allport and L. K. Frank. Each in his own fashion contributed to and, in some cases, was influenced by the thinking of Harry Stack Sullivan.

We must remind ourselves of our original purpose, the presentation of Sullivan's theory of anxiety. But, for at least two reasons, this is not a simple matter. The first source of difficulty is that of distinguishing between his theory of anxiety and his theory as a whole. A good case could be made for the assertion that maintains that the totality of Sullivan's thought is, in fact, a statement of the conditions for and the consequences of anxiety. The second obstacle has to do with the levels at which the theory can be grasped. Patrick Mullahy (1955) puts the problem well when he states, "at first blush it appears that the statement that psychiatry is the study of the processes that involve or go on between people, interpersonal relations, is simple and obvious. Yet, it is the most complicated psychiatric theory known to us" (1955, p. 279).

The Interpersonal Theory of Psychiatry (1953) constitutes "the last complete statement which Sullivan made of his conceptions of psychiatry" (1953,

p. vii). It is, in fact, the relatively unabridged version of the lectures that he gave at the Washington School of Psychiatry during the winter of 1946–1947. In it, he explicitly sets forth his idea of the developmental approach, his basic assumptions and postulates, his conceptions of the stages of human development, and his formulations regarding the causes, types, and consequences of mental illness.

According to Sullivan, the meaning and purpose of the developmental approach is to understand how

from birth onward, a very capable animal becomes a person—something very different from an animal; and as to how this transformation of a very gifted animal —who is always there but who cannot be defined because he is constantly being transformed—is brought about, step by step, from very, very early in life, through the influence of other people, and solely for the purpose of living with other people in some sort of social organization (1953, p. 5).

From the perspective of a psychopathologist, Sullivan states:

if we go with almost microscopic care over how everybody comes to be what he is at chronological adulthood, then perhaps we can learn a good deal of what is highly probable about living and difficulties in living (1953, p. 4).

The reader should immediately note, particularly from the first excerpt, Sullivan's fundamental divergence from Freud. For the latter, the animal is always explicitly there, behind the ego, and development is conceived in terms of the ego's ability both to tame and yet to provide the animal with sufficient gratification. For the former, one begins as an animal, but development is understood as a transformation of that animal into a human person. It is not merely the growth and tribulations of a facade behind which the instinct oriented creature remains intact. Further, this transformation occurs exclusively in an interpersonal context. Thus the aims of society and its representatives are grasped as facilitating the humanization, however conceived, of the growing individual. Development is not simply a series of conflicts and compromises; it is also a process of ripening and coming to fruit. One of the most important implications of this conception is that the human form of living is understood as something to be achieved, always in the framework of human relations. Humanness is not just given fait accompli through the inheritance of some instinctual or drive makeup. It is, rather, an interrelated network of possible feelings and actions that significant others attempt to foster in the individual and which the individual continually attempts to realize so that he may take his place in a society of people. When we specifically focus upon Sullivan's conception of anxiety, we shall come to grips with the full impact of this implication.

In contrast to Freud's implicit acceptance of a bifurcated, Cartesian ontological system, Sullivan understands the living human person as existing in a series of necessary relations with his environment. The precise meaning of this state of affairs is expressed in a statement of three principles appropriated from twentieth-century biological thought. They are as follows.

1. The Principle of Communal Existence. This refers to the fact that:

the living cannot live when separated from what may be described as their necessary environment. . . . It is possible to think of man as distinguished from plants and animals by the fact that human life—in a very real and not only a purely literary or imaginary sense—requires interchange with an environment which includes culture. . . . Man requires interpersonal relationships, or interchange with others (1953, pp. 31–32).

2. The Principle of Organization. This refers to the fact that the human being, understood bodily, is dynamically structured in such a way as to facilitate its communal existence with the environment. It should be noted that Sullivan is not merely referring to microscopic sensory nervous system structures. Rather, he is pointing to the macroscopic, functionally interrelated units of the body (eyes, ears, mouth, hands, feet, etc.) that both structure and make possible an individual's relations with the environment.

3. The Principle of Functional Activity. This refers to the fact that the human being, at any given moment and in any particular situation, brings to his communal existence with the environment various sets of interests and orientations, each of which facilitate and determine relatedness. There is a strong suggestion of teleology here, and Sullivan clearly implies that human behavior is purposeful and goal-directed.

What, one may ask, are some of the consequences of Sullivan's appropriation of these principles? First, and perhaps of greatest importance, is the fact that the proper object of psychiatric and psychological study ceases to be the psyche or isolated mental apparatus. The person is no longer conceived to be cut off from the allegedly external world. Rather, the scientist must now focus his attention upon the person-necessary environment complex, keeping in mind that the most significant aspects of the necessary environment are other people and the culture that they express. As Sullivan himself states:

the general science of psychiatry seems to me to cover much the same field as that which is studied by social psychology, because scientific psychiatry has to be defined as the study of interpersonal relations, and this in the end calls for the use of the kind of conceptual framework that we now call field theory. From such a standpoint, personality is taken to be hypothetical. That which can be studied is the pattern of processes which characterize the interaction of personalities in particular recurrent situations or fields . . . (1953, pp. 367–368).

A second consequence of these principles is that the psychiatrist himself, when he functions as such, becomes an object of study and a source of information.

The actions or operations from which psychiatric information is derived are events in interpersonal fields which include the psychiatrist. The events which contribute information for the development of psychiatry and psychiatric theory are events in which the psychiatrist participates; they are not events that he looks at from atop ivory towers (1953, pp. 13–14).

Unlike the Freudian analyst who conceives himself to be little else but a screen upon which the patient projects transferences, the Sullivanian therapist is there as a participating person in the treatment situation.

Finally, human experience and action must now be understood as emerging from the ground of communal existence. It is no longer appropriate to think of meanings as coming from the person's psyche or mental apparatus, somehow being projected upon an external world. Nor can we grasp meanings as originating in an independent, pristinely pure, external environment. Rather, the human experience of meaning, as well as the actions that express that experience, can be understood only in terms of the dialogue that continually unfolds between the person and his necessary environment.

If we now combine Sullivan's sense of development with the principles he appropriated from biology, we realize that his theory is concerned with and oriented toward the evolution of person-necessary environment processes. Further, it is this evolution that constitutes the transformation of the gifted human animal into the culturally meaningful human being. According to Sullivan, there are seven reasonably well-defined stages in this transformation. However, before we enumerate and describe them, we should like to stress that they are stages of person-necessary environment change; they are not developments whose locus is to be found "in" either the person or the environment. Thus, consistent with Sullivan's thought, we are emphasizing, even to the point of redundancy, that the unit of focus is always the person-necessary environment complex, taken as an unbreachable totality; person and necessary environment constitute poles of a continuously unfolding network of relationships. This is Sullivan's conception of development.

The stages that mark milestones in this unfolding process may be described as follows:

1. Infancy. This period extends from "a few minutes after birth to the appearance of articulate speech, however uncommunicative or meaningless (1953, p. 33). It is the relationship that the infant enjoys with the mother or mothering one. Further, it is characterized primarily by what Sullivan terms the "Theorem of Tenderness."

2. Childhood. This period "extends from the appearance of the ability to utter articulate sounds of or pertaining to speech, to the appearance of the need for playmates—that is, companions, cooperative beings of approximately one's own status in all sorts of respects" (1953, p. 33). It is the relationship between the child and his parents and is primarily characterized by what Sullivan terms the "Theorem of Reciprocal Emotion."

3. Juvenile Era. This period "extends through most of the grammar-school years to the eruption, due to maturation, of a need for intimate relation with another person of comparable status" (1953, p. 33). This stage is actually a matrix of relationships: the individual with his peers, the individual with his parents, and the individual with other socially sanctioned authorities (teachers, policemen, clergymen, etc.). It is primarily characterized by what Sullivan calls "Competition," "Compromise," and "Social Accommodation."

4. Preadolescence. This is "an exceedingly important but chronologically brief period that ordinarily ends with the eruption of genital sexuality and puberty, but psychologically or psychiatrically ends with the movement of strong interest from a person of one's own sex to a person of the other sex" (1953, p. 33). For Sullivan, this is one of the most important periods of life. It is the relationship between the person and his chum and constitutes the first opportunity for a genuine expression of love.

5. Early Adolescence. This is the period "which in this culture (it varies, however, from culture to culture) continues until one has patterned some type of performance which satisfies one's lust, one's genital drives" (1953, pp. 33–34). Essentially it is the relationship with members of the opposite sex in which the individual attempts to establish for himself a comfortable pattern of heterosexual relating.

6. Late Adolescence. This is the period in which the individual, through his increasingly varied relationships, brings other aspects of his life, i.e., personal ambitions, lifelong goals, etc., into harmony with his sexual interests and patterns of relating.

7. Adulthood. This is the period when the individual searches to "establish relationships of love for some other person, in which relationship the other person is as significant, or nearly as significant, as one's self" (1953, p. 34).

To trace the patterns of interpersonal processes as they unfold throughout these stages of development is, for Sullivan, the proper object of psychiatric theory. In general, these processes revolve around two fundamental concerns: the pursuit of satisfactions that pertain to the various bodily needs of the individual, and the pursuit of security that pertains to the individual's interest in avoiding anxiety. As has been suggested above, the person-necessary environment complex is conceived as a field. As such, it can be grasped as existing in degrees of equilibrium or disequilibrium. A state of complete equilibrium is, for Sullivan, hypothetical. The closest thing to it would be the state of sleep as it exists in the young, satisfied infant. Usually, however, this field is, to some degree, in a state of disequilibrium.

Sullivan conceives of two major sources of disequilibrium: tensions associated with bodily needs and tensions associated with anxiety. The latter arise solely from and express disjunctions in one's interpersonal relations. In other words, for this theorist, anxiety is exclusively a function of one's relations with other people. It occurs insofar as a significant other is anticipated as likely to condemn or actually does condemn one's manner of achieving satisfactions. The remainder of this exposition will be devoted to an elaboration of this statement.

In our initial discussion of Sullivan's conception of development, we suggested that the growing individual is continually confronted with the task of achieving humanness and of being affirmed by others as being an acceptable human being. At each developmental level, this achievement and affirmation involves different modes of acting and feeling. For example, in infancy it may mean smiling at mother when she nears the crib; in the juvenile era, it may mean being athletically competent and competitive. In early adolescence, it may involve having a date or being popular with the opposite sex. The particular requirements vary from level to level, but their essential meaning is always the same: being aware that one is experienced as and feeling one's self to be an adequate human being.

Obviously, there are different degrees of being anxious. Sullivan recognizes this continuum, although he speaks only of two points along it: mild anxiety that is, perhaps, an everyday occurrence for most people, and sudden, severe anxiety that occurs for the most part during infancy and in striking pathological states. In any event, the degree of anxiety that the individual experiences is a function of two factors: the significance of the other—either real or fantasied—who disapproves of one's manner of being, and the severity with which this disapproval is expressed and communicated. Sullivan calls the general class of disapproving communications "forbidding gestures." As we have just stated, mild anxiety is understood to be an everyday occurrence for most people. In a rather picturesque affirmation of this fact, Sullivan describes behavior in interpersonal situations as "picking one's way through the raindrops of anxiety." In other words, in their everyday relations with others, people modify their expressions and actions in accordance with their experience of their partner's reactions to them. Severe anxiety, on the other hand, is like receiving a "blow on the head, in that it simply wipes out what is immediately proximal to its occurrence. If you have a severe blow on the head, you are quite apt later to have an incurable, absolute amnesia covering the few moments before your head was struck" (1953, p. 152). Thus, at best, people have difficulty and in most cases cannot orient themselves in situations in which severe anxiety occurs. It is problematical to anticipate and almost impossible to cope with.

Such characterizations as we have stated lead us to our next point: the specific manner in which the experience of forbidding gestures induces anxiety. In a certain sense, we find it rather surprising that Sullivan's disciples and/or followers feel the necessity of apologizing for his formulations regarding this issue. An example of this is given by Mabel Cohen in her Introduction to The Interpersonal Theory of Psychiatry. She writes:

The question of the method of communication of anxiety from mother to child (as well as from person to person in general) has been left largely unanswered by Sullivan. He lumped such communicative experiences under the category of "empathy"; but by empathy he did not mean anything resembling extrasensory perception (1953, p. xvi).

We should like to suggest that Sullivan's choice of the term "empathy" was deliberate; it was not a lumping together of something that was not understood, although we recognize that he may not have been able explicitly to justify the choice of this term to the natural scientist. The word empathy refers to the possibility of experiencing another's feelings about some situation or state of affairs. It seems to us that Sullivan was trying to point to the fact that in anticipation or in actuality, we can, at times, experience ourselves through the affirming or condemning eyes and gestures of the other. We can "see" ourselves as others "see" us and we can feel about ourselves as we experience others as feeling about us. This, for Sullivan, permits the induction of anxiety. If we could not "step outside" of our own perspective, if we could not view and feel about ourselves as we experience others as doing, we could not be anxious.

Understood as a particular form of tension and hence as a source of disequilibrium, anxiety is always unpalatable according to Sullivan. In fact, he claims that anxiety, as a tension, works in direct opposition to the satisfaction of other tensions, i.e., the tensions pertaining to bodily needs and the tensions associated with the need for sleep. Because of the unpleasant, obstacle character of anxiety, people are impelled to develop elaborate systems and processes that enable them to avoid this experience. The most important of these is the so-called self-system. Of this Sullivan says:

the self-system is derived wholly from the interpersonal aspects of the necessary environment of the human being; it is organized because of the extremely unpalatable, extremely uncomfortable experience of anxiety; and it is organized in such a way as to avoid or minimize existent or foreseen anxiety (1953, p. 190).

The self-system has its origins in infancy when certain gestures, expression, tones of voice, etc., of the mother come to be grasped by the infant as signs of impending distress. The organization of such experiences is the beginning of the self-system, which then utilizes the recall of such earlier experiences to function as a warning or foresight of anxiety. The self-system operates mainly through a control of focal awareness. That is to say, we develop skill in attending to those aspects of a situation that are not anxiety inducing; we do not notice or we ignore experiences that would promote anxiety. Thus the self-system has what Sullivan calls "unfortunate aspects" in that we frequently are not able to experience and make use of information that might be beneficial, even though it is anxiety arousing. Before the reader assumes that Sullivan is speaking here about some actual entity, presumably located within a psyche or brain, let us cite the theorist's own comments about this interpretation. Referring to the self-system as a part of the personality, he notes: "when I speak of 'parts of personality,' it must be understood that 'personality' is a hypothesis, so this is a hypothetical part of a hypothesis" (1964, p. 217). In other words, Sullivan grasps the entire idea of personality as a construct, the purpose of which is both to describe and to account for the events that occur at one pole of the person-necessary environment relationship. A major aspect of this construct is the self-system, a hypothetical conceptual structure that serves as a unifying reference point *for the theorist* in organizing peoples' statements about themselves as well as their anxiety-avoiding actions. As the self-system controls focal awareness—that is, as self-concious, explicit experience tends to be limited to that which is consistent with the organization of meanings of the self-system—Sullivan can speak of the techniques (he calls them dynamisms or security operations) with which the self-system precludes focal awareness of certain anxiety-arousing meanings. We shall now discuss these operations in some detail.

According to Sullivan, there are four reasonably distinct security operations through which individuals avoid coming to grips with the fundamental meaning—"I am not an adequate human being"—of anxiety-provoking situations. These dynamisms of self-defense he calls sublimation, selective inattention, substitution, and dissociation. The reader should note that, for Sullivan, it makes no sense to ask if an individual employs security operations at all. Interpersonal living, by its very nature, means vulnerability to anxiety. Thus it becomes more meaningful to ask: Upon which defensive tactic does an individual tend to rely, and to what extent—that is, how frequently and in what variety of situations—does the individual rely upon this tactic? As we shall see, it is possible to grasp both the specific meaning of each operation as well as the differences that exist between them if we guide our thinking with the following questions:

1. To what extent does the use of a particular security operation permit focal awareness of the anxiety-provoking situation?
2. If the operation does permit focal awareness, how is this handled so as to minimize its implications?
3. If the operation does not permit focal awareness, how is this accomplished?
4. In what senses does the individual's behavior express his explicit experience or lack thereof of the anxiety-provoking situation?

In his discussion of the events of early childhood, Sullivan depicts the developing individual as pursuing the satisfaction of both bodily and activity needs. Sooner or later, the manner in which this is done meets with disapproval, particularly from the mothering one, and when this happens, the pursuit of satisfaction becomes problematical for the child. By far and away the most frequently manifested, compromise solution is one that utilizes sublimation. Comparing his sense of this phenomenon with that of Freud, Sullivan states:

As I have already indicated, when I talk about sublimation I am not discussing exactly what Freud had in mind when he set up the terms; my thinking about sublimation makes it a very much more inclusive process than a study of classical psychoanalysis might suggest. The manifestations of what I shall continue to call sublimation, for want of a better term, appear in late infancy, become conspicuous in childhood, and become very conspicuous indeed in the succeeding period. . . . Sublimation is the unwitting substitution, for a behavior pattern which encounters anxiety or collides with the self-system, of a socially more acceptable activity pattern which satisfies part of the motivational system that caused trouble (1953, p. 193).

In other words, sublimation is the process through which a given situation no longer means "do this," which would lead to anxiety, but now means "do that"—which partially satisfies the motive in question and does not lead to anxiety. Further, this process is unwitting, that is, the individual is unaware of the fact that the meaning of the situation has changed for him; he is unaware that he is settling for partial satisfaction.

If we now apply our previously stated questions to this process, we find that in sublimation the individual does not become focally aware of the anxiety-provoking situation as such. Rather, the meaning of the situation is altered. For example, the sensation of pressure in one's rectum no longer means relax and defecate. Instead, it means constrict the anal orifice and get to a bathroom. Further, this alteration of meaning is not realized as a change. Finally, the individual's behavior—running to a bathroom—expresses the altered, compromise meaning of the situation for him. Insofar as it allows some satisfaction, it inhibits self-conscious awareness of the change that has occurred.

As the developing individual moves into the juvenile era, he finds that his parents, teachers, and peers all expect him to attend to that which is socially relevant and appropriate. Violations of this requirement frequently meet with crude criticism, ridicule, and disparagement. As a result, the juvenile is educated, primarily by anxiety, to control his focal awareness. He learns not to notice, not to question the implications of, and certainly not to express that which his necessary environment deems to be irrelevant, immature, and/or less human. To do any of these things would mean to run the risk of being made anxious, and that, by definition, is undesirable. The process of not noticing and of concentrating only on that which is to some extent socially acceptable, Sullivan calls selective inattention.

As the theorist himself realizes and states, the ability to focus one's attention on only that which appears to be relevant is a mixed blessing. On the positive side of the ledger, we can speak of concentration, and of being able to put aside, at least for the moment, details that are not immediately relevant to one's pursuits. Sullivan's description of the marksman and his ability to suspend reactions to all extraneous stimuli is quite apt here. On the negative side of the ledger, however, we must acknowledge unfortunate consequences of this process. When some of the salient meanings of a given situation are, in fact, important for our growth, but also provoke anxiety, they too must be defended against. Thus Sullivan states:

selective inattention is, more than any other of the inappropriate and inadequate performances of life, the classic means by which we do not profit from experience which falls within the areas of our particular handicap. We don't have the experience from which we might profit—that is, although it occurs, we may never notice what it must mean . . . (1953, p. 319).

A further clarification of this ubiquitous and extremely important process seems necessary. Sullivan claims that in selective inattention we notice the event as such; we are aware that it is happening. But with that awareness we do nothing; we ignore its implications and ramifications; we do not ask about its meaning for our lives as human beings. The event is just there, noticed and then dismissed. In this way its anxiety-provoking meanings and consequences are suavely avoided.

When we apply our guiding questions to this process, we find that, unlike the situation of sublimation, in selective inattention the event is grasped as such in focal awareness. Its meaning has not been altered. However, the full meaning of the event remains opaque: "the drawing out of inferences—the education of relations, as Spearman would say—simply does not follow" (1956, p. 76). As a result, there is no behavior directly expressive of the anxiety-provoking experience. The observer, if he is extremely sensitive, only sees or hears something missing—some meaning or implication of the situation has been left out.

Occasionally, perhaps too frequently, a child lives and grows in a home in which

no matter what aggression anyone perpetrates on another—no matter what outrages the parents perpetrate on each other, or the elder siblings perpetrate on each other, on the parents, or on little Willie—there is always some worthy principle lying about to which appeal is made. And the fact that an appeal to an entirely contradictory principle was made 15 minutes earlier does not seem to disturb anybody. . . . Here is a situation where it has been found that it is better to have this limited verbal magic than only the other thing one could have—an awful lot of fairly open hostility and dislike and hatred (1956, pp. 230–231).

In such a home, the child learns that focusing his attention upon some verbal thought or statement—whenever things get frightening or whenever he feels that he might say something that would bring the world down upon him—alleviates the unbearable sense of danger. This, according to Sullivan, is the prototype of substitution. It involves a dramatic shift in one's focal awareness. That which was originally experienced as thematic and anxiety-provoking is, with great effort, the object of flight. There is no question as to the meaning of what was experienced. It is not altered, nor are its implications ignored. Rather, the individual flees to focus his attention upon some socially acceptable, though rarely appropriate-to-the-situation, truism. In a succinct phrase, a piece of verbal magic is substituted for an anxiety-provoking thought. As one might expect, this security operation works only occasionally and even when it does, the individual never achieves the sense of safety that is given through sublimation or selective inattention. Further, as the clinician must already realize, continued and intense dependence upon this particular security operation leads to an obsessional way of life.

From the above, we immediately realize that substitution, in contrast to sublimation, does not insulate the individual against anxiety-provoking experiences. Focal awareness of that which is to be fled occurs explicitly, if only for a moment. Further, although this is followed by a radical shift in attention, the meaning of that which was originally experienced is not forgotten, lost, or nihilated. Thus both in and after the shift, the individual remains vaguely apprehensive, uncertainly secure. The behavior that expresses the fact of the initial anxiety-provoking experience is the intensity with which it is fled, the tenaciousness with which the individual clings to and pronounces his verbal magic.

Although he ascribed considerable significance to it in his earlier works, Sullivan later came to grasp dissociation as relatively less frequent in its occurrence and primarily confined to matters schizophrenic. As has been stated above, the self-system has its origins in infancy. More specifically, it comes into being in order to facilitate the infant's pursuit of satisfaction, while, at the same time, safeguarding him from anxiety.

Although we originally described the self-system as an organization of the developing individual's experiences that were related to anxiety, we now require a further clarification of this hypothetical structure. Actually, the self-system is composed of three interrelated organizations of experience. One of these Sullivan calls "good me" in that it is an organization of those need-activity-satisfaction sequences that were also socially approved. In other words, "good me" is that portion of the individual's sense of self that is constituted by his experiences with actions that led not only to unencumbered satisfaction but also to tender cooperation from significant others. The second aspect of the self-system is termed "bad me." This is an organization of experienced sequences that may be characterized as need-activity-satisfaction with mild anxiety. In other words, although the individual may have achieved satisfaction of certain needs through his actions, he also incurred the slight-to-moderate disapproval of significant others in the process. Finally, there is that aspect of the self-system that Sullivan labels "not me." This is an extremely crude organization of the infant's experience. It is constituted by sequences that involved need-activity-nonsatisfaction together with sudden and severe anxiety induced by the mothering one.

By the time the infant reaches childhood, the "not me" component of the self-system can no longer be granted access to awareness. Insofar as any aspect of it comes into awareness, the child experiences "uncanny emotion" and an unreal, out-of-this-world sense of awe, loathing, dread, disgust, and/or horror. The process through which this original component of the self-system is, as it were, exorcised, Sullivan terms dissociation. That is to say, any referent to those needs or activities that had previously led to sudden and severe anxiety are banished from the rest of the personality. They are defended against through various performances and orientations that make their focal awareness an impossibility. Thus in dissociation "the patient simply hasn't any of this business of being aware of events. You know from his subsequent behavior that an event has simply sidetracked itself, for it was part of his life, even though it is not part of his known experience" (1956, p. 76). There is neither direct nor altered focal awareness of the anxiety-provoking event. Further, although certain actions, i.e., tics, automated behavior, and the like, may suggest to the observer that the individual is experiencing something, the latter, when asked, can relate nothing about such experiences and is even frequently unaware of the behavior that expresses them.

Before we attempt to summarize Sullivan's conception of anxiety, it might be helpful to mention briefly his formulations regarding fear. Unlike most of the theorists discussed in this book—an exception would be the existentialists—Sullivan radically distinguishes fear from anxiety. While he acknowledges that the two phenomena are similar in that they both consist

of a very severe drop in euphoria . . . fear . . . is a very widely distributed device of living organisms for the purposes of self-preservation. Thus it is not so exclusively human or preternaturally social as anxiety. Perhaps fear and anxiety feel much the same. But fear, as it is ordinarily manifested, is that "bundle" of processes called out either by the great novelty of a situation or by something in a situation that is really dangerous, or at least very unpleasant in the sense of causing pain or severe discomfort. [Further] fear is ordinarily mediated by some of the distance receptors. . . . Fear causes an increasing alertness and creates changes in the internal "economy" of the body, so that the supply of energy available for muscular action is increased (1956, pp. 91–92).

Elsewhere, Sullivan states: "fear, from its mildest to its most extreme form, that of terror, is to be considered to be the felt aspect of tension arising from danger to the existence or biological integrity of the organism" (1953, p. 50).

If we pull all these assertions together, we find that Sullivan conceives of fear as being an adaptive response of man and other animals. It is elicited by either an actually dangerous entity or by a situation so novel that it, too, constitutes a danger to the organism. In both cases, it is evident that fear must be understood as a spatial event. Further, the danger to which fear refers is one of bodily integrity. The fearing creature fears for his continued biological existence. Finally, unless fearing reaches the point of absolute terror, its effect is to heighten the organism's sensitivity to its necessary environment. With this increased acuity there emerge further possibilities of adaptive action and self-preservation.

In contrast to the processes characteristic of fear, anxiety is conceived to be an exclusively human, social phenomenon. As such, it is elicited by the experienced disapproval and/or condemnation of significant others. It expresses the individual's anticipation or actual sense of being a failure in his most fundamental task, that of becoming a human being. Anxiety, for Sullivan, is not adaptive; it is disjunctive; it temporarily cuts the individual off from his necessary environment and renders him helpless. There is no increased acuity; there is no mobilization of the body for action; there is only the pathetic cry of distress and a desperate need to flee. But unlike fear, that which is fled is not some environmental situation or object. Rather, in anxiety the individual flees from his own experience; he flees from himself. Thus, we can see that for Sullivan, fear and anxiety, although they may share some felt characteristics, are, in fact, fundamentally divergent.

Comments

From the previous exposition and discussion, it should be clear that Sullivan's thought is rich, incisive, and certainly provocative. He has freed himself from most of the constricting conceptions that an acceptance of Cartesian ontology imposes on a theorist (see, for example, Freud). He has realized the significance of both developmental and experiential factors in the project of understanding human living. Of greatest importance, perhaps, he has grasped the problematical nature of human becoming, the fact that humanness is not given in any fait accompli manner, but is, instead, a state of affairs always to be achieved. Further, such achieving is never once and for all, for as life unfolds, the states of affairs to be achieved and the conditions of their achievement (the developmental epochs) change.

Anxiety is the intermittent, occasionally chronic sense of being a failure as a human being. Thus it is inextricably tied to the fact that one lives with other human beings in a culture that, among other things, presents criteria of humanness. This is certainly a thought-provoking conception. It suggests that psychology should be concerned with the study of interpersonal processes, not simply intrapsychic events. It implies the necessity of cross-cultural comparisons, of analyses of human being both in and across different societies. Finally, but certainly not of least importance, it affirms the meaningfulness and significance of everyday life experience.

Unfortunately, from our point of view, there are limitations to Sullivan's thought. He is still grounded, at least to some extent, in a natural-science conception of man. He still conceives of people as energy or tension systems, striving to achieve homeostasis. He still wants to reduce experience and activity to transformations of energy. Finally, despite his acknowledged sensitivity and empathy, he still understands human experience only from an observer's perspective.

In general, however, we find ourselves to be exceedingly enriched by our reading of Sullivan. As will be evident in our "integration" chapters, we shall utilize many of his ideas in formulating our own conception of anxiety.

REFERENCES

Cohen, Mabel B. *Introduction to the interpersonal theory of psychiatry.* New York: Norton, 1953.

Hall, C., & Lindzey, G. *Theories of personality.* New York: Wiley, 1957.

Mullahy, P. *Oedipus: myth and complex.* New York: Grove, 1955.

Perry, Helen S. *Introduction to schizophrenia as a human process.* New York: Norton, 1961, by permission.

Sullivan, H. S. *The interpersonal theory of psychiatry.* New York: Norton, 1953 (London: Tavistock Publications Ltd.), by permission.

Sullivan, H. S. *Clinical studies in psychiatry.* New York: Norton, 1956, by permission.

Sullivan, H. S. *The fusion of psychiatry and social science.* New York: Norton, 1964, by permission.

Wyss, D. *Depth psychology: a critical history.* New York: Norton, 1966.

3

The Ego-Psychological
Approach: Edith Jacobson

In *Ego Psychology and the Problem of Adaptation* (1939), Heinz Hartmann wrote:

Psychoanalysis . . . started out with the study of pathology and of phenomena which are on the border of normal psychology and psychopathology. At that time its work centered on the id and the instinctual drives. But soon there arose new problems, concepts, formulations, and new needs for explanation, which reached beyond this narrower field towards a general theory of mental life. A decisive, and perhaps the most clearly delineated, step in this direction is our recent ego psychology . . . (1961, p. 4).

In this chapter we have a dual purpose. On the one hand, it would seem worthwhile to trace in some depth the development of the ego-psychology perspective. In so doing, we would like to specify carefully the manner in which this orientation represents a particular modification—some would say a realization—of Freud's original formulations. On the other hand, we would also like to present a representative ego-psychological theory of anxiety. Thus we shall eventually focus upon the work of Edith Jacobson. We begin, however, with an examination of history, that is, with the evolution of the ego-psychological perspective.

The reader may recall from our earlier discussion of the orthodox Freudian approach (see Chapter 1) that we characterized this version of psychoanalysis as an archeology. That is to say, we claimed that Freud attempted to uncover, specify, and trace the ontological as well as genetic foundations of all human living. As we noted in our exposition, the founder of psychoanalysis was guided in this enterprise by commitments to both Darwinian and natural scientific thought. Thus human reality, in all its aspects, was ultimately grasped as being reducible to physical, biologically given determinants. In other words, the source and essential agent of all human acts, relationships, and affects was, on a priori grounds, understood to be the animal—the instinctual or the id.

The ego, or that aspect of the person that is directly concerned with external objects and events, as well as with social and cultural values, was conceived in the manner of a veneer or facade. Further, it was said both to cover and yet to derive from the original animal wellspring. Thus, as a product of and mediator for the relations of the animal with repressive society, the ego was portrayed as developing and surviving primarily for the purpose of keeping peace. It had little, if any, true life of its own.

In a very real sense, the pivotal issue around which the whole ego-psychological movement has evolved is this characterization of the ego. Specifically, such thinkers as Anna Freud, Heinz Hartmann, Ernest Kris, Paul Federn, and Erik Erikson, to mention only a few, have been concerned with the status, derived or equioriginal, of the ego. They have carefully analyzed its functions or apparatuses and have questioned its reduction to unfolding instinctual processes. They have pointed to Freud's own later works in an effort to demonstrate that the founder of psychoanalysis had himself realized the problem. Hence, they insist that the direction of contemporary psychoanalytic ego-psychology is, in fact, a genuine realization of Freud's earlier formulations. However, before we sketch the nature of their argument, particularly as it is presented by Rapaport (1959), we need to ask: Why is the status of the ego so critical to psychoanalytic theory?

As has been suggested above, a psychoanalytic psychology that awards the status of ultimate reality exclusively to instinctual id processes must, of necessity, reduce and define all human phenomena in terms of these processes. Ego, or external world phenomena, on the other hand, can be accorded only a secondary, contingent, and/or derived status. Objects, events, and values of the external world come into existence and can be acknowledged only insofar as they relate in some manner to the instinctual strivings. Further, various forms of "mental health" and "psychopathology" must be conceived and articulated primarily as functions of instinctual gratification and/or frustration. Otherwise, they cannot be considered real.

That this position as described was, in fact, Freud's orientation may be clearly seen in the following excerpt from *Types of Onset of Neurosis* (1912):

The most obvious, the most easily discoverable, and the most intelligible precipitating cause of an onset of neurosis is to be seen in the external factor which may be described in general terms as [instinctual] frustration. The subject was healthy so long as his need for love was satisfied by a real object in the external world; he becomes neurotic as soon as this object is withdrawn from him without a substitute taking its place. Here happiness coincides with health [instinctual gratification], unhappiness with neurosis [instinctual frustration] (1958, Vol. XII, p. 231).

Inherent in this position is a rather fundamental problem. Instinctual gratification or satisfaction is a biological value. That is to say, the hypothesized instincts or drives are biological processes that allegedly seek certain states of affairs, i.e., discharges of energy through relationships with external objects. These states of affairs are values; they are certainly not preordained necessities. The instincts value certain kinds of relationships with certain types of objects. According to Freud, failure to attain these relationships results in neurosis. However, friendship, honesty, professional success, marriage, loyalty, courage, courteousness, personal achievement, and dignity are also values in human life. They, too, are states of affairs for which most people expend considerable energy. Are they to be grasped as nothing but disguised derivations, sublimations, and displacements of instinctual processes? Are these values, because they refer primarily to the ego and its relations with the world, to be understood as mere epiphenomena? Is "mental health" nothing but a question of sexual or aggressive instinctual gratification? This is the ultimate logical conclusion to which the orthodox analyst must come. As is commonly stated by such people, the purpose of psychoanalysis is to reduce or eliminate intrapsychic (ego, id, and superego) conflict, thereby facilitating gratification.

It is this position to which the ego psychologists take exception. Their argument, as we shall see, is that *both* id instinctual values and ego social values are equiprimordial. Only when their respective developments are grasped as equally real, equally constitutive of human life, can psychologists and psychiatrists fully understand the meaning of a given individual's life and situation.

According to Rapaport (1959) there are four phases in the development of psychoanalytic ego psychology. The first, which essentially coincided with Freud's prepsychoanalytic period, that is, prior to 1897, revealed an already existing concern with the ego. However, at that time, this structure sometimes stood for the "person," sometimes for the "self," and sometimes for "consciousness." Nonetheless, the founder of psychoanalysis apparently recognized, even at this point in his thinking, that man could not be completely understood solely in terms of an inherited instinctual endowment. There were also structures or processes that concerned themselves with defense against both internal and external dangers. Everything could not be reduced to types and vicissitudes of gratification maneuvers. Still, the precise nature of these defensive phenomena was left unexplored. Further, they, too, were frequently spoken of as being instinctual, i.e., "ego instincts."

During the second phase, which extended from 1897 to 1923, Freud presented his first systematic version of psychoanalytic thought. However, his major concern even at this time was still with the vicissitudes of the instincts, particularly with repression. As Rapaport states: "the question arose: what is the repressive (defensive) force? This question was answered by the assumption that repression (defense) is effected by ego instincts. . . . Thus in this phase of the theory even crucial ego functions were conceived of in terms of instinctual drives" (1959, p. 7). Still, the question of defense was sustained, even if it was tentatively answered in biological terms.

The most important events of the second phase, however, were to be found in the later conception of secondary process and the reality principle. The former referred to the fact that the ego, in its subservience to the id, had to sustain accurate and realistic relations with the external world. It had to be able to locate instinct-gratifying objects in the world as well as assess the feasibility of their procurement. The latter, that is, the reality principle, expressed the modus operandi of the ego—one that was fundamentally different from the pleasure-seeking id. Thus, even though the secondary processes were not grasped as autonomous, that is, as independent of instinctual strivings, they "provided a conception of reality relations and involved a concept of consciousness which was independent of the topographical conception simultaneously introduced" (Rapaport, 1959, p. 8). In other words, a foundation was laid for a subsequent ego-psychology that could orient itself toward the individual's involvements with external objects and events. Further, the idea of a reality principle and the notion of reality testing further specified the original conception of secondary process and sustained interest in the relationship of the mental apparatus to the external world.

Finally, with Freud's analysis of the process of repression (1915), the inadequacy of the topographical model was revealed. Distinct psychic functions could no longer be located in hypothetical containers called the conscious and the unconscious. The economic model seemed more feasible, and repression "proved to be a matter neither of topography nor of ego instincts" (Rapaport, 1959, p. 8). Instead, repression was now understood in terms of permanent, unconscious defense against instinctual drives. Thus at least some aspects of the ego had to be unconscious and the simple equations: ego equals consciousness, id equals unconsciousness, had to be modified.

The third phase in the development of psychoanalytic ego-psychology began with the publication of *The Ego and the Id* (1923). In this work the ego was characterized as a coherent organization of mental processes that were said to be constituted by identifications with abandoned instinctual objects. While the organization revolved primarily around the system perception-consciousness, it also included those unconscious structures and processes that were involved in defensive maneuvers. Further, for the first time the ego was accorded energies of its own, such energies being the neutralized transformations of instinctual drives. Thus, with this conception, the ego attained genetic roots, the system perception-consciousness. Its power was increasing and its functioning was not exhausted by mere perception in the service of the instincts.

Still, the ego was denied autonomy. Its development as well as its form was ultimately understood in terms of id, superego, and external world demands. Its perceptual functions were still primarily for the sake of the instincts, and its origin was still conceived to be the primordial id. Further, the fundamental task of the ego was seen to be that of a weak keeper of the peace —it was never free of its three harsh masters. Finally, although the ego was entrusted with the task of defense, no specific characterization of this project was undertaken.

Three years after the publication of *The Ego and the Id*, Freud radically altered his conception of defense and, thus, his portrayal of the ego. This change was, according to Rapaport, clearly expressed in the paper "Inhibitions, Symptoms and Anxiety" (1926).

Here Freud repudiated the conception that the ego is totally subservient to the id. . . . The ego autonomously initiates defense by the anxiety signal . . . , becomes increasingly able, in the course of development, to turn passively experienced anxiety into a form of active anticipation . . . , makes use of the pleasure principle in pursuing its own ends . . . , has a great variety of defenses at its disposal . . . , is ultimately concerned with reality relationships . . . , and therefore curbs instinctual drives when action prompted by them would lead into reality danger . . . (Rapaport, 1959, p. 10).

With this modification of the theory, Freud is claimed to have accomplished the following: (1) the problem of the individual's relations with external reality is again made central to the theory; (2) the relations of instinctual drives to external reality is thematized; and (3) the role of the ego is now grasped as primarily adaptive, that is, its major function is to mediate, according to its own principles of functioning, between the instinctual drives on the one hand, and external reality on the other. Nonetheless, with all this the ego still lacked the prestige of autonomy. Although there were hints and suggestions of epigenesis or independent ego development, no definitive characterization was to be found.

Still, Rapaport insists that a solid foundation had been laid. The possibility of explicating a thorough reality and object-relations psychology within the general framework of Freudian theory had emerged. The stage was set for the fourth phase, beginning with the writings of Hartmann, Kris, Lowenstein, and Erikson. As far as others, such as Horney, Kardiner, and Sullivan were concerned, the old foundations were still inadequate. Rapaport acknowledges these workers' contributions, but at the same time, chides them for having left the fold, for having discarded the basic framework of Freudian psychoanalysis.

Because Hartmann's conceptualization of the ego and its functions is generally acknowledged to be the articulated foundation of subsequent psychoanalytic ego-psychologies, it might be useful to outline the major tenets of his theory. First and foremost, the ego is not grasped as developing out of the id.

Rather, both are understood as differentiating from a common matrix—the earliest undifferentiated state of psychic development. It is this step that marks the beginnings of postnatal existence. Further, the apparatuses of motility, perception, and memory, which will eventually become the ego's major means of control and executive functioning, are said to exist already in the undifferentiated state. They are equiprimordial with the instinctual drives and herald the equioriginality of the ego.

The existence of these apparatuses as equiprimordial with the instinctual drives Hartmann attributed to evolutionary processes, e.g., natural selection. In other words, it was claimed that this was nature's means of phylogenetically guaranteeing a coordination between the organism's instinctual endowment and its probable environment.

Second, Hartmann offered a conceptual explanation for the autonomy of other ego functions, even those defensive structures originally born of conflict with either the instinctual drives or with external reality. In so doing, he stressed the adaptive character of all ego processes and "laid the foundation for the psychoanalytic concept and theory of adaptation" (Rapaport, 1959, p. 13). Further, through this conceptual innovation, Hartmann "outlined the first generalized theory of reality relations in psychoanalytic ego psychology" (Rapaport, 1959, p. 13).

Finally, with regard to the question of the origins of ego energies, Hartmann (1950, 1955) and Kris (1950, 1955) conceived of hypothetical means through which the ego could neutralize and subsequently appropriate libidinal and/or aggressive instinctual energies. Thus for the first time, a conception of autonomous, adaptive, reality-oriented ego development was articulated, at least in its essential outline. It remained for Erikson (1937, 1950, 1956) to elaborate upon an epigenetic theory of ego development, a theory of reality relationships, and especially a psychosocial theory of development.

We have already spoken of one fundamental problem that was inherent in the orthodox psychoanalytic position, i.e., the necessity of reducing all social and personal values to biological ones. With the establishment of the autonomous, concurrently unfolding ego, contemporary ego-psychology overcame this difficulty, at least to some extent. The structures and processes of the ego, as well as their relations with external reality, no longer required translation or interpretation to a level of instinctual meaning. They were real in themselves—at least, equally as real as the hypothesized instinctual strivings.

But, as we shall now examine, there was an even more thorny issue in the original psychoanalytic formulation. If, as Freud claimed, the ultimate source and meaning of human reality was instinctual—i.e., if all objects, relations, and events were really nothing more than manifestations of instinctual strivings, and if these strivings were always unconscious—then all human experience had to be suspect. Reasons were rationalizations; objects and events were merely disguised, displaced, and/or sublimated expressions of libidinal or aggressive impulses. In other words, reality as we experience it is a convenient illusion, a product of assorted defense mechanisms. Even the analyst himself could never be sure that his thoughts and perceptions were not really the compromise production of his own psyche. To put the matter most succinctly, the original orthodox Freudian psychoanalysis expressed a theoretical solipsism. There could never be any guarantee as to the reality of an individual's experience, no matter how many years of analysis he had undergone.

With the establishment of a theory of reality relations, with the emancipation of the ego and its functions from alleged underlying instinctual meanings, it would appear that ego-psychology had, in fact, overcome the solipsistic tendencies of Freud's formulations. Still, as we shall comment upon after presenting Jacobson's theoretical conceptions, some difficulties remain.

As a contemporary representative of the fourth phase in the history of psychoanalytic ego-psychology, Edith Jacobson has been concerned with the differentiation and diversification of the ego through reality relations. Further, within this general area, one of her major interests has been the manner in which ego development facilitates and/or hinders the dynamics of affective growth and expression. In this section of the chapter, we shall attempt to sketch Jacobson's theory of affects and, specifically, her interpretation of anxiety.

Consistent with the general orientation of contemporary psychoanalytic ego-psychology, Jacobson's discussion of affective phenomena is couched almost exclusively in terms of the economic and structural points of view (see Chapter 1, p. 5). However, while she accepts the usual assumption of an ultimate energy substructure for all psychic processes, that is, that mental phenomena are alleged to be expressions of bound or discharged energy, she departs from Freud's emphasis on the primordiality of the libidinal and aggressive instinctual forces. Further, she modifies to a considerable extent the original conceptions of psychic homeostatic functioning and the pleasure principle. Therefore, she is compelled to reinterpret the meanings of such phenomena as affect, pleasure, and unpleasure.

With regard to the qualitative characteristics of the original instinctual endowment, Jacobson assumes with Hartmann that at the beginning of life, instinctual energy is in an undifferentiated state; it is neither libidinal nor aggressive. Only later do these two types of "psychic drive" differentiate, emerge, and develop. Further, with this differentiation, various preferred discharge pathways gradually make their appearance.

If one asks about the factors that are involved in the transformation of undifferentiated instinctual energy into libidinal and aggressive drives, Jacobson replies that the process is psychobiologically determined. In other words, there is said to be a biologically given predisposition for this transformation, but, its actual occurrence, as well as related issues of strength and quantity, depend upon the types of internal and external stimulation to which the mental apparatus is exposed. Moreover, in the course of structural differentiation, that is, in the course of id, ego, and superego genesis, the previously noted libidinal and aggressive drives undergo a process of fusion and partial neutralization. The resulting neutralized energies become invested in the systems ego and superego, thereby guaranteeing their relative autonomy from the id.

In this view, which conceptualizes id instinctual unfolding and ego development as concurrent and equiprimordial, anxiety is understood as both a signal and as an adaptive, equilibrium-seeking phenomenon. It can function as a signal in that the ego uses it to mobilize defenses against instinctual promptings for which it is unprepared. It can function as an adaptive, equilibrium-seeking phenomenon in that its occurrence facilitates the development of new discharge pathways and new means of ego control. An example that demonstrates these possibilities is cited by Jacobson. When the early adolescent is faced with genital promptings, the ego, which is still concerned with solidifying previous achievements, responds with signal anxiety. It mobilizes defenses against these new urges in an effort at delaying their uncontrolled expression. Later, when faced with these same instinctual promptings, the mature ego tends not to be overwhelmed and anxiety is not provoked. Hence, the developmentally earlier response of anxiety can be grasped as a function of the ego's inability to reinstate previous means of discharge. Eventually, when it has found new techniques of control and new avenues of discharge—ones that lead to optimal instinctual as well as emotional freedom—it no longer experiences anxiety in the face of these drives.

As has already been suggested, Jacobson retains the Freudian commitment to the economic and structural points of view. However, she abandons the orthodox psychoanalytic conception of the mental apparatus as continually striving to achieve a state of minimal, if not negligible, excitation. Although she understands the early organism's psychoeconomic state as one that is characterized by a low level of tension and by a generally diffuse dispersion of undifferentiated energy, her model of the mature psychic apparatus is radically different from Freud's closed-energy system.

A brief review may be helpful here. In the original Freudian formulation, the whole mental apparatus was alleged to be constantly seeking states of minimal excitation. This constituted homeostatic equilibrium and was, supposedly, preferred by the organism. The pleasure principle referred to the tendency of the psyche as a whole and the id instincts in particular to discharge increases in tension level as soon as possible, regardless of the consequences. Thus the notion of the pleasure principle followed directly from the original conception of homeostasis. The reality principle, on the other hand, referred to the qualifying tendency, characteristic of the ego, to delay indiscriminate energy discharge, especially if this activity would prove to be dangerous to the organism. Nonetheless, the ego with its reality principle functioned in the long-term service of the pleasure principle and the principle of homeostasis. That is to say, the ego required delay only insofar as it was deemed necessary for the organism's safety—and even then it continually searched for opportunities to facilitate discharge eventually. If permanent delay was required, then pain as well as lack of gratification were the consequences.

Jacobson, instead of accepting these principles that equated homeostasis with minimal tension and pleasure with the process of tension reduction, proposes a "preferred state" thesis. In this view, homeostasis involves a medium or optimal level of tension equilibrium. This condition, not one of negligible excitation, is claimed to be the organism's preferred state. Further, pleasure is not simply a matter of tension reduction or, for that matter, tension arousal. Rather, it involves actions that express the individual's preference for a particular tension-discharge pattern, for particular modes of energy discharge. Thus cycles of pleasure can occur through alternate experiences of excitement and relief, corresponding to the shifting biological states of the individual. Pleasure can be attached to swings on either side of the optimal, preferred level of organismic tension. The only requirement is that discharge processes can utilize selected, preferred pathways.

We may now ask: To what, concretely, does the pleasure principle refer? Jacobson's answer is that the specific work of the pleasure principle is to enforce the return of the tension pendulum to a medium line, to the organism's optimal and preferred level of general excitation. Further, this is to be accomplished through preferred discharge pathways. Thus, we may specify the relationship of pleasure to the pleasure principle. The former refers to an affect that accompanies discharge through a particular preferred pattern, i.e., through particular ways of responding to some situation. The latter refers to the general tendency of the organism to maintain a medium, optimal level of excitation through the use of preferred discharge pathways.

A moment's reflection reveals the new meaning of the reality principle. The concept now refers to the ego's need to sustain the organism's homeostasis, its optimal level of excitation, regardless of whether preferred discharge pathways are available. In other words, the necessity of maintaining homeostasis takes priority over questions of pleasure. If preferred pathways are not present or utilizable, then the ego, in the service of organismic equilibrium, will use other channels of discharge—behaviors that will not necessarily be accompanied by pleasurable affect.

In an effort to exemplify her conceptions, Jacobson cites the experiences and behaviors involved in sexual foreplay. Here, initial increases in tension level as a result of necking and petting can be experienced as pleasurable, especially if the individual is handling his sexual promptings in a manner that he himself prefers. Alternatively, increases in tension level can be experienced as unpleasant if the individual is, for example, necking but not petting. (We are assuming, of course, that he would prefer to pet, but for some reason cannot.)

In either case, the desire for change can arise. With the first, that is, with the individual who is necking and petting, sexual intercourse and orgasm as a preferred means of tension discharge and relief from heightened excitation could be experienced as pleasurable. With the second, a change in foreplay that involved both preferred modes of discharge as well as still higher levels of excitation could also be experienced as pleasurable. To put the matter most succinctly, then, pleasure is not merely a question of tension arousal and of tension reduction. Rather, it is a matter of preferred modes of behavior, of preferred patterns of energy discharge, and of the maintenance of a general organismic equilibrium.

Consistent with the line of reasoning just described, Jacobson argues that affects in general cannot be defined or distinguished by their tensional qualities. Many affects are associated with normal ego functioning and their tensional qualities do not automatically make them pleasant or unpleasant, disruptive or disturbing. Still less are affects necessarily the result of conflict. Thus direct instinctual discharge as well as defensive tactics may be accompanied by affect.

Although all affects both develop in and are expressed by the ego, Jacobson claims that some structural differentiation is necessary as well as valid. In other words, as affects cannot be distinguished in terms of their tensional qualities and as all affects are not, by definition, disruptive or unpleasant, it is important to specify their respective bases. That is to say, it is important to understand them as functions of the ego's relations with the id, the superego, and the external world. On this point, Jacobson asserts the following:

one of their [the affects'] qualitative determinants must be the site of the underlying energetic tension by which they have been induced and which may arise anywhere within the psychic organization (1953, p. 46).

With this as her working assumption, Jacobson goes on to distinguish:

1. Simple and compound affects arising from *intrasystemic* tensions:
   (a) Affects representing the instinctual drives proper—those that arise directly from tension in the id, e.g., sex, excitement, and rage.
   (b) Affects developing directly from tensions in the ego, e.g., reality fear, physical pain, complexes of more enduring feelings and feeling attitudes—objects of love and hate.
2. Simple and compound affects induced by *intersystemic* tensions:
   (a) Affects induced by tensions between the ego and the id, e.g., fear of id, anxiety, complexes of disgust, shame, and pity.
   (b) Affects induced by tensions between the ego and the superego, e.g., guilt feelings, depression.

Comparing her structural model with the one proposed by Rapaport, Jacobson claims that hers has the advantage of including pleasurable affects.

These, she insists, Rapaport must ignore because he conceptualizes affect as libido dammed up by repression. Further, she regards his theory, as well as others that suggest that affects are modes of energy discharge under adverse conditions, as not only inadequate but also dangerous. For Jacobson, affects do not arise from dammed-up psychic energy. Instead, they correspond to processes of discharge, to dynamic processes in the organism, to the flux of mobile psychic energy released, to the rise and fall of the organism's tension level, and to the amounts of excitation that move the general tension level above or below the organism's optimal medium.

If we keep in mind the formulations described earlier, particularly those regarding pleasure, the pleasure principle, and the reality principle, we may grasp some of the specifics of Jacobson's conception of anxiety. In so doing, we should not be surprised to find that this theorist's modified structural and economic model ultimately determines and limits what she can posit about this affect. She begins with a general characterization reminiscent of the orthodox Freudian view. Thus anxiety is said to develop in the system ego. As such, it is understood to be a specific state of unpleasure induced by intersystemic tensions—those between the ego and the id. Further, anxiety is seen as the motor of repression.

While Jacobson acknowledges that later, postinfantile anxiety functions for the most part as a signal for the ego, she insists that it is also a discharge phenomenon. In this regard, it is not confined to infancy, during which period excessive quantities of excitation are rather automatically discharged in the service of the newborn's psycho-organismic equilibrium. It also occurs in later life when the ego, operating in terms of the reality principle, requires a return to the medium, optimal level of general excitation. And this requirement is instituted despite the fact that the preferred discharge pathways, preferred behaviors, are unavailable or are as yet undeveloped. Thus anxiety can accompany later discharges of tension through nonpreferred pathways in the service of homeostasis. It is in these types of situations that anxiety can become libidinized, that is, used as an auxilliary outlet for sexual energy.

With regard to the signal function of anxiety, Jacobson understands this affect as having a special role in the individual's search for adjustment *with* gratification. In general, anxiety communicates to the ego that a state of danger either exists or is impending. If one asks about the specific nature of this danger, an economically couched description of three general types is given. The first is that which was originally depicted by Freud when he himself spoke of the signal function of anxiety. It is the danger of the ego being overwhelmed with unmastered and undischargeable quantities of excitation. It is the problem that the ego faces when it has not developed preferred or even satisfactory discharge pathways for certain types of instinctual promptings. Finally, it is in this situation that the ego responds with a mobilization of its defenses, thereby forestalling disorganization and potentially impulsive discharge.

The second type of peril that the ego utilizes as an anxiety signal occurs when the level of organismic excitation is too low. In this case the problem is not one of being overwhelmed or disorganized. Rather, it is the danger that the ego experiences as either an internal deadening or a loss of contact with external reality. In either event, the task is not to mobilize more defenses, but, on the contrary, to loosen up—to find new pathways for discharge and contact.

Finally, the third type of danger that can function as an anxiety signal for the ego occurs when a tension-discharge pattern is not allowed to take its preferred course. In such a situation, the individual experiences anxiety over his inability to achieve pleasure, to behave in ways that are satisfying to him. Further, this inability is somehow inexplicable, e.g., he doesn't understand why he can't handle his promptings in a gratifying manner. The reader may have already surmised that such a situation occurs when the ego is in conflict with itself, i.e., when it has mutually incompatible interests. At such times, a reappraisal of its values are necessary.

It should be evident that these two latter conceptions of signal anxiety are original with Jacobson. They would not have been possible within the orthodox Freudian framework because excessively low levels of excitation were alleged to be desirable and because no consideration was given to preferred discharge pathways. Thus, for Jacobson, anxiety is grasped primarily as an adaptive phenomenon, one that the ego utilizes in its continuing development and differentiation. While anxiety means danger to the ego, it also provides an opportunity for the development of new and more appropriate discharge pathways, i.e., new behaviors.

Before evaluating Jacobson's thought, let us briefly summarize her conception. For her, anxiety is both a structural and economic phenomenon. It is that affect which emerges when there are intersystemic tensional problems between the ego and the id, or when the ego is forced, through the reality principle, to discharge excessive excitation through nonpreferred pathways. Anxiety is primarily a signal, one which the ego utilizes to sustain and further adaptation. Finally, anxiety is a discharge phenomenon that permits it to be easily libidinized or fused with other affects.

Evaluation and Comments

As was noted in the first section of this chapter, Jacobson and the other ego-psychologists have overcome two of the most serious deficiencies of the orthodox Freudian framework. There is no longer a reduction of ego and external world values to inner, unconscious, instinctual ones. Further, external world objects and events and relations are given the same ontological status as instinctual strivings. They are grasped as equally real and the danger of solipsism seems to be avoided.

In her own thinking, Jacobson has also overcome the general psychoanalytic—both id- and ego-oriented—prejudice that limits understanding of affective phenomena primarily to terms of conflict and disruption. For Jacobson, affects accompany all psychic energy processes. They are sometimes pleasurable, sometimes unpleasurable, but always adaptive.

Finally, Jacobson's energy model, which underlies her theory of affects, represents a decisive improvement over the Freudian closed-energy system. Her conception allows the organism to seek tension, to expand tension tolerance, and to enjoy and benefit from what it once experienced as intolerable, or, at least, unpleasurable. She depicts and speaks of an ongoing organism, one which gradually becomes aware of both the external world and the self. Further, her conceptualized psychic system seems to be one that is genuinely capable of new levels of integration.

There are still two major criticisms that this writer should like to make regarding Jacobson's theory. First and foremost, Jacobson either ignores (or more probably presupposes) the experienced meaning of anxiety. In any case, it is never made explicit, except to say that it is an affect that functions as a signal. In a very real sense, then, Jacobson's conceptual framework dictates to the phenomenon; it decides in advance what it can be.

The second criticism is not only directed at Jacobson. It applies to the whole ego-psychological perspective. For these thinkers, the reality of the concepts ego, id, and superego is taken for granted, as is the assumption of an "external world" and underlying energies. Thus affect becomes the conscious, perceived accompaniment of the flux of energy processes. While adaptation does not mean a return to some static state, it still implies a physicalistic, tension equilibrium. While the organism is grasped as capable of seeking tension and integrating it, and while the organism is dynamic, it is still mechanical. The energy is still the underlying reality and man is ultimately *Homo natura*.

REFERENCES

Erikson, E. H. Configurations in play—clinical notes. *Psychoanalytic Quarterly*, 1937, 6, 139–214.

Erikson, E. H. *Childhood and Society*. New York: Norton, 1950.

Erikson, E. H. The problem of ego identity. *Journal of the American Psychoanalytic Association*, 1956, 4, 56–121.

Freud, S. Types of onset of neurosis (quoted text written in 1912). In the *Standard edition of the complete works of Sigmund Freud*. (Trans. by James Strachey). London: Hogarth, 1958, vol. XII, pp. 231–238 (New York: Basic Books).

Freud, S. Inhibitions, symptoms and anxiety (quoted text written in 1926). In the *Standard edition of the complete works of Sigmund Freud*. (Trans. by

James Strachey). London: Hogarth, 1959, vol. XX, pp. 77–175.

Freud, S. *The ego and the id* (quoted text written in 1923). In the *Standard edition of the complete works of Sigmund Freud.* (Trans. by James Strachey). London: Hogarth, 1961, vol. XIX, pp. 12–66.

Hartmann, H. Comments on the psychoanalytic theory of the ego. *The Psychoanalytic Study of the Child,* 1950, *5,* 74–96. New York: International Universities Press.

Hartmann, H. Notes on the theory of sublimation. *The Psychoanalytic Study of the Child,* 1955, *10,* 9–29. New York: International Universities Press.

Hartmann, H. *Ego Psychology and the Problem of Adaptation* (Trans. by David Rapaport). New York: International Universities Press, 1961.

Kris, E. On preconscious mental processes. *Psychoanalytic Quarterly,* 1950, *19,* 540–560.

Kris, E. Neutralization and sublimation: observations on young children. *The Psychoanalytic Study of the Child,* 1955, *10,* 30–46. New York: International Universities Press.

Jacobson, E. The affects and their pleasure-unpleasure qualities in relation to the psychic discharge processes. In Rudolph M. Lowenstein, ed. *Drives, affects, and behavior.* New York: International Universities Press, 1953.

Jacobson, E. *The self and the object world.* New York: International Universities Press, 1964.

Rapaport, D. Introduction. In E. Erikson, *Identity and the life cycle.* Psychological Issues, Monograph 1, Vol. 1, No. 1, New York: International Universities Press, 1959, by permission.

4

The Physiological Approaches

In the opening paragraphs of a chapter entitled, "The Physiology of Anxiety," Levitt (1967) immediately acknowledges that "few people need experimental investigation or a learned text to be aware that the experience of a strong emotion like anxiety, anger, or sexual excitement has marked physiological accompaniments" (1967, p. 91). The man on the street accepts the pounding of his heart, the sweating of his hands, and the dryness of his mouth as constitutive, that is, as natural components of his anxious condition. However, the scientist, given his particular purview, finds these phenomena to be somewhat enigmatic. As Levitt states, the scientist wonders "Why do these emotional states have physiological concomitants? . . . Does the pattern of physiological reaction differ among emotional states; can these patterns be used to differentiate any emotions?" (1967, p. 91).

In order for Levitt and others to raise these questions, they must have already accepted certain metaphysical assumptions concerning the nature of man. Unfortunately, these ideas are rarely made explicit. Nonetheless, if we are to grasp the meaning of the physiological approaches to anxiety, they must be clarified and understood. Only in this way can we adequately make sense of and fully appreciate the investigations of and speculations about bodily processes in affective states.

Ultimately, there are three sources of data for the physiologically oriented researcher and/or theoretician. The first is the subject's report—if he or it can make one—of his own feeling state. This report may be given in direct response to questioning, or it may be inferred from responses to such measuring instruments as the Taylor Manifest Anxiety Scale. A second source is the experimenter's observations of physiological changes in his subjects. This is accomplished through the use of a vast and ingenious array of instruments and procedures that are designed to measure such phenomena as heart rate, cardiac output, respiration rate, frontalis muscle tension, palmar conductance, salivary output, finger temperature, blood-sugar level, endocrine activity, and the like. Finally, to such sources as have been noted, we can add the experimenter's perceptions and evaluations of the stimuli or stimulus conditions to which his subjects are allegedly responding. In other words, the experimenter, because of his presumed objectivity (Bergmann and Spence, 1944), decides what it is in the situation that is arousing the emotional reaction of his subjects.

When we speak of making explicit the metaphysical foundations of the physiological approaches to anxiety, we are addressing ourselves to those implicit principles that guide the manner in which these three sources of data are usually questioned, grasped, and related. In order for Levitt and other natural scientists to ask why emotional states have physiological concomitants, they must have already accepted, albeit silently, a mind- or experience-body split. In our discussion of the learning-theory approach to anxiety, we will trace this philosophical stance back to the thinking of René Descartes. Thus, in this chapter, it should be sufficient to point out that the physiological approaches to emotion locate the specific affective state in the experiential realm, the *res cogitans*, the mind. The bodily realm, which is assumed to be part of the external, corporeal, quantitative world, the *res extensa*, is grasped as independent of the mind. Still, observation contradicts this assumed division; at least, it demonstrates that experiential phenomena are, in fact, accompanied by bodily processes. How can this be so if the two are truly independent? This is the question that puzzles the scientist. This is the inquiry with which Levitt introduces his discussion of the physiology of anxiety.

If we are to understand the answers that various natural scientists have given to this question, we must first grasp the conceptions of mind and body with which these investigators have worked. For at least three centuries, the psyche or mind has been understood to be a sort of ethereal, purely private realm. It was—and is, if you will—conceived of as being a container, the essential contents of which are ideas. Whether these contents are objective, that is, whether they accurately reflect "reality," has always been a subject of debate. In general, however, it has usually been maintained that ideas are continuously vulnerable to contamination. The body, on the other hand, has consistently been understood to be a mechanism, or, as a conglomeration of mechanisms. As such, it has been described in terms of analogies to machines, steam engines, hydraulic systems, even computers. The most definitive presentation of these two conceptions has been given by Descartes and, we submit, it is because of the uncritical acceptance of these formulations that the natural scientist is faced with such questions as we have noted.

Rather than reflect upon and alter the unquestioned mechanistic conception of body, or the ethereal, purely private portrayal of mind, the contemporary scientist of nature does one of three things: (1) he may accept the observed concomitance of mental and physical processes as a kind of unexplained parallelism; (2) he may reject their assumed independence and adopt an interactionist position; or (3) he may claim an epiphenomenal orientation. In the case of the first, no assertion is made as to the more fundamental reality of either the mental or the physical events. The natural scientist, however, chooses to focus upon the physiological phenomena because he believes them to be more amenable to scientific procedure and constructs. Thus such phrases as "the physiological correlates of" follow quite logically. Further, in keeping with his assumption of a deterministic universe, the scientist imposes a causal framework upon the various sources of his data. The stimulus conditions that he, the experimenter, believes to be significant in the situation are grasped as the causes of the subject's emotional reactions, both physiologically and psychologically. Finally, he sometimes extends the causal chain and asserts that the stimulus conditions initially arouse specific central nervous system structures, which, in turn, provoke concurrent physiological and psychological reactions.

In the case of the interactionist position, the theoretician grants the reality of both the physiological and psychological phenomena, but denies their independence. Thus the stimulus conditions provoke both physiological and psychological reactions that then interact. The result of this interaction is the phenomenon to be explained. As we shall see, however, the final product, if it is some state like an emotion, is still understood as existing only on the psychological level.

Finally, in the case of the epiphenomenal orientation, the theoretician expands the causal chain, denies the independence of the physiological and psychological realms, and insists that the latter is "nothing but" an incomplete shadow or reflection of the former. Hence, the external stimulus conditions are grasped as the cause of a series of physiological reactions that, in turn, both cause and are vaguely mirrored by the experiential or psychological state. Compared with the more real events that occur within the body, grasped as a physiological mechanism, the experienced emotions are epiphenomena, essentially extrinsic to the major focus of the scientific enterprise.

Regardless of which metaphysical stance the theoretician takes, the procedural principles that essentially constitute the physiological approach may be summarized as follows. First, the emotional state, in this case anxiety, is conceptualized as a psychological construct, i.e., it belongs to the experiential realm and its scientific existence must be grounded in physical, quantitative phenomena. Second, as a construct, anxiety is understood to be an effect, the ultimate cause of which is to be found in the stimulus conditions of the environment, the external world. Mediating between this cause-effect relationship and essentially foundational to it are the various physiological processes and mechanisms of the body. Thus we can understand the sense of such statements as "the neurophysiological bases of." Finally, it is the natural scientist's task to delineate those causally conceived, psychophysical relations that constitute the scientific meaning of anxiety. This means that he is concerned with clarifying the sequences of and correlations between external stimulation, physiological processes, and affective experience.

One of the earliest attempts at a precise formulation of these sequences and correlations was advanced by William James and Carl Lange in the late 1880s. Their conception, which came to be known as the James-Lange theory, stated that "the bodily changes follow directly the perception of the exciting fact, and . . . our feeling of the same changes as they occur is the emotion" (James, 1890, p. 449). In other words, experience of both visible (sweating, crying, etc.) and sensible (pounding heart, rapid breathing, etc.) bodily phenomena were said to be synonymous with emotion. For James and Lange, experienced physiological phenomena do not cause emotion—nor are they the results thereof. Rather, visible and sensible bodily changes make possible and are the stuff of emotional experience.

Inherent in this theoretical formulation are a number of critical assumptions. First, in equating the experience of bodily change with emotional experience, James and Lange implied that different emotions are constituted by the perception of recognizably different bodily states. This would suggest that through the manipulation of such states, one should, at least theoretically, be able to manipulate the affective experience. Second, it is assumed that autonomic reactivity is essential for emotional experience. This is so because the bodily changes of which James and Lange speak are, in fact, controlled by the autonomic nervous system. Third, it is claimed that the perception of the exciting fact leads only to autonomic arousal and that this, in turn, makes possible the visible and sensible changes that constitute the stuff of the emotional experience. As we shall see, each of these assumptions has become questionable in the light of subsequent research. Before presenting this material, however, we should like to note that the James-Lange theory is essentially an interactionist one. The exciting fact or external stimulus causes the bodily changes, which, when perceived by the mind or psyche, make possible emotional experience. We would also like to suggest that, in fact, the James-Lange theory was not a conception of emotions, but, rather, was a formulation regarding the process by which individuals become aware of their already being emotionally involved in some situation. More of that later.

By demonstrating that animals surgically deprived of all autonomic reactivity were still capable of manifesting emotional behavior, Canon (1927, 1929) cast significant doubt upon the James-Lange theory. Specifically, Canon and Bard showed that affective experiencing and the behavior that clearly expressed its occurrence were not directly a function of autonomically induced bodily changes. As Schachter (1964) states in his review of these theories:

research, on the whole, provided little support for a purely visceral formulation of emotion, and led Canon to his brilliant and devastating critique of the James-Lange theory . . . a critique based upon these points:

1. The total separation of the viscera from the central nervous system does not alter emotional behavior.
2. The same visceral changes occur in very different emotional states and in non-emotional states.
3. The viscera are relatively insensitive structures.
4. Visceral changes are too slow to be a source of emotional feeling.
5. The artificial induction of visceral changes that are typical of strong emotions do not produce the emotions (1964, pp. 138–139).

As we shall soon see, these facts led Schachter and others to formulate an alternative interactionist conception of emotion. Canon and Bard, however, after rejecting the James-Lange theory, offered their own alternative. They suggested that both affective experience and autonomic reactivity arise concurrently (the parallelist position). That is to say, the two are relatively independent of each other; they are not causally or interactively related. Further, both types of phenomena are said to be mediated by particular lower brain centers—specifically, the thalamus and the hypothalamus. Thus in terms of the procedural principles outlined earlier in this chapter, the Canon and Bard theory asserts that anxiety and, for that matter, all emotions, are the effects of stimulus conditions originating in the environment and mediated through specific structures of the central nervous system.

Current attempts to further clarify and specify the relations of external stimulation, physiological processes, and affective experience have focused upon particular areas or structures of the central nervous system, the process of general bodily arousal and its relation to cognitive or experiential factors, particular patterns of bodily change believed to be expressive of anxiety, and endocrinological factors involved in the activation of these expressive features. We will present a partial summary of the research findings and speculations in each of these areas.

With regard to the particular areas or structures of the central nervous system involved in the occurrence of anxiety, research has demonstrated that, aside from the thalamus and hypothalamus, an organization of the brain composed primarily of paleocortex and known as the limbic system is incontrovertibly integral to the experience of pain or pleasure. By implanting electrodes directly into the brains of living animals and people, Olds and Milner (1954), Brady (1958), Heath (1964), and Bishop et al. (1964) have shown that a temporary "immunization" to pain and fear is possible when the limbic system areas are stimulated. Because, for experimental purposes, fear is equated with anxiety, and because fear is assumed to be a response to actual or anticipated pain, it is argued that this system of the brain is, in fact, functionally involved in the occurrence of anxiety.

Another area of the brain, the reticular formation, which is thought to be intimately related to the level of cortical functioning, was originally claimed by Lindsley (1951) to be significant for any theory of emotion. In essence, he hypothesized that the greater the level of cortical activity, the greater the state of emotional arousal. Subsequently, Malmo (1957) proposed that this system —now usually referred to as the reticular activating system (RAS)—controls the possibility of the experience of anxiety. He suggests that this particular affective experience "is a result of a weakening of the inhibitory aspect of the RAS. This permits too many facilitative impulses to be discharged in the cortex, leading to an arousal level beyond the optimal" (Malmo, 1967, p. 96). Just why the inhibitory functioning of the RAS should become weakened is not clear, although there is some suggestion that this may be caused either by constitutional factors or by periods of prolonged overstimulation. The speculative reader may, at this point, see an analogy between this conception of anxiety and that of Freud, especially from the latter's economic perspective. In the theories of the founder of psychoanalysis, the ego experiences anxiety when it cannot inhibit and is therefore overwhelmed with stimulation from either the id or the external world.

Related to and somewhat consistent with the RAS formulation is the theory of general arousal. This position, as propounded by Duffy (1941), Malmo (1959), Schachter and Wheeler (1962), Schachter and Singer (1962), Levi (1963), Korchin (1964), and Schachter (1964), holds that physiological arousal is emotionally nonspecific and that there are no particular physiological patterns correlative to particular emotional states. Rather: "the physiological reaction is simply a general arousal or activation. The subjective experience of a specific emotion exists solely on the cognitive or psychological level" (Levitt, 1967, p. 100). To put the matter more precisely, it is claimed that while the level of bodily arousal corresponds to the degree of emotionality being experienced, the particular direction of that arousal—that is, the particular emotion being experienced—is a function of the perceptual, cognitive activity of the subject. Thus two people could be equally aroused, but one could be experiencing anger while the other is feeling joy. Here, then, is a concrete example of an interactionist theory. Further, because it is more explicitly formulated than the others, we shall attempt to examine it in detail. The reader should note, however, that when these theorists speak of bodily arousal, they conceive of the body as a kind of engine that can function at different levels of RPM. Levels of bodily arousal have only quantitative meaning.

In any event, the substance of this theory is clearly expressed in the following excerpt:

Given such a state of arousal, it is suggested that one labels, interprets, and identifies this state in terms of the characteristics of the precipitating situation and one's apperceptive mass. This suggests, then, that an emotional state may be considered a function of a state of physiological arousal. . . . The cognition, in a sense, exerts a steering function. Cognitions arising from the immediate situation as interpreted by past experience, provide the framework within which one understands and labels one's feelings. It is the cognition which determines whether the state of physiological arousal will be labelled "anger," "joy," or whatever (Schachter, 1964, p. 139).

An example of how this theory actually applies to a concrete situation is also given by Schachter.

Imagine a man walking alone down a dark alley when a figure with a gun suddenly appears. The perception-cognition "figure with gun" in some fashion initiates a state of physiological arousal; this state of arousal is interpreted in terms of knowledge about dark alleys and guns, and the state of arousal is labelled "fear" (1964, p. 140).

Before we present Schachter's explicit formulation of the process through which the cognitive and arousal components interact, we might raise several questions about his example. Why is it necessary to assume that the perception-cognition "figure with gun" initiates "in some fashion" only a state of physiological arousal? Why couldn't it be the case that this perception-cognition immediately gives rise to the meaning "My God, I'm being robbed," which then functions as the ground for both the explicit experience of fear and the bodily manifestations of that experience? Or, alternatively, why is the body's reaction only quantitative, only a question of degree of arousal? Why can't the body react qualitatively, with fear, a reaction that may or may not be labeled subsequently? Is it possible that Schachter's commitment to a view of the body as mechanistic and foundational to experience interferes with his observations and formulations about affective sequences? We shall elaborate upon this alternative in the chapters that attempt an integration of the theories.

According to Schachter, the interaction of cognitive and physiological arousal components of emotion can be conceptualized as follows:

1. Given a state of physiological arousal for which an individual has no immediate explanation, he will "label" this state and describe his feelings in terms of the cognitions available to him. To the extent that cognitive factors are potent determiners of emotional states, one might anticipate that precisely the same state of physiological arousal would be labelled "joy" or "fury" or any of a great number of emotional labels, depending on the cognitive aspects of the situation (1964, p. 142).

2. Given a state of physiological arousal for which an individual has a completely appropriate explanation (e.g., "I feel this way because I have just received an injection of adrenalin"), no evaluative needs will arise and the individual is unlikely to label his feelings in terms of alternative cognitions available. Finally, consider a condition in which emotion-inducing cognitions are present but there is no state of physiological arousal. For example, an individual might be completely aware that he is in great danger but for some reason (drug or surgical) might remain in a state of physiological quiescence. [The] formulation of emotion as a joint function of a state of physiological arousal and appropriate cognition

would . . . suggest that he does not [feel any emotion]. This . . . leads to my final proposition (1964, p. 142).

3. Given the same cognitive circumstances, the individual will react emotionally or describe his feelings as emotions only to the extent that he experiences a state of physiological arousal (1964, p. 142). One final point. If it is correct that the labels attached to feeling states are cognitively, situationally, or socially determined, then it is clearly possible that an uncommon or inappropriate label can be attached to a feeling state. Where such is the case, we may anticipate bizarre and pathological behavior (1964, p. 170).

As has been suggested earlier, a number of investigators have endeavored to differentiate the particular patterns of bodily processes expressive of anxiety. Martin (1961), for example, presents a rather clear picture of these phenomena. He bases his work on that of Ax (1953) and assumes, as do most researchers in this field, that anxiety is equivalent to or is a subclass of fear. Hence, anxiety is said to involve increases in heart rate, systolic blood pressure, cardiac output, respiration rate, frontalis muscle tension, forehead temperature, palmar conductance, central nervous system activity, and blood-sugar level. Accompanying these changes are decreases in peripheral resistance, diastolic blood pressure, hand temperature, and salivary output.

Related to the work and findings of Martin and Ax are the findings of researchers who have attempted to uncover specific endocrinological patterns that could be grasped as underlying the particular patterns of bodily processes expressive of anxiety. Martin (1961) and Breggin (1964) have suggested that these patterns of bodily process are primarily a function of increased adrenalin (epinephrine) secretion. Still, the causal chain is, as yet, quite unclear and, as Buss (1961) points out, some of the most important studies are questionable on methodological grounds.

Comments

Within the contextual framework of the physiological approach, outlined in the opening of this chapter, we are no longer seeking to grasp the characteristics of anxiety as a human experience. Certainly, theoreticians of this orientation have not directed themselves to any analysis of the stimulus conditions —that situation in the face of which one is anxious. With regard to the question of that about which people are anxious, it has been assumed that anxiety can be equated with fear and that, as such, one is anxious about impending pain. On the other hand, as was suggested at the outset, physiological theory and research are directed to those anatomical, physiological, and cognitive factors that are essential to the possibility of the anxiety experience. In this regard, it has been found that anxiety, reports of anxiety, or anxious behaviors involve the activity of particular areas of the central nervous system, the secretion of hormonal substance, and the arousal of probably the entire organism (conceived as a mechanistic thing).

What then, is the significance of these findings? For those who have already adopted a conception of man that constitutes him as the Other—an organism whose ultimate reality is anatomical and physiological process; a passive, reactive thing that I can observe but with whom I do not relate—such research and speculation leads to an exhaustive natural scientific definition and explanation of anxiety. Correlations between various external stimuli, physiological process, and reported experiences, *causally related*, constitute a definitive analysis. As Heath (1964) has suggested, with such information it is theoretically possible to intervene in and control the life experiences of an individual, primarily by altering his physiology. In this way, people can be "immunized" to painful external events and/or internal ideational stimulation.

However, there are some who still believe that an individual's experience, even if it has not been educated by natural scientific training, is valid in its own right. This experience needs to be understood on its own terms, not necessarily reducing it to one side of a psychophysical equation. Further, there are those who would even go so far as to understand the human body as something other than a complex mechanism, as something that experiences the world meaningfully and responds to that world prior to any cognitive formulation of such experiences. For these theoreticians and researchers, the approaches described in this chapter need revision and the research findings require reinterpretation. We shall have more to say about these and other issues later when we attempt to integrate the various approaches described in this book.

REFERENCES

Ax, A. F. The physiological differentiation between fear and anger in humans. *Psychosomatic Medicine*, 1953, *15*, 433–442.

Bergmann, G., and Spence, K. W. The logic of psychophysical measurement. *Psychological Review*, 1944, *51*, 1–24.

Bishop, M. P., Elder, S. T., & Heath, R. G. Attempted control of operant behavior in man with intracranial self-stimulation. In R. G. Heath, ed. *The role of pleasure in behavior*. New York: Hoeber, 1964.

Brady, J. V. The paleocortex and behavioral motivation. In H. F. Harlow and C. N. Woosely, eds., *Biological and biochemical bases of behavior*. Madison: University of Wisconsin Press, 1958.

Breggin, P. R. The psychophysiology of anxiety. *Journal of Nervous and Mental Disease*, 1964, *139*, 558–568.

Buss, A. *The psychology of aggression*. New York: Wiley, 1961.

Canon, W. B. The James-Lange theory of emotions: a critical examination and an alternative theory. *American Psychologist*, 1927, *39*, 106–124.

Canon, W. B. *Bodily changes in pain, hunger, fear, and rage.* Boston: Branford, 1929 (new ed., New York: Harper & Row, 1963).

Duffy, E. The conceptual categories of psychology: a suggestion for revision. *Psychological Review,* 1941, *48,* 177–203.

Heath, R. G. Pleasure response of human subjects to direct stimulation of the brain: physiologic and psychodynamic considerations. In R. G. Heath, ed., *The role of pleasure in behavior.* New York: Hoeber, 1964.

James, W. *The principles of psychology.* New York: Holt, 1890.

Korchin, S. J. Anxiety and cognition. In C. Sheerer, ed., *Cognition: theory, research, promise.* New York: Harper & Row, 1964.

Levi, L. The urinary output of adrenalin and noradrenalin during different experimentally induced pleasant and unpleasant states. Acta Psychotherapeutica et Psychosomatica, 1963, *11,* 218–227.

Levitt, E. *The psychology of anxiety.* Indianapolis: Bobbs-Merrill, 1967.

Lindsley, D. B. Emotion. In S. S. Stevens, ed., *Handbook of experimental psychology.* New York: Wiley, 1951.

Malmo, R. B. Experimental approach to the symptom mechanisms in psychiatric patients. *Psychiatric Research Reports,* 7, American Psychiatric Assoc., 1957, 33–49.

Malmo, R. B. Activation: a neuropsychological dimension. *Psychological Review,* 1959, *66,* 367–386.

Martin, B. The assessment of anxiety by physiological behavioral measures. *Psychological Bulletin,* 1961, *58,* 234–255.

Olds, J., and Milner, T. Positive reinforcement produced by electrical stimulation of septal area and other regions of rat brain. *Journal of Comparative and Physiological Psychology,* 1954, *47,* 419–427.

Schachter, S. The interaction of cognitive and physiological determinants of emotional states. In P. H. Leiderman & D. Shapiro, eds., *Psychobiological approaches to social behavior.* Stanford: Stanford University Press, 1964, by permission.

Schachter, S., and Wheeler, L. Epinephrine, chlorpromazine, and amusement. *Journal of Abnormal and Social Psychology,* 1962, *65,* 121–128.

Schachter, S., and Singer, J. Cognitive, social and psychological determinants of emotional states. *Psychological Review,* 1962, *69,* 379–399.

5

The Learning-Theory Approach

Although most introductory texts usually date the inception of modern experimental psychology with the opening of the Leipzig laboratory in 1879, the philosophical and methodological underpinnings of this enterprise have a considerably longer history. In fact, they go back at least to the seventeenth-century French philosopher, René Descartes (1596–1650). While accepting as valid the knowledge already gathered by the physical sciences, Descartes pursued a firmer basis for philosophy. A major consequence of this endeavor was that the final logical wedge was driven between mind and matter, between mental and physical, between subject and object, between experience and action, between man and world. The domain of mind, the *res cogitans*, and the world of matter, the *res extensa*, were said to be co-existing, fundamentally different, and mutually exclusive realms of the universe. That which characterized the mind were ideas, subjective in their origin, always susceptible to error except when clear and distinct, and relatively independent of any necessary correspondence to objects in the world. That which characterized the world, on the other hand, was extension, substantiality—always mathematical in nature. In the Cartesian view, the world, which included the human body, was a corporeal, quantitative mechanism. While Descartes granted equiprimordiality to both mind and matter, he was concerned with grasping the nature of the latter and concluded that objective knowledge thereof could be obtained only through the methods of the physical sciences.

Subsequent philosophers then turned their attention to the delineation of the path to objective knowledge. John Locke (1632–1704) asserted that only the primary qualities of objects were objective. By the phrase "primary qualities," he referred to those sensible characteristics that could be perceived by more than one sense modality, such as extension, form, and motion. These qualities were to be distinguished from "secondary qualities," which were characteristic of experience through any one sense modality. They were labeled as merely subjective. Thus, for Locke, as well as Descartes, the ordinary experiences of everyday life in which man unquestionably believes, must, by and large, be dismissed as contaminated. Knowledge and sensory qualities are objective only insofar as a real world emits stimuli that influence the senses. The world is the source of all that is real, and experience is objective only when it mirrors or accurately reflects the world.

From the above foundations, it was but a brief step to the empiricism of David Hume (1711–1776). In the spirit of Locke and of Newtonian physics, the objective physical world was claimed to be the one fundamental reality and philosophy was to be transformed into a natural science. Hume wrote: "As the science of man is the only solid foundation for the other sciences, so the only solid foundation we can give science itself must be laid on experience (i.e., sense experience) and observation" (1956, pp. 124–125). Experience, passively received through the impingement of stimuli emitted by the real world, is the source of all knowledge and action. Eventually it was to be claimed that if the scientist already knows the stimuli, he need not bother with such intermediaries as experience, however conceived.

The establishment of psychology in the halls of natural science was not easily accomplished, for serious difficulties were immediately encountered. For example, the content of psychology in the late nineteenth and early twentieth centuries was, in fact, the study of Descartes' *res cogitans*, consciousness. This was precisely that which was rejected by natural science as subjective at best, probably epiphenomenal, and certainly not amenable to the methods of science. Treating consciousness as an object of the world, as was done by the Introspectionists, did not help very much. This problem was solved, however, through a redefinition of the subject matter of psychology, introduced by the founder of Behaviorism, John B. Watson. Guided by the assumption that a person's experienced needs and drives can only be studied by repeatable observations made by an objective other, Watson decreed that consciousness was unamenable to investigation and unnecessary as a scientific construct (1947, p. 23). The psychologist must direct himself exclusively to what can be observed, to the *res extensa*. For the purposes of the scientific enterprise, man shall be conceived as an object of nature. Consequently, "psychology, as the behaviorist views it [is] a purely objective experimental branch of natural science" (1965, p. xi).

There was, however, another major hurdle to overcome. To put the matter in its most succinct form, the experimenter, who was also a human being, had to assume the validity of his own experiences and perceptions. In other words, the behavior of the scientist, as a scientist, had to be given a privileged position. In his work as an experimenter, the psychologist could not question the objectivity of his own perceptions, although he was bound to assume, in keeping with Cartesian and scientific thought, the susceptibility to error of his subjects' perceptions. As Bergmann and Spence state:

scientific empiricism holds to the position that all sciences, including psychology, deal with the same events, namely, the experiences or perceptions of the scientist himself. The behavior scientist who claims to study such perceptual behavior in his subjects is thus asked to start uncritically from his own perceptions (1944, p. 3).

As a justification for this privileged position, they continue:

The empiricist scientist should realize that his behavior, symbolic or otherwise, does not lie on the same methodological level as the responses of his subjects, and consequently that he should not in reporting the latter use any mentalistic terms which have not been introduced from a physicalistic meaning basis (1944, p. 4).

Thus the solution to the problem of what to do with the experimenter's experience is simply to assume its validity, its accurate correspondence to the facts of the world. The experimenter is directed to the Other and his experiences of the Other are taken as objective. S. S. Stevens, in an article addressed to the very same problem, states the solution even more explicitly:

What becomes acceptable psychology accrues only when all observations, including those which a psychologist makes upon himself, are treated as though made upon "the other one." Thus, we make explicit the distinction between the experimenter and the thing observed (1939, p. 228).

Unfortunately, this solution results in a form of uncritical dictating to the data.

In summary then, the foundation has been laid for an objective, natural science of the Other. Experimental psychology shall attempt to grasp and explain the observable behavior of the Other, conceived as an object of nature, passively receiving and responding to stimuli emitted by the real world. These stimuli, as well as the responses thereto, shall be conceptualized in terms of the procedures and constructs of physical science and the experimenter shall take for granted the validity of his own perceptions.

A direct heir to this conceptual framework is contemporary learning theory, the basic assumption of which is that the greater part of human behavior is acquired through empiricistically conceived conditioning. Further, it is also assumed that the processes involved in this phenomenon, like all natural events, display certain consistencies that can be formulated in terms of causal laws. As shall become evident, the approach of learning theory to psychopathology is consistent with these assumptions.

In 1894 Freud first delineated anxiety neurosis as a discrete clinical syndrome to be distinguished from neurasthenia. At about the same time, the noted American philosopher-psychologist William James expressed the view that anxiety was an instinctive reaction, phylogenetically fixed and unlearned. This claim was not seriously challenged by American psychologists until the appearance and papers of John B. Watson, who, in his classic "little Albert" experiment, demonstrated that fears were specifically related to individual learning histories. Watson's discovery, coupled with Pavlov's research on experimental neurosis in dogs, one year earlier, served as the initial impetus for turning scientific psychology to the phenomenon of anxiety.

Undoubtedly, the first truly significant movement toward the *rapprochement* of experimental and abnormal psychology occurred with the publication of "A Stimulus Response Analysis of Anxiety and Its Role As a Reinforcing Agent" by O. H. Mowrer (1939). This paper, firmly grounded in the thought of Clark Hull (1921, 1943, 1952), expressed views that have left an indelible mark upon the learning theoretical approach to the phenomenon of anxiety. For this reason, both the general orientation of Hull and the specific proposals set forth in Mowrer's paper will be considered at this time.

Clark Hull is the author of the first systematically delineated, stimulus-response theory of learning. The assumptions and conceptions that both ground and orient the substance of his formulations may be stated as follows:

1. All organisms seek to maintain a constant, relatively minimal level of excitation. This is called the principle of homeostasis.

2. An increase in the level of organismic excitation, whether caused by internal or external stimulation, arouses a state of drive. The latter, consistent with the principle of homeostasis and in a manner analogous to other theorists' conceptions of motive, impels the organism to act (respond). Eventually, the activity (responses) of the organism produce a state of affairs that leads to a reduction in the level of excitation, thereby reducing drive. An obvious example would be hunger. The increase in the organism's level of excitation is caused by internal stimulation (peristaltic contractions of the stomach). Drive is then operative and when the activity that ensues results in the incorporation of food, the peristaltic contractions diminish. The drive (hunger) is thus said to be *reduced*.

3. Learning is the process in which a particular response, because of its power to produce a reduction in the excitation potential of a particular stimulus (or configuration of stimuli), becomes linked with or associated to that stimulus.

4. The linkage or association between a particular stimulus and a particular response is called *habit*, and the effectiveness of that linkage is described in units of *habit strength*.

5. The rate at which habit strength is accrued, that is, the rate at which learning takes place, is directly a function of the number of times the particular response involved in the habit has, in association with the particular stimulus, led to drive reduction.

6. The phenomenon of drive reduction—that is, reduction of the excitation potential of a particular stimulus and, therefore, a return to the homeostatic state—is synonymous with the phenomenon of *reinforcement*. Any object or event that materially leads to or is the cause of drive reduction is called "reinforcement."

7. The tendency of an organism to respond in a particular manner at a particular time is a multiplicative function of drive and habit strength. In other words, if there is a tendency to respond, there must be a drive operative.

Hull's students, including such distinguished workers as John Dollard, Neal Miller, Kenneth Spence, and O. H. Mowrer, have furthered, tested, and refined the conceptions just outlined. The theory of Dollard and Miller (1950), which we shall soon discuss, is a logical child of both Hull's thought and Mowrer's pioneering paper.

In a footnote early in the paper, Mowrer (1939) explicitly states his conception of anxiety: "Psychoanalytic writers sometimes differentiate between fear and anxiety on the grounds that fear has a consciously perceived object and anxiety does not. Although this distinction may be useful for some purposes, these two terms will be used in the present paper as strictly synonymous" (1939, p. 184). This emphatic identification of anxiety with fear has never since been seriously questioned by learning theorists in psychology. Even today, it serves as the first principle in the experimental study of anxiety.

Also expressed in Mowrer's paper was a conclusion as to the precise nature of anxiety. He postulated that this phenomenon is, to a large extent, learned; that it can serve to motivate trial-and-error behavior; and that its reduction reinforces the learning of new habits. Subsequently, these three postulates have come to constitute the essential features of the learned-drive conception of anxiety, a conception that learning theorists have almost universally accepted.

In this chapter, two contemporary learning theories of anxiety will be presented at length. The first, that of John Dollard and Neal Miller, best exemplifies the development of Mowrer's postulates. The second, that of Hans J. Eysenck, is embedded in a learning-psychobiological approach to personality.

Dollard and Miller

An explicit statement of the Dollard and Miller (1950) theory is given in their book, *Personality and Psychotherapy*. This work has been widely received, referred to, and its concepts utilized. In it, the authors argue that learning occurs when a drive, acting upon the individual in the form of a stimulus, is reduced as a consequence of some response. This state of affairs, drive reduction following a particular response, tends to reinforce that response and thereby increase its probability of reoccurring. Dollard and Miller point out that the assumption that is fundamental to their entire theory is "that a sudden reduction in strong drive acts as a reinforcement" (1950, p. 42).

In their approach to the phenomena of psychopathology, these theoreticians have generally accepted the observations and postulates of Freudian psychology. Yet, like Mowrer before them, they have translated the fundamental principles of psychoanalytic theory into the conceptual framework of a stimulus-response learning system. The basic elements of this translation are as follows:

[1] The principle of reinforcement has been substituted for Freud's pleasure principle (1950, p. 9).

[2 The concept of] ego strength has been elaborated in two directions; first . . . a careful account of the higher mental processes; second . . . the description of the culturally valuable, learned drives and skills (1950, p. 9–10).

[3] A naturalistic account is given of the immensely important mechanism of repression . . . as the inhibition of cue producing responses (1950, p. 10).

[4] The dynamics of conflict behavior are systematically deduced from more basic principles (1950, p. 10). [The more basic principles to which Dollard and Miller refer are those of drive, habit strength, response tendency, goal gradient phenomena, and stimulus generalization.]

[5] The somewhat vague concept of "reality" is elaborated in terms of the physical and social conditions of learning (1950, p. 10).

We are now ready to begin our concrete examination of the Dollard and Miller theory of anxiety. Further discussion of the concepts of drive, habit, and reinforcement, as well as specific elaborations of such concepts as cue, approach-avoidance conflict, and generalization will occur in the course of the exposition.

As has already been stated, Dollard and Miller ground their formulations in the conceptual framework advanced by Clark Hull. This means that all behaviors (responses) are understood as being drive-impelled and that all learning (habit acquisition) is held to be a function of reinforcement. However, while any stimulus is capable of arousing the organism and functioning as a drive, certain classes of stimuli are said to form a base for most human motivation. The most prominent representatives of these classes are hunger, sex, and pain. The drives to which these stimuli give rise and represent are described as primary and innate. On the other hand, however, the conditions of our social existence have necessitated the formation of a secondary class of drives that are, essentially, elaborations of the primary ones. To refer to them as "secondary" is to assert that they are learned and that they constitute facades behind which the primary drives are at work. According to Dollard and Miller, fear is classified as an extremely important secondary or learned drive.

Following the thought of Mowrer, these authors claim that anxiety, if not equatable to fear, is a particular form of it. In fact, the definition given in the

Miller and Dollard book makes this quite explicit: "When the source of fear is vague or obscured by repression, it is often called anxiety" (1950, p. 63). But what does it mean to call fear a learned drive? What is its source and how is it learned? Further, how does repression function within the context of this system such that the source of fear can be obscured? The answers to these questions constitute the essence of the Dollard and Miller theory.

As anxiety is to be understood as a particular variety of fear, it seems appropriate carefully to review Miller's (1948) classic demonstration of the lat-

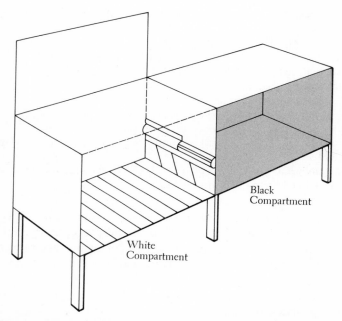

Black Compartment

White Compartment

Fig. 1. Apparatus for studying fear as a learned drive. (From Dollard and Miller, 1950.)

ter's behavioral properties. The apparatus utilized in this research is depicted in Fig. 1. During the first stage of the experiment, rats were placed in the white compartment and administered shock through the floor grid. They escaped this aversive stimulus only by fleeing through the open door into the black compartment. Miller explains the behavioral pattern in the following manner: The shock caused pain that, in its capacity as a stimulus capable of arousing a primary drive, innately elicited a fear response; the manifestation of this fear response was the rat's flight from the white compartment. In Stage two of the experiment, the shock was omitted in order to eliminate the primary drive of pain. With the door between the two compartments closed, the rats, when placed in the white compartment, showed distinct signs of agitation and fear. This fear response of Stage two was said to have been learned in association to the cues of the white compartment.

To digress for a moment, a *cue* is defined by Dollard and Miller as a stimulus that, although not strong enough to impel the organism to action (that is, not strong enough to arouse a drive) does determine where and when the organism will respond and which response it will make. A stimulus is said to have cue value insofar as it is distinctive. Thus, in this situation, the features of the white compartment, acting as cues, determined that the fear response would be made in their presence.

In Stage three of the experiment, the conditions were identical to those of Stage two except that a wheel-turning-response opened the door into the black compartment. The rats, in their exploratory, trial-and-error behavior, motivated by the fear drive, did in fact, learn to open the door by turning the wheel. On the basis of this experiment, Dollard and Miller describe and justify their conceptions of fear in the following manner:

> We say that fear is *learned* because it can be attached to previously neutral cues, such as those of the white compartment; we say that it is a *drive* because it can motivate, and its reduction can reinforce, the learning of new responses, such as turning the wheel. . . . Therefore, we call fear of a previously neutral cue a *learned drive* (1950, pp. 67–68).

The pliability of fear as a learned drive, within the context of stimulus-response theory, greatly contributes to its functional importance. In its occurrence as a process, it conforms to the basic laws of a stimulus: it can serve either as a cue or as a drive. Likewise, fear conforms to the basic laws of a response: it can be learned, inhibited, and/or generalized to cues similar to those of the original learning situation. Further, as a response, it tends to be reinforced by the very same stimuli that elicit it.

We will now turn our attention to the events and processes through which the source of fear can become obscured; that is, through which fear becomes anxiety. In order to do this, we must enter the realm of psychopathology, for Dollard and Miller conceive of anxiety as emerging only under conditions of neurotic conflict. In fact, for these authors, all neurotic fear is, by definition, anxiety. Further, that which makes fear neurotic is that its source is obscured—in a word, unconscious.

The role of fear in neurosis is a central one in the Dollard and Miller theory of psychopathology. A diagram of the basic factors involved in neurosis, presented in Fig. 2, graphically illustrates this point. As indicated, guilt and similarly learned drives occupy the same position as does fear. However, Dollard and Miller refer to fear as "the strongest and most basic" of these drives and elsewhere, they even refer to guilt and shame as "composed to a considerable extent of fear" (1950, p. 90). In its capacity as a drive, fear serves as the prime motivating factor in conflict, symptom formation, and repression. The precise nature of its role in these phenomena will shortly be discussed. It is, however, already clear that fear, because of its drive properties, appears as the prime causal factor in the genesis of neurosis.

In considering the etiology of psychopathology, Dollard and Miller state

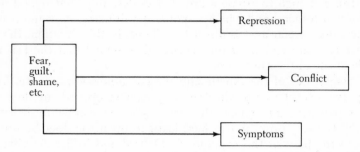

Fig. 2. Some basic factors involved in neurosis. (Adapted from Dollard and Miller, 1950.)

that "an intense emotional conflict is the necessary basis for neurotic behavior. The conflict must further be unconscious. As a usual thing, such conflicts are created only in childhood" (1950, p. 127). While the authors acknowledge the possibility of four basic forms of conflict—approach-approach, approach-avoidance, avoidance-avoidance, and double approach-avoidance (see Fig. 3) —the second possibility, approach-avoidance, is most important for their

Fig. 3. The basic forms of conflict.

theory. This type of conflict is the one that is most frequent in human life and, further, it is the difficulty that usually lies at the heart of neurosis.

As can be seen in Fig. 3, in the approach-avoidance conflict there are two competing, mutually exclusive response tendencies with reference to the same goal object. On the one hand, there has already been some accretion of habit involving movement toward the goal object because it has been associated with drive reduction (reinforcement). The tendency to keep away from or flee the goal object has also been reinforced because the latter has, at times, been associated with pain, fear, or one of their derivatives. A simple example of this, one that would not involve anxiety and therefore would not constitute neurotic conflict, would be the situation of the person who wants to go swimming, but upon entering the water, finds it too cold. The reasons for stating that this situation would not involve anxiety and hence would not constitute a neurotic conflict are the following: Although the response of swimming-in-the-water is inhibited by the fear of its coldness, the would-be-swimmer perceives the cues associated with his drive to swim as well as the cues associated with his fear of the water; he perceives and can label the source of his fear—the coldness of the water and the discomfort of his body. This, then, is a situation of "normal" fear and "normal conflict."

How does the source of fear—that is, the cues associated with its arousal as a drive and implementation as a response—become obscured? Another way of asking this question is: How does repression take place? This is what Dollard and Miller mean by repression: the inhibition of cue perception and labeling, thereby preventing the verbalization of the cue thought or percept, though not inhibiting the cue-determined response. Although Dollard and Miller state, "We must admit that we do not know the exact conditions under which the common conflict-producing circumstances of life generate severe (neurotic) conflicts in some and not-so-severe conflicts in others" (1950, p. 155), they do generally suggest how this might occur.

Imagine the situation of little Jimmy who has discovered that fondling his penis when it "tingles" is pleasurable. Here, the sex drive, aroused and manifested by the tingling sensations in his penis, is effectively reduced by the manual response of fondling. The habit—fondle my penis when it tingles—has been reinforced and thereby strengthened. Now, consider what happens when Jimmy's mother frequently catches him in the act. Let us suppose that each time this happens, she spanks his hand with increasing severity. According to the Dollard and Miller formulation, the pain of the spanking would innately arouse the fear response of pulling the hand away from the penis. As the number of spankings increase, both in their frequency and severity, the strength of the fear drive is increased, as is the strength of the habit constituted by pulling the hand away when the penis tingles. This occurs because mother tells him that she won't spank him when he doesn't touch it. The pulling-the-hand-away response is also strengthened because each time he evades a spanking by performing this act his fear is markedly reduced. Finally, however, through repeated spankings, the fear drive becomes so strong that it is aroused even at the perception of the tingling of the penis (the original cue for the fondling response). As a consequence of such strength, there is an inhibition of the labeling of this cue and hence it operates at a nonverbal level. Thus not only is the fondling response inhibited but the verbalization and hence awareness of the cues involved in the arousal of fear is also repressed. Jimmy is fearful when his penis tingles, but he no longer perceives why. In a word, he is anxious—caught in the throes of a neurotic conflict.

One outcome of neurotic, unconscious conflict is the development of symptoms. As we might expect, here, too, anxiety plays a central role. According to Dollard and Miller, there are basically two types of symptoms: those learned and those unlearned. An example of an unlearned symptom would be the heart palpitations or "nervousness" that tend to accompany chronic anxiety. If these behaviors serve to diminish the fear drive, probably through eliciting sympathy and comforting behavior from others, there is no need to develop further fear-impelled responses.

Learned symptoms are formed when, in the course of behavior during a high drive state, some maladaptive response serves to bring about a reduction of the drive level and is thereby reinforced. In their discussion of what drives can motivate the learning of symptoms, Dollard and Miller cite fear as the most important. They support this claim with three reasons: "because it is so strong, because it can be attached to new cues so easily through learning, and because it is the motivation that produces the inhibiting responses in most conflicts" (1950, p. 190). The list of pathological symptoms to which these authors attribute fear as the usual motivating factor covers the whole spectrum of possibilities; it ranges from phobias and compulsions to hallucinations and delusions.

Let us return to the situation of little Jimmy and see how he might develop a symptom. When we left him he was in the throes of a neurotic conflict. That is to say, while the tingling sensations in his penis aroused and represented a condition of high drive, a competing drive (fear of pain) associated with the cues involved in explicitly perceiving and labeling these tingling sensations caused the perceiving-labeling process to be inhibited or repressed. Thus, while the high drive state continued to exist, it did so at an unconscious (unverbalized) level. Further, each time Jimmy approached perception of these tingling sensations (the cues for labeling the sexual interest and determining the fondling response), or each time his hand wandered near his genitals, he became fearful—even though he could not say why. To put it succinctly, he was anxious.

Now, let us imagine that one day, while Jimmy is in a condition of high drive, he discovers that sitting upon a chair causes him to be more acutely aware of his genitals. Immediately, he becomes even more anxious and stands up. Later, at dinner, his mother asks him to be seated and while trembling in anxiousness, he tells her, "I'm afraid to." When asked why, he can only look bewildered and say, "I don't know. I feel better when I stand." Clearly, what has happened here is that Jimmy now has to go to greater lengths to avoid perceiving the original, fear-producing cues (tingling sensations in his penis). Eventually, he may become fearful of any object upon which he might sit. He even could begin to avoid wearing underwear, for this, too, stimulates his penis.

The phenomenon we are describing is known as *stimulus generalization*. Specifically, objects, events, or states of affairs (all of these are stimuli) that are perceived as stimuli or arouse perceptions of some original stimulus situation (in this case the cues of tingling sensations in the penis) elicit the original conditioned response—avoidance or flight. Further, and this is what makes these behaviors neurotic symptoms, there is no awareness of why these avoidance behaviors make little Jimmy feel better, i.e., reduce his fear drive. Nonetheless, they do so and are hence reinforced.

Finally, then, we can see that anxiety is something we learn. Further, once it has been learned, it can motivate maladaptive behavior. It is in this latter capacity that anxiety becomes the prime causal factor in the development of neurotic conflict, symptom formation, and still more repression—the basic elements of neurosis.

Comments

Given the perspective from which Dollard and Miller view human phenomena in general and anxiety in particular, their theoretical formulations follow quite logically. However, it should be recalled from the introductory remarks made at the beginning of this section that these authors have adopted an empiricistic, natural scientific approach to psychology. This means that they have concerned themselves with conceptualizing and explaining the behavior of the Other, understood as an object of nature, passively receiving and responding to stimuli of both internal and external origin. The derivation of anxiety from fear is perfectly reasonable if one only concerns oneself with the subject's overt behavior and not with his experience. The use of such terms as drive, habit, stimulus, response, and reinforcement are completely consistent with a thorough-going, physicalistic determinism. However, the terms' ontological status may require further clarification. What is the difference between an object and a stimulus? Why, when we perceive objects does the behavioristic theorist insist that we are responding to stimuli? Is all perception illusory? What, then, may we say about the perceptions of the theorist or experimenter? Such matters are problematic for any theory of the organism conceived along empiricistic lines.

One may ask: Of what value is the Dollard and Miller formulation to our general understanding of anxiety? Certainly, if one's preferred conceptual framework is of an S-R variety, then the above specifications may well be quite useful. On the other hand, if one is not already committed to this mode of explaining phenomena, then alternative formulations that focus upon experiential aspects of anxiety might prove to be descriptively richer and more enlightening. One must remember that Dollard and Miller began their exercise with a general acceptance of the psychoanalytic conception of anxiety. In essence, their whole endeavor can be grasped as a translation, however successfully accomplished, of the psychoanalytic idiom into that of modern stimulus-response learning theory.

Hans J. Eysenck

Hans Jurgen Eysenck was born in Germany on March 4, 1916. Educated in France and England, as well as in Germany, he received his Ph.D. in psychology from the University of London in 1940. Since then he has occupied the following positions: senior research psychologist at the Mill Hill Emergency Hospital; visiting professor in the United States, first at the University of Pennsylvania and later at the University of California; professor of psychology at the Institute of Psychiatry, University of London; and director of the psychology department at Maudsley Hospital. In all, he has published more than two hundred articles, not to mention books, in British, German, American, and French journals of psychology.

The breadth of Eysenck's interests, as expressed in his writings, is considerable. It includes such topics as body types, handwriting, neurotic and psychotic behavior, personality dynamics, the effects of heredity (in twin studies), tranquilizing drugs, and humor. The style of his writing is aggressive —some would say antagonistic. Major targets of his books and articles are projective test theorists and users, psychiatrists, Sheldon, Freud, nonempiricist and non-natural scientific thinkers, and most psychotherapists (especially proponents of psychoanalysis). Speaking about the founder of psychoanalysis, Eysenck wrote, "I not only abjure Freud and all his works, but have tried to put a rational method of diagnosis and treatment in the place of psychoanalysis, i.e., Behavior Therapy. This is an important part of my system" (1964, p. 607).

If one asks about the thinkers who have significantly yet positively influenced Eysenck's work, the names of Watson, Jung, and Kretschmer must be given priority. The founder of Behaviorism, to whom Eysenck dedicated *Behavior Therapy and the Neuroses* (1960), found a receptive and enthusiastic follower in the person of this prolific scientist. From Jung, Eysenck appropriated the dimensions of introversion and extraversion which, as we shall see, are basic to his conceptions of personality. Finally, from Kretschmer, he developed and utilized a critical interest in the problems of constitution, heredity, and temperament.

The problem of placing or situating Eysenck's thought within the field of general experimental-learning psychology is mitigated to some extent if we realize that, unlike his cohorts, he has been overwhelmingly concerned with the study of personality. While others have been content to define this term in an omnibus fashion, that is, as the sum total of one's learned behavior, Eysenck has found this approach to be an inadequate brushing aside of a vastly important and useful concept. It is a recognized fact, he claims, that the classical S-R paradigm of learning has given way to the more contemporary idea that O, the organism, intervenes between S and R. Further, "organisms differ both with respect to past reinforcement schedules and also with respect to innate potentiality" (1965, p. 15). Thus Eysenck considers the study of O, which constitutes the study of personality, to be an essential factor in the learning theoretical approach to the phenomena of psychopathology.

In his review of the history of psychiatry, Eysenck delineates two major concerns: the classification of personality disorders and dynamic analyses of them. It is to the former task, that of nosology, that he devoted most of his early work. In his later writings, the questions of dynamics and therapy have been of foremost concern. As his theory has such a decidedly deductive flavor

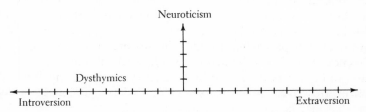

Fig. 4. Personality dimensions of neuroticism and introversion–extraversion. (Adapted from Eysenck, 1965.)

and because, like Dollard and Miller, he conceptualizes anxiety in the context of psychopathology, we shall, of necessity, enter into a description and analysis of his theoretical approach to the behavior disorders. A "secondary gain" to be derived from this exploration is the opportunity to compare and contrast Eysenck's formulations with those of more traditional learning theory (e.g., Dollard and Miller's concepts).

Through the use of laboratory experimention and factor analysis, both of which he believes to be necessary in order to achieve natural scientific validity, Eysenck postulated two major dimensions of personality: neuroticism and introversion-extraversion. This conception of dimensions can, perhaps, be best understood by analogy to a graph (Fig. 4), in which each dimension is represented by an independent axis.

Just as one could plot a point when given the calibrated axes of a graph, so, according to Eysenck, one can locate any particular, nonpsychotic, individual's personality with respect to the two dimensions depicted. In other words, any nonpsychotic individual partakes, in the makeup of his personality, of both some degree of neuroticism and some characteristics of either introversion and/or extraversion. Nosologically speaking, Eysenck asserts that almost all the major neurotic behavior patterns can be analyzed in terms of the interplay of neuroticism and introversion-extraversion.

At a descriptive level, the meanings of these dimensions can be most easily grasped through characterizations. Thus the person who ranks high on the neuroticism dimension is likely to be an overly emotional individual, one whose affective reaction to stimuli, particularly anxiety-provoking stimuli, would be relatively quick, strong, and lasting. As far as the introversion-extraversion dimension is concerned, the typical extravert "is sociable . . . has many friends . . . needs to have people to talk to . . . craves excitement . . . is generally an impulsive individual"; the typical introvert, on the other hand, "is quiet . . . introspective . . . reserved and distant . . . keeps his feelings under close control" (1965, p. 19).

In considering the dynamic properties of these two dimensions, their causes, and their possibilities of interplay, we must carefully approach Eysenck's conception of anxiety and learn how he believes it is learned and/or inherited. As was suggested above, the major characteristic of the neurotic individual is his emotional lability. That is to say, he is excessively sensitive and responsive to anxiety-provoking stimuli. This feature of his behavior is, according to Eysenck, based upon the neurotic's inherited autonomic nervous system tendencies. In other words, such an individual is genetically predisposed to be affectively overreactive. This is one source of anxiety and, strictly speaking, it results in what may be termed anxiety-proneness.

The second source of anxiety is learning or conditioning. The paradigm for its acquisition involves two stages. Initially, there is a single traumatic event, or a series of subtraumatic events, either of which produces strong, unconditioned, autonomic fear responses. Obviously, these traumatic events function in a manner that is analogous to Dollard and Miller's pain stimuli. Though they may serve to disrupt behavior, such a disruption by itself should not in any sense be considered neurotic. In the second stage, however, conditioning takes place.

From now on it will be found that the conditioned stimulus (Dollard and Miller's cues contiguously associated with the traumatic events), as well as the unconditioned stimulus (the traumatic events or the pain stimuli), produce the original maladaptive emotional behavior. This, it seems is the essential learning process which takes place in the learning of (anxiety) neurosis (1965, p. 4).

In pointing to conditioning as a second source of anxiety, Eysenck agrees with Mowrer, as well as with Dollard and Miller, in conceptualizing it as an acquired drive. However, he is not concerned with the subject's ability to verbalize anxiety's source and he does not deal with the issue of repression. In other words, anxiety, for Eysenck, is conditioned fear. Further, rather than accepting the Hullian notion of drive reduction (reinforcement) as essential for the acquisition of anxiety, Eysenck posits that both conditioned fear and neurotic behavior are learned through simple Pavlovian conditioning. Schematically, a previously neutral stimulus (the traumatic event) comes to elicit the autonomic fear response through contiguous association.

We may now begin to examine the dynamic properties of these dimensions as well as the consequences of their interplay. Actually, we have already presented Eysenck's assumption as to the fundamentally genetic basis of neuroticism. That is, we have noted his claim that neuroticism is primarily manifested by emotional lability and oversensitivity, and that these characteristics are, in turn, based upon inherited tendencies of the individual's autonomic nervous system. With regard to the introversion-extraversion dimension, the reasoning is somewhat more complex.

Both poles of the continuum (both introversion and extraversion) as well as the shadings between them are, according to Eysenck, learned. However, after acknowledging this common feature, we must now attend to the uniquenesses. Eysenck assumes that the extravert is the way he is because of his deficient socialization. That is to say, he is a slow learner who has failed to acquire adequately the rules of society; he has not been conditioned to the inhibitions and modulations of behavior that society values. Consequently, he tends to be immature and impulsive in his acts.

The introvert, on the other hand, has been oversocialized. He is easily conditioned and has, in fact, learned the rules of society too well. As a result, he is inhibited, constricted, and overly meditative and conscientious. He tends to deliberate excessively and is frequently unable to act.

If Eysenck had stopped there, his introversion-extraversion dimension would still be essentially descriptive. Asked why people are either introverts or extraverts, he would have to answer: Because they've learned to be that way. But Eysenck went further. He asked: Is there anything in the constitutional or hereditary endowment of these people that determined the courses of the (previously described) learning processes? To this question he gave the provisional answer, "yes," and immediately set out to prove its truth.

It has been Eysenck's belief that psychology has been too preoccupied with environmental influences upon personality and behavior. As a consequence, there has been an unfortunate exclusion of the hereditary and constitutional factors. To fill this void, to uncover the biological roots of personality and hence behavior, has been a major goal of Eysenck's work. But, as he himself states, "any proof for the existence of a biological basis of personality must begin with a discussion of the influence of hereditary factors" (1965, p. 29). Upon experimental findings of the type presented below, Eysenck justifies his search for such a basis.

Shields (1962) administered questionnaires on intelligence, neuroticism, and extraversion to 28 pairs of dizygotic twins (DZ), 44 pairs of monozygotic twins raised together (C), and 44 pairs of monozygotic twins raised apart (S).

The correlations of their scores on the various questionnaires is presented below.

Comparison of Scores for Groups DZ, S, and C on Intelligence, Neuroticism, and Extraversion

	C	S	DZ
Intelligence	0.76	0.77	0.51
Extraversion	0.42	0.61	0.17
Neuroticism	0.38	0.53	0.11

Adapted from Eysenck, 1965, by permission.

With respect to all factors measured, the monozygotic twins, raised both apart and together, were found to be more similar than were the dizygotic twins. Eysenck interpreted these and similar results as conclusive evidence for including hereditary factors in his formulations about the causes of neuroticism as well as introversion-extraversion.

The next step was to determine, if possible, the specific influences or manifestations of these hereditary factors. Granted that heredity plays a role in the formation of personality, what is (are) the actual mechanism(s) through which this role is effected? As his starting point in this inquiry, Eysenck utilized the work of Pavlov (1927) on experimental neuroses in dogs. In this work, the Russian physiologist had noticed that either of two types of neurosis could develop, depending upon the temperament of his subject. He concluded that his dogs would develop neurasthenic or hysterical neuroses as a function of the dominance of the excitatory or inhibitory actions of their central nervous systems. In Eysenck's interpretation and elaboration of Pavlov's thinking (as well as further refinements made by Hull), he generated what proved to be an extremely important element of his theory. He states:

It is easy to see what Pavlov and Hull had in mind in advocating this concept of inhibition. Whenever a stimulus-response connection is made in the nervous system, there are created both excitatory and inhibitory potentials. The algebraic sum of these determines the amount of learning which takes place, and through it the particular reaction the organism makes when the stimulus in question is presented again (1955, p. 29).

To put this somewhat differently, Eysenck is asserting that the ease and degree to which learning occurs is a function of two complementary processes: on the one hand, the rapidity and strength with which excitatory potentials build up along nerve fibers, and on the other hand, the rapidity and strength with which inhibition tendencies are accumulated and dissipated by the nerve fibers.

Eysenck asks, What if it were the case that each individual inherits an "excitation-inhibition balance" peculiar to his nervous system? In other words, what if it were true that each individual is genetically endowed with a specific rate at which his nerve fibers build up and dissipate both excitation and inhibition potentials? If this were so, then it would also be true that each person's sensitivity to stimuli, accessibility to and speed of conditioning, would be constitutionally determined. Further, if it is true that introverts and extraverts differ in and because of the degree to which they have been socially conditioned, then, one could argue that tendencies that determine the bases of introversion and/or extraversion are genetically transmitted. These assumptions do, in fact, constitute significant components of Eysenck's theory. He posits an innately given "excitation-inhibition balance" that, he argues, lies at the root of each personality. Further, it ultimately determines the individual's position along the introversion-extraversion dimension.

Eysenck cites two crucial experiments in support of these assumptions. The first, performed by Franks (1956), tested the hypothesis that introverts do, in fact, condition more easily and rapidly than extraverts. The second, evidently performed by either Eysenck himself or one of his collaborators, tested for the existence and differential manner of functioning of the excitation-inhibition balance in both introverts and extraverts.

Utilizing 20 introverts, 20 extraverts, and 20 normals, Franks compared these subjects on the acquisition and extinction of several conditioned responses. His results showed the introverts to give significantly more learned responses than did either the normals or the extraverts. Thus Eysenck found support for his hypothesis, which asserted that introverts are more easily conditioned.

Originally, the excitation-inhibition balance, which Eysenck assumes is inherited, was dealt with as a construct. Nonetheless, Eysenck always believed that there were specific physiological phenomena in which this construct could be grounded. Consistent with this belief, he suggested that impulses arising from the different parts of the reticular formation may be responsible for excitation and inhibition. The former, he hypothesized, occurs because of facilitating impulses that arise from the synchronizing and recruiting systems of the thalamic reticular formation. Inhibitory impulses are directed at the cortex and are antagonistic in effect to the influence of the excitatory activating system.

Using the following rationale, Eysenck has obtained some support for his assumptions about this excitation-inhibition balance in introverts and extraverts. If stimulant drugs, such as the amphetamines, and depressive drugs, such as the barbiturates, act through the ascending reticular formation, and if some people are introverts because of a dominance of excitation potentials while others are extraverts because of a dominance of inhibition potentials, then the performances of extraverts when compared to those of introverts should be directly proportional to the performance of depressed individuals when compared to stimulated ones. This hypothesis may be stated in the form of an equation: E/I equals D/S (where E equals performance by extraverts, I equals performance by introverts, D equals performance by people given depressants, and S equals performance by people given stimulants). As Eysenck states, the equation predicts that "on experimental tests relevant to the excitation-inhibition balance, extraverted people, when compared to introverted people, score in the same way as people administered depressant drugs when compared to people administered stimulant drugs" (1965, p. 49–50). When this experiment was, in fact performed, the results were consistent with Eysenck's equation.

Fortified with these assumptions and findings, Eysenck has produced a theory of personality dynamics, the core of which may be stated in the form of one equation and two postulates. First, the equation: P_b equals $P_c \times E$, where P_b refers to behavior personality, that is, the degree to which neurotic, introversive, and/or extraversive tendencies are expressed, and where P_c refers to constitutional (genetically determined) aspects of the personality, and where E refers to environmental influences upon the personality. As the formula indicates, the phenotypic (expressive) behavior patterns are generated by an interaction of environmental affects, schedules of reinforcement and punishment that the person has encountered in his life, and the constitutional or biological predispositions of the personality. In other words, the behavioral personality of an individual is a function of his genetic endowment and personal history. This emphasis upon heredity as a major explanatory basis of behavior is in sharp contrast with the almost totally environmentalist position of Dollard and Miller, not to mention other learning theorists.

The two postulates presented below specify concretely the relations of the excitation-inhibition balance to behavioral personality. Further, they point to the type of pathology which can occur if it is also true that the individual has inherited a strong neurotic tendency.

The Postulate of Individual Differences.   Human beings differ with respect to the speed with which excitation and inhibition are produced, the strength of the excitation and inhibition produced, and the speed with which excitation and inhibition are dissipated. These differences are properties of the physical structures involved in making stimulus-response connections (1957, p. 114).

The Typological Postulate.   Individuals in whom excitatory potentials are developed slowly, and in whom excitatory potentials so developed are relatively weak (or in whom strong inhibitory potentials are developed quickly), are thereby predisposed to develop extraverted patterns of behavior and to develop hysterical psychopathic disorders in the case of neurotic breakdown; individuals in whom excitatory potentials are generated quickly, and in whom excitatory potentials so developed are relatively strong (or in whom weak inhibitory potentials are generated slowly), are thereby predisposed to develop introverted patterns of behavior and to develop dysthymic disorders in the case of neurotic breakdown . . . (1957, p. 114).

From these assumptions, dimensions, postulates, and equations, Eysenck is able to derive the standard neurotic syndromes (anxiety reaction, obsessive-compulsive neurosis, depression, phobia, etc.). Further, he is able to give a dynamic explanation of these syndromes' etiology in terms of constitutional and conditioning factors. For example, dysthymia (anxiety reaction) is a consequence of strong introversive and neurotic tendencies. The former are based upon the inheritance of dominant excitation potentials that have facilitated the overlearning of societal values and prohibitions. The latter are based upon the inheritance of sensitive, overly reactive autonomic nervous system tendencies that have led to excessive emotional lability and general anxiousness.

Comments

As the central concern of this book is to present, evaluate, and integrate different theories of anxiety, we shall confine our remarks to Eysenck's conception of this particular phenomenon. This is not to dismiss in any way his formulations regarding the dynamics of psychopathology. Rather, it is to return to our original project, keeping in mind that tangentially related topics can be addressed elsewhere and at other times.

Eysenck's theory of anxiety can be succinctly summarized if we first orient ourselves by concretely asking three questions: What it it? Why is it? What are its consequences? In answering the first of these inquiries (What is anxiety?), we must not confuse the general stimulus-response approach to this phenomenon with Eysenck's unique hypotheses as to its sources and dynamics. Thus, for this theorist, anxiety is a learned drive; more specifically, it is conditioned fear. Unlike Dollard and Miller, however, Eysenck does not concretely distinguish between the "whatness" of fear and anxiety. There is no expressed concern with the subject's ability to perceive or verbalize the source of the fear; there is no attempt to comprehend the process of repression. Viewing this phenomenon strictly from the perspective of an observer, Eysenck, to all intents and purposes, equates fearing behavior with anxious behavior.

In his answer to the question of why there is anxiety, Eysenck distinguishes his approach from all other learning theories. Essentially, there are two sources of this phenomenon, both of which are ultimately grounded in the constitution or biological endowment of the person. The first, which is a major component of the trait, neuroticism, is the inherited lability of the subject's autonomic nervous system. To be more specific, Eysenck assumes that the neurotic is neurotic because of his genetically determined sensitivity and overresponsiveness to noxious (anxiety-provoking) stimuli. This is a direct and fundamental source of anxiety—the tendency of the individual, because of his constitutional makeup, to be susceptible to anxiety-provoking stimuli.

The second major source of anxiety is less direct in its influence. Eysenck assumes that individuals inherit what he calls an excitation-inhibition balance. The net result of this, depending upon the dominance of either excitation or inhibition tendencies, is that individuals are either unusually given to or insulated from the conditioning processes involved in socialization. The former group—those who are most accessible to social learning procedures—become introverts and are characterized by excessive guilt, shame, social consciousness, and anxiety. The latter, who are least accessible to social learning influences, become extraverts and are characterized as childish, impulsive, and generally unsocialized. Thus the second source of anxiety is learning: specifically, it is the impact of a repressively conceived society, which in turn is mediated by inherited excitation or inhibition nervous system tendencies.

What may we say about the consequences of anxiety in Eysenck's system? The answer is clear and distinct: it is neurosis, the acquisition of neurotic symptoms. While the particular syndrome acquired will be a function of the particular learning history of the individual, the ultimate result will, by definition, be neurosis.

We may now ask, What has Eysenck told us about anxiety? If we wish to understand what anxiety is, we are told that, by definition, it is fear. If we then ask what is fear, we are given a description, from the perspective of an observer, of a cluster of behaviors defined as fear responses. This we cannot question, nor can we ask how the observer knew these responses were, in fact, manifestations of fear. Finally, if we relinquish our inquiry into the whatness of anxiety, or conditioned fear, and orient ourselves to the question of its bases or causes, we are told the following: anxiety has two major sources, both of which are ultimately a function of heredity. The first is direct, in the sense that some people inherit a lability of the autonomic nervous system that predisposes them to be overly sensitive and reactive to anxiety-provoking stimuli. These people are anxiety prone and, by definition, neurotic. The second source is also hereditary, but less direct in its manifestation. It involves the degree to which individuals are accessible to repressive social learning. This accessibility is a function of a genetically transmitted characteristic of the nervous system, probably the reticular activating system. Thus, if we ask why some people are more anxious than others, we are finally told that they are constitutionally predisposed to be so.

REFERENCES

Bergmann, G., and Spence, K. W. The logic of psychophysical measurement. *Psychological Review*, 1944, *51*, 1–24.

Bischof, L. J. *Interpreting personality theories*. New York: Harper & Row, 1964.

Dollard, J., and Miller, N. *Personality and psychotherapy*. New York: McGraw-Hill, 1950, by permission.

Eysenck, H. J. *Dimensions of personality*. London: Routledge and Kegan Paul, 1947.

Eysenck, H. J. A dynamic theory of anxiety and hysteria. *Journal of Mental Science*, 1955, *101*, 28–51.

Eysenck, H. J. The dynamics of anxiety and hysteria. New York: Praeger, 1957.

Eysenck, H. J. Behavior therapy and the neuroses. London: Pergamon, 1960.

Eysenck, H. J., & Rachman, S. The causes and cures of neuroses. San Diego: Knapp, 1965, by permission.

Franks, C. M. Conditioning and personality: A study of normal and neurotic subjects. *Journal of Abnormal and Social Psychology*, 1956, *52*, 147–150.

Hull, C. L. Quantitative aspects of the evolution of concepts: An experimental study. Psychological Monographs, 28 (Whole No. 23), 1921.

Hull, C. L. *Principles of behavior*. New York: Appleton-Century-Crofts, 1943.

Hull, C. L. A *behavior system*. New Haven: Yale, 1952.

Hume, D. A treatise on human nature (quoted text written in 1739). In *The age of enlightenment*, ed. by Sir Isaiah Berlin. New York: New American Library, 1956.

Miller, N. Studies of fear as an acquirable drive: I. Fear as motivation and fear-reduction as reinforcement in learning of new responses. *Journal of Experimental Psychology*, 1948, 38, 89–101.

Mowrer, O. H. A stimulus response analysis of anxiety and its role as a reinforcing agent. In *Readings in learning*, ed. by L. M. Stolurow. Englewood-Cliffs, N.J.: Prentice Hall, 1953.

Pavlov, I. Conditioned reflexes (trans. by G. V. Anrep). London: Oxford, 1927.

Shields, J. Monozygotic twins brought up apart and brought up together. London: Oxford University Press, 1962.

Stevens, S. S. Psychology and the science of science. *Psychological Bulletin*, 1939. *36*, 221–263.

6

The Existential Approach

In the introduction to his book *The Worlds of Existentialism*, Maurice Friedman writes:

Give me a one sentence definition of existentialism. This statement is often more a ritual defense against the insecurity aroused by not being *au courant* than a genuine desire for knowledge. It typifies more than any other the phenomenal popularization and distortion that the movement called existentialism has undergone since Jean-Paul Sartre's widely publicized visit to the United States in 1946. The very notion that existentialism is something that can be defined in a catch phrase, or that one can merely know about it without understanding it from within, has made it for some people into an intellectual fad and robbed it of its proper seriousness. Yet, existentialism is not merely a fad any more than it is a single well-defined movement within philosophy. It is a powerful stream welling up from underground sources, converging and diverging, but flowing forward and carrying with it many of the most important intellectual tendencies and literary and cultural manifestations of our day (1964, p. 3).

Through the following pages, we shall present and discuss the theories of two existentialistically oriented thinkers. Further, insofar as it is feasible, an attempt will be made to portray some of the history and character of this "powerful stream" to which Friedman refers. In this way, it may be possible to illuminate both the "what" and the "why" of the phenomenon of existentialism. Basically, however, our primary purpose will be to examine the particular contribution that each of these theorists has made to our understanding of anxiety.

Although it has recently become quite fashionable to discover the seeds or roots of an existential perspective in almost all philosophies, not to mention many schools of psychology, the clear emergence of this point of view is usually felt to have occurred with the writings of the nineteenth-century Danish philosopher Sören Kierkegaard. While passionately pursuing the meaning of being a Christian, Kierkegaard opposed himself to a long and venerable tradition of philosophical assumptions and modes of inquiry. Prior to his time, philosophers had by and large devoted themselves to the search for immutable, eternal truths. In so doing, they had consistently assumed that the universe and everything in it, including man, could be grasped through reason. Everything was potentially capable of rational explication. Of course, such an explication called for objectivity, an avoidance of the subjective thoughts and feelings of people, and a focusing upon the permanent, the consensually valid, the reasonable.

Kierkegaard began the revolt against these conceptions of man and the universe. He argued that truth is in man, not in nature. He rejected Hegel's attempted rejection of subjectivity and insisted that the individual's thoughts and feelings are the keys to his existence. Further, he dismissed the Cartesian separation of man and world and asserted that the existent individual is continually concerned with and relating himself to the world. Finally, Kierkegaard raised to a position of central importance the questions of freedom, choice, and possibility. This attitude, it should be noted, was in direct opposition to Hegel and others who had in effect translated freedom into the understanding of or even the love of necessity.

From the Kierkegaardian spring, two major streams have flowed. On the one hand, there are the theologically oriented writers, Berdyev, Buber, Tillich, and Marcel, each of whom has tried to speak to the spiritual crisis of contemporary man, especially in his relation to a deity. On the other hand, there have been and are both philosophers and psychologists who have addressed themselves to the human world of everyday life without any particular concern for theological issues. These men have taken up Kierkegaard's concern with the meaning of human existence and the individual experience of freedom. Further, they have, as we shall see, rejected the constricted, exclusively rational understanding of man as nothing but a brief moment in the lawful unfolding of nature. Prominent members of this latter group are Heidegger, Sartre, Merleau-Ponty, Straus, Binswanger, Boss, May, and Farber. The list is by no means exhaustive. However, regardless of any theological commitment, that which brings these thinkers all under the same roof and that which unites them despite their considerable differences in level of discussion and focus of attention is their agreement upon the central significance of the following activities and characteristics that are seen as fundamental to human life.

1. To be man is to exist, to stand out amongst the entities of the universe and to be concerned with their being. Man is not just another object of nature, not just a *Homo natura*, a thing among things governed by "natural laws." Rather, and we must be quite clear in our grasp of this assertion, he is that through which there is a universe. This is not to say that man creates by some magic the entities that he discovers. Nor is it to fall into an idealistic

position and claim that the universe is nothing but a product of man's thought and/or imagination. Instead, it is to acknowledge and affirm the fact that man, in his pursuit of understanding, grasps that which is in human terms. Man co-constitutes through his way of living the meaning of both himself and the entities he encounters. Finally, once one realizes the finite character of man's power to co-constitute meaning, one has grasped the sense of the existential concept of existence. (We shall concretely exemplify this process in our exposition of the thinking of Martin Heidegger.)

2. If man exists—that is, co-constitutes the meanings of both himself and the entities of the universe—then that which is grasped as real is always real for someone. There is nothing, either real or imaginary, which is completely independent of human experience. Someone or something *is* only insofar as human beings comprehend it (him) as existing. Further, the realness or reality of some object or person is not a function of its reliability or repeatability. I do not ask others if they, too, see the typewriter before I sit down to use it. In fact, just the reverse is true. It is just because I see the typewriter as real that I can and do expect others to experience it in the same way. Finally, while there are no humanly grasped beings independent of man, there are, alternatively, no men independent of other beings. Man and universe are mutually interdependent and co-defining. The Cartesian split of subject and object is utterly rejected.

3. Correlative to this notion of existence is the realization that man lives, understands both himself and others, and dies in a world that he experiences as meaningful. Thus any attempt to understand human living must begin with the human experience of meaning. Further, this affirmation of human experience cannot be exclusively confined to that of the experimenter or the scientist. The latter cannot presuppose the alleged objectivity and veracity of his perceptions, thoughts, etc., while at the same time, insisting that his subjects' experiences are "merely subjective"—deceived, unnecessary for scientific explanation.

4. Man experiences some freedom, some opportunity for choice. When he reflects upon it, his life unfolds before him, both transparent and opaque, and he stands able to grasp the decisions he has made and the possibilities that loom before him. Insofar as such experiences occur to an individual, they are real for him. Thus he is confronted both with the power and the responsibility of choice.

In our sampling of the existential perspective, we shall direct our attention to the work of two thinkers who perhaps most strikingly epitomize this point of view. They are Sören Kierkegaard, the innovator of the movement, and Martin Heidegger, its most prominent synthesizer.

Kierkegaard

As has just been suggested above, of all the people whose names are associated with existential philosophy and psychology, there is probably no one who is more frequently mentioned than Sören Kierkegaard. Despite the controversy that continually surrounds the French writer Jean-Paul Sartre, or the almost mystical reverence that is paid to the German ontologist Martin Heidegger, the nineteenth-century Dane emerges as the fountainhead of all the divergent lines of existentialistic thought.

Born in Copenhagen in 1813, Kierkegaard's most productive years were spent thinking and writing in this center of Danish intellectual life. A literary, poetic satirist, he had no desire to be either a philosopher or a theologian. Nonetheless, his life and his works can accurately be seen as a continuing struggle with the meaning of being a Christian. Thus, despite the fact that he lived only forty-two years, he wrote many books—most of which dealt with morality, religion, philosophy, and aesthetics. In the process of writing, Kierkegaard attacked the hypocrisy of conventional religion, the anonymity of middle-class man (with his institutionalized, impersonal life), and the idealistic rationalizations of the Christian tradition presented in Hegelian dialectics. In place of these, he offered a conception of the indvidual as an individual, a call to man to return to his most fundamental concern: his personal responsibility for his life and actions. Some of the outstanding representatives of Kierkegaard's work are *Either/Or* (1843), *Fear and Trembling* (1843), *Repetition* (1843), *Philosophical Fragments* (1844), *The Concept of Dread* (1844), *Concluding Unscientific Postscript* (1846), *The Sickness Unto Death* (1849), and *The Attack Upon Christendom* (1854–55).

While it is not the intention of this section to present and discuss Kierkegaard's thought in its entirety, some general characterization is necessary. This is so not only because an understanding of Kierkegaard's conception of anxiety would be impossible without it but also because the philosophers who harkened to his call continually borrowed from this innovator's understanding of the human condition.

In his writing, Kierkegaard tries to show that there are two constitutive characteristics of man that distinguish him from all other animals. On the one hand, he is caught between freedom and the necessity to make of his life what he will, while on the other hand he is potentially capable of being self-consciously aware of his possibilities for freedom. In other words, while each person is faced with the problem of carving out a life amidst the dialogue of necessity and choice, he is also condemned to be aware of himself as, at least to some extent, a self-determining being. Man is a creature who must grasp himself by a direct, self-conscious apprehension and always in the face of possibility. Further, this continuing grasp of oneself in the context of beckoning possibilities demands an ever-attentive appreciation of the difference between conception and actuality. For Kierkegaard, the freedom to envision alternatives, to choose among them, and to actualize certain possibilities is the goal of the individual's development. Man becomes man in his increasing ability to reflect upon his situation, confront his options, select among them, and realize his responsibilty for that selection.

Anxiety, according to this thinker, can be located in the gap that exists between comprehension of possibility and the choice that leads to its actualization. It is to be found in the movement from "I might" to "I will and am responsible for." Further, it is unavoidable if man is to fulfill his development. Anxiety is inherent in the confrontation of alternatives, the realization of freedom. In fact, it can be described as the self-awareness of the possibility of freedom: "dread (anxiety) is freedom's reality as possibility for possibility" (1944, p. 38). The anxious person is one who grasps the following: there is something about this possibility that is desirable; it could occur, but that would depend, at least in part, upon me; if I choose to try to make it occur, then I will be responsible for both the choice and the event, should it be realized. We may further clarify this conception of anxiety by presenting Kierkegaard's distinction between original and later characteristics of this phenomenon.

According to Rollo May, Kierkegaard's notion of original anxiety can be understood as a "seeking after adventure, a thirst for the prodigious, the mysterious" (1950, p. 34). The person does not experience his separateness from the environment. He does not envision himself as an active force, capable of directing his own life and bringing possibilities into existence. He does not confront his freedom as such. The anxiety that he feels is not grounded in his grasp of some personal responsibility for the future. Instead, it is merely the awareness of something that might happen: "This dread (anxiety) belongs to the child so essentially that he cannot do without it; even though it alarms him, it captivates him nevertheless by its sweet feeling of apprehension" (Kierkegaard, 1944, p. 38). His own part in its actualization does not occur to him. Hence, he feels powerless and in such a state can only wait and wonder.

The crucial factor that determines a shift from the original anxiety of young children to the distress suffered by adults is the coming to pass of self-awareness, the realization of one's individuality and separateness from others and the environment. Obviously, once a person perceives himself as a separate entity, a being who is not completely embedded in his surroundings, he can no longer conceive of possibility or any course of events in the same manner as before. He is no longer completely at the mercy of either a supportive or a threatening environment. For the first time, he realizes his capacity to act upon his own initiative, his possibility of changing his situation, and even, perhaps, the course of his life. With this realization comes the problem of choice. Awareness of the possibility of willful action brings with it an understanding of the fact of choice and the responsibility therefore. To comprehend one's possibilities of choice is to face the necessity of negating certain alternatives, as well as the likelihood of coming into conflict with one's environment. Anxiety arises with this confrontation of freedom in that the agent who must choose and who has no guarantee of the final outcome, must also bear the full responsibility of his choice.

The whole problem of choice, which the individual faces as a finitely free being, accounts for the "inner conflict" that Kierkegaard considers basic to an understanding of anxiety. If the person were not free, conflict would not and could not occur. That it does, in fact, characterize anxiety can be seen in the following description of the phenomenon. As Kierkegaard asserts, anxiety "is afraid, yet it maintains a sly intercourse with its object, cannot look away from it, indeed will not" (1944, p. 92). Further, "anxiety is a desire for what one dreads, a sympathetic antipathy. Anxiety is an alien power that lays hold of an individual and yet one cannot tear oneself away, nor has a will to do so; for one fears, but what one fears one desires" (1944, p. xii). From these observations, it appears that Kierkegaard has conceived of the anxious person as being caught between two mutually exclusive possibilities, as yet unable to abandon one for the other. In such a situation he is impotent and stands paralyzed in his freedom. It should be noted that, while Kierkegaard contrasts the terms fear and anxiety to explain this situation, he does not believe that they are interchangeable. We shall discuss his manner of distinguishing between them later.

Any discussion of Kierkegaard's theory of anxiety would be incomplete without some mention of its implications for the philosopher's major concern, i.e., the problem of how an individual can will to be himself, which is his true vocation. This is a problem for each person, to be decided by each person, because no one can forsee or specify exactly what this self is that he is supposed to will to be. Whether a person attains selfhood will depend upon his willingness and ability to confront the anxiety inherent in his possibilities and further, to move ahead despite it. A person cannot be free and responsible without encountering his anxiety. Thus, if he evades it, he is evading being himself; he has refused to recognize his possibilities; he has refused to make his choice. For the moment, at least, he has negated the human condition and his own humanity in the process.

It should be evident by now that Kierkegaard considers anxiety to be both inherent in and necessary for growth. He states: "He who is educated by anxiety is educated by possibility, and only the man who is educated by possibility is educated in accordance with his infinity. . . . The greater the anxiety, the greater the man" (1944, pp. 139–140). These statements follow logically from Kierkegaard's belief that the process of becoming a self (individuation), which is every person's essential task as a person, proceeds through the confrontation with anxiety. But how, we may ask, can anxiety help an individual to grow, to become himself? Kierkegaard claims that each experience of anxiety enables the person to free himself from the finite, petty constrictions of everyday life, constrictions that close the individual off to his freedom and ultimately to his possibilities as a responsible self. Confronted with his anxiety the person realizes that he himself is personally involved in his world. He is not lost in the anonymity of what people in general do; he has not surrendered his freedom to others, or to public opinion. He is confronted by himself as a free being who is personally responsible for his decisions and actions.

When an individual has undergone and moved through anxiety, he finds himself freer to face it again. Kierkegaard suggests that as this process repeats itself in the course of life, the individual will teach himself faith and inward fortitude. Then one has "courage to renounce anxiety without any anxiety which only faith is capable of—not that it annihilates anxiety, but remaining ever young, it is continually developing itself out of the death throe of anxiety" (1944, p. 104). This state, then, would be characteristic of the man who has attained selfhood by willing to be himself. Through experiencing anxiety, he will have come to the point at which his main concern is with the possibilities of his life, rather than with evading individual experiences of anxiety. The latter is never abolished, but the person with faith, whether this be placed in a deity or in one's future, is able to sense anxiety's value without surrendering to the temptation to renounce his freedom, his responsibility, and thus his selfhood in the face of it.

As was previously suggested, Kierkegaard does not use the words "fear" and "anxiety" interchangeably, although he recognizes their similarity. The basis of his distinction between them is in terms of their relations with objects. In fear, there is a definite feared object and the person moves away from it. In anxiety, on the other hand, the object is not experienced as so clearly repelling and the person's reaction is not, therefore, to move in any specific direction. The conflict within himself prevents him from settling upon any specific course of action. Thus his relation to that which he is anxious about is uncertain. Primarily, he is concerned with and caught up in his inner conflict.

Summary and Comment

Kierkegaard claims that anxiety is the experiential state that arises when an individual responsibly confronts his freedom for certain possibilities. A distinction must be made between original and later anxiety, or the anxiety of the very immature (in which there is no realization of one's individuality or the power of choice) and the anxiety that can only occur after the individual has reached a state of self-awareness, with its recognition of possibility and responsibility for personal action. Only through this later form of anxiety can a person attain selfhood, for encounters with it enable one to be freed from the petty constrictions of everyday conformity and personal anonymity. Finally, fear is said to differ from anxiety in that the fearful man moves away from the feared object that is clearly and specifically grasped; the anxious man, to the contrary, is conflicted and uncertain about the object of his distress.

As with the other theorists presented in this book, we must first be clear as to the perspectives from which Kierkegaard's interpretations and assertions emerge. Then we can adequately evaluate his contribution to our understanding of the phenomenon of anxiety. Thus it is important to realize that this thinker's approach to the human condition in general, and anxiety in particular, is from the standpoint of an existentially oriented thinker—i.e., one who is concerned with the development of certain individual experiences in a social context. For these reasons, the reader should not expect, nor will he find statements as to the causes of behavior, theoretical discussions of various bodily states, or postulates concerning the alleged functioning of an assortment of hypothetical drives, instincts, or needs.

To say that Kierkegaard is an existentially oriented thinker is to realize that he is concerned with the problems of freedom, choice, and personal responsibility. Man is not understood as an empiricistically conceived passive recipient of stimuli. Nor is he merely a respondent to his environment. Man and world are co-defining, and through an individual's choices, he makes both himself and his world.

When we claim that Kierkegaard is concerned with the development of certain individual experiences, we are asserting that he has already grasped human development as a process of becoming. In this movement, that which is of paramount importance is the experience of the individual as he undergoes and realizes it. It is not "sensory experience" to which Kierkegaard is addressing himself. It is not the transmission of various excitations from afferent to efferent nerve systems. Rather, it is experience as it is understood in the everyday sense of the term. It includes perceiving, thinking, imagining, etc.

Finally, to claim that Kierkegaard is aware of the social significance of these experiences is to say that he sees the individual as struggling to affirm his experience as his own, to realize the uniqueness of his own feelings and understandings, and to resist the pressure of society's demand that he experience something else.

With this in mind, we may now ask about Kierkegaard's formulations regarding the phenomenon of anxiety. From the exposition, we can see that he grasps anxiety as an experiential state, constituted by the individual's awareness of his own possibilities, by his realization that he has no objective justification for choosing among them, and by his limited capacity to foresee all the consequences of a possible choice. To complicate matters further, the individual may realize that if he enacts certain choices, he will be individualized as a separate entity, potentially in conflict with his fellow citizens and personally responsible for all the consequences. On these grounds anxiety inevitably occurs and, according to Kierkegaard, must be wholeheartedly faced and conquered.

Heidegger

The German philosopher, Martin Heidegger, is probably one of the most famous as well as influential proponents of existentialistic thought. Born in 1889 at Messkirch in Baden, Heidegger received his doctorate from the University of Freiburg, where he studied mathematics, physics, and philosophy. Soon afterwards, in 1920, he became the assistant of Edmund Husserl, the founder of phenomenology, and the two worked in close cooperation until 1923. At that time, Heidegger was offered and accepted the rank of professor ordinarius at the University of Marburg. There he stayed until 1928, when upon Husserl's request, he succeeded his former teacher as chairman of philosophy at Freiburg. Today, he continues to live and write at his retreat, a ski hut in Todtnau near Freiburg.

The central problem to which Heidegger has devoted his entire professional career is that of ontology, the study of the Being process. As far as such thinkers as Medard Boss, Ludwig Binswanger, Jean-Paul Sartre, and Maurice Merleau-Ponty are concerned, Heidegger's opus magnum, *Being and Time* (1927), constituted the basis and/or the point of departure for most of their work. In this section we shall attempt to outline some of Heidegger's thinking, especially as it related to the nature of anxiety. By no means should the reader conclude that what follows is an exhaustive or comprehensive discussion of this man's brilliant work. Those who would seek a more profound understanding of both his method and his thought should acquaint themselves with his writings, which are, for the most part, available in English. If this seems too difficult or time-consuming, the scholarly expositions of William Richardson (1963) could be quite helpful.

As has been suggested above, Heidegger's whole philosophical effort has been to illuminate the Being process, that by which there are beings (entities) rather than nothing. For the reader who has not been initiated into the problems of philosophy, it might be helpful to digress for a moment and elaborate upon such terms as Being, beings, and ontology. Even prior to the days of Socrates and Plato, philosophers such as Parmenides and Heraclitus questioned the nature of the universe, the existence of entities, and the characteristics of man. They asked, "Why is there anything rather than nothing?"; "What is the ultimate ground or origin of all beings?"; and "As all beings exist in some form, what is this attribute or process that they share as beings?" Generally, the raising of these questions has continued throughout human history and the answers offered have constituted two distinct, yet obviously related disciplines. On the one hand, these questions have been expressed in the form of theological inquiry. Here the emphasis has been on some original or Supreme Being who is alleged to have created all other beings. On the other hand, these questions have been expressed in the form of ontological inquiry, and reflections upon the common attributes, qualities, or processes characteristic of all beings have been preferred. The fruits of these reflections have been stated in terms of immutable essences, eternal Ideas, and Being processes by which particular beings are made manifest. Although he originally revealed some interest in theology, Heidegger soon turned to ontology and a requestioning of the Being process.

In *Being and Time*, Heidegger starts his analysis with an explicit acknowledgement of the indisputable fact that man uses the word "is." He says "the tree is tall," "the cup is on the table," "the sky is blue," "the woman is beautiful," etc., and in so doing, he demonstrates his power to comprehend and affirm the existence of beings as particular beings. How is this possible? What is the nature or Being of man that he can and does, in fact, perceive existing entities as such? Heidegger argues that everyday experience (he calls it ontic experience), which is a necessary prerequisite for the kinds of assertions just noted, can occur only because man has ontological knowledge. Man can affirm and articulate the existence of entities, including himself, only because he already possesses an understanding, albeit vague and unquestioned, of the process by which entities are what they are. This is ontological knowledge.

An example at this point might be helpful. If I place a pen in front of a student and ask him to tell me what it is, he would presumably be able to say, "It's a pen." In so doing, he would be demonstrating his power to grasp the fact that this entity exists for him as an entity. Further, he can label it as such. But now, if I ask him what must he already know such that he is able to recognize the pen as a pen, he may be puzzled. Usually, he will say, "What do you mean? I learned a long time ago that this is a pen." That's probably true, but it does not adequately account for the fact that he can recognize the pen as a pen at this time. The conditions under which a fact was learned are not synonymous with or sufficient to explain the conditions under which the learned fact is manifested. In other words, if one has previously learned that certain objects with certain characteristics are called pens, this, by itself, does not account for the expression and utilization of this learning in the present. One must also ask, What is the nature of the present situation? and, most importantly, How is this previous learning alive and operative in the present? What my student had once learned is a knowledge of what makes a pen a pen —ontological knowledge of the Being of a pen. Further, only because this knowledge is now a present as well as a past part of the student's life, is he capable of recognizing and labeling this particular entity.

The problems that Heidegger poses in *Being and Time* may be stated as follows: (1) What is man that he demonstrates ontological comprehension?

and (2) How does this ontological comprehension operate such that there is a unity to experience? In answer to the first of these questions, Heidegger suggests that there is some central aspect or process "in" man, there is a dimension of man's being, his Self, understood ontologically and presubjectively, which constitutes his power to grasp the fact that entities exist. This process or Self he denotes by the term Dasein and his analytic of Dasein is the basis of the Daseinsanalysis of both Binswanger and Boss.

A further explication of the meaning of Dasein would be most helpful if we are clearly to understand Heidegger's conception of anxiety. Literally translated, Dasein would mean "the There-being." Although this seems awkward and certainly jars the reader, there is some merit in its use. Heidegger is trying to point to that aspect or process, most central to man, which constitutes his ontological dimension. By referring to this process as the There-being, we are consistent with the conception of Dasein as a being whose essential nature is to be "there"—that is, alongside of and in intimate relations with the entities of the world. Dasein is, among other things, the manner in which man's ontological comprehension of the entities of world is organized. Dasein or the There-being is not locked up inside of itself or without reference to anything but itself. It is not like a mental apparatus, or a psyche, or a *res cogitans* (à la Descartes). Rather, it is that process in man that underlies his recognition of and familiarity with the beings of the world.

Continuing our clarification of the meaning of Dasein, we might indicate that to which it does not refer. Dasein is not a thing; it is not some entity or attribute of man that he happens to possess, such as brown eyes or big feet. Nor is Dasein some faculty or cognitive process such as thinking, memory, imagination, etc. To say that it is the Self, understood ontologically and presubjectively, is to say that it is essential to the Being of man, that it is, in fact, the most salient feature of the Being of man. Dasein is that which must already exist—already in the sense of ground or foundation, not in the temporal sense of prior—for such a phenomenon as subjectivity (experience of both objects and oneself) even to occur. Dasein is the most significant process that man manifests; it is his power to grasp and comprehend the fact that he and other entities exist; it is that which makes him the distinctive being he is.

What may we say about the relationships that exist between Dasein as ontological foundation and man as subject who thinks, feels, experiences, and understands himself and events? As a process as well as a realm of man's Being, Dasein is a continually unfolding frame of reference or matrix of meanings. Further, the elements or ingredients of this frame or matrix are ontological comprehensions and these, in turn, are the ground upon which man experiences both himself as a subject and other entities. Paraphrasing Richardson, we could say that Dasein is the center of the entire man; it is that which makes possible all that characterizes him as man.

The reader who has at least some familiarity with the history of philosophical thought will, by now, have realized that Heidegger has rejected or undercut the traditional dichotomy of man and world as the starting point for his analysis. There is no mind or mental apparatus on the one hand and external world on the other as there is, for example, in Freud. There is no Cartesian separation of *res cogitans* and *res extensa* (see the introduction to the chapter on the learning-theory approach to anxiety). Consistent with his rejection of this traditional starting point, Heidegger denies the philosophies of Idealism and Realism, which derive from Cartesian thinking. He insists that both man and world, as they are experienced, arise from a common ground of possibility and meaning. This common ground is Dasein.

Some of the extremely important consequences of this view may be stated in the following manner: man and the human world, the world as it is experienced and lived by human beings, are co-defining; there is no world without man and there is no man without a world—insofar as something exists, it exists for someone who grasps it as such, whether this be in perception, imagination, thought, etc. The human world is not only a conglomerate or collection of entities to be found within some larger whole called nature or the universe. It is also and most primordially that wherein man lives and dies; it is the context in which he strives to accomplish his goals and realize the meanings that are significant to him. The human world is a network of involvements, meanings, and significances that revolve around man. Man, on the other hand, is an evolving system of projects and understanding, continually struggling to understand himself as well as that which he encounters in his activities. Thus it can be said that man also is a process and not a thing.

There are certain modes of being—Heidegger calls them existentials— that are characteristic of Dasein. Another way of saying this is that there are certain typical forms of living that are constitutive of man as man. One of these, Richardson translates with the term "disposition." In so doing, the translator claims that by this term Heidegger is trying to point to the fact that Dasein is perpetually finding itself in some situation with some affective involvement. Characteristic of affective involvements is the fact that Dasein discovers them already there; it does not create them through any cognitive or volitional act. Further, it is for the most part unaware of how it got to be in such a state or to where that state is leading. Another characteristic of affective involvements or states is that they color and influence the manner in which Dasein illuminates objects and events to be experienced. As is well known, in sadness or depression we find that the world is gray and undifferentiated while in joy or enthusiasm, the world is vivid, alive, and inviting. Whatever the affective state, the world is revealed in that state's light.

Another mode of being that is characteristic of Dasein, Richardson translates with the term, "fallen-ness." With this term Heidegger is not trying to imply some negative value on human life or action, as might be the case with certain theologies. Rather, he is referring to the fact that Dasein is continually preoccupied with the world of things, the world of "they" or "people in general," the world of anonymity. This preoccupation Heidegger describes as a flight from Dasein's foremost concern: its own individuality, its own existence.

We may now begin to approach Heidegger's conception of the phenomenon of anxiety. However, in order to do this more adequately, it will be necessary to contrast anxiety with fear. The philosopher himself states that they are kindred phenomena and that a clear distinction between them is required because "for the most part they have not been distinguished from one another; that which is fear gets designated as 'anxiety,' while that which has the character of anxiety gets called fear" (1963, p. 230).

For Heidegger, it is not enough merely to differentiate between fear and anxiety. It is not enough to describe two possibilities of being and label one of them fear and the other anxiety. Adequate analyses of these phenomena must not only show how they are different but must also reveal why they have been confused and what, if any, is their relationship to each other. Heidegger tries to do just this and begins with the fact that fear as well as anxiety is a dispositional mode of being of Dasein. Both are affective states through which Dasein and its situation are revealed. As such, Dasein discovers itself already there, thrust into a state by no act of choice and frequently unaware of how it got there or to where it will lead. Further, as affective states, both fear and anxiety have an "in the face of which" and an "about which" they are so involved. Finally, with these phenomena there is an element of "fleeing away from" that is constitutive of their being.

In the case of fear, that in the face of which Dasein is fearful is the fearsome, a specific entity that can be clearly located within the world. The fearsome, radiating its character of injurious detrimentality, comes from a definite place or region. In its coming, there is the question of whether it will reach Dasein. This uncertainty, rather than assuaging the fearing, only intensifies it. That about which Dasein is fearful is always some particular potentiality of its being. Finally, the element of fleeing away from, which Heidegger insists is always present, becomes in the case of fear, a shrinking back in the face of the fearsome. An example may help to clarify this. Consider the situation of a child who is about to receive an injection. That in the face of which he is fearful, the fearsome, is the syringe that the doctor is bringing toward his arm. That about which he is fearful is himself, grasped as a being who can experience pain. And the fact that it usually takes the persuasions, if not the physical coercions, of his mother to hold him testifies strikingly to the element of shrinking away.

In the case of anxiety, Heidegger claims: "that in the face of which Dasein is anxious is not any being within the world at all, nor is it injurious in any determined or determinable way, nor is it here nor there nor anywhere. It is no-being and no-where" (Richardson, 1963, p. 72). In other words, that in the face of which Dasein is anxious is not a specific entity. It cannot be located; it has no place or origin from which it comes. But it is not nothing. What is this something that cannot be located, and that cannot be defined in terms of its detrimental possibilities? Heidegger's answer is that Dasein is anxious in the face of the collapse of its world, the gradual dissolution into insignificance of the totality of its involvements. Dasein is anxious in the face of the meaninglessness of its activities and understandings.

That about which Dasein is anxious is itself, the continuing viability of its possibilities of self-understanding. Those ways in which Dasein had previously grasped itself, even taken itself for granted, no longer make sense. Dasein is a stranger to itself and its world. The element of fleeing away from, which is constitutive of anxiety, is a turning away from oneself and an intensified preoccupation with the entities of the world. In anxiety Dasein flees from itself and makes even more urgent efforts to be at home with the entities of the world.

Can we find a helpful example to put flesh on this skeleton? My students tell me, and I have only little trouble remembering myself, that the phenomenon usually referred to as "test anxiety" is most suitable for our purposes. In this state, that in the face of which one is anxious is not the test per se, but rather its meaning. If one pursues the matter fully and faithfully, one will find that the whole world of the student is at stake. The situation of being anxious about a test illuminates not only the student's relations with some possible grade, but also his involvements with his parents, teachers, peers, and, of course, his future goals and ambitions. That about which the student is anxious is clearly himself. The whole meaning of his life, as he currently grasps it, is in question. Can he continue? Is he viable? Finally, as is well known, when the intensity of this state reaches even a moderate level, he can no longer face it. Instead, the questions are abandoned and he absorbs himself in a frenzy of makeshift and unrelated-to-the-test activities.

Let us recapitulate and summarize Heidegger's analyses. Both fear and anxiety are dispositional or affective states. Both involve, as constitutive elements of their respective modes of being, an "in the face of which" and an "about which" they are so affectively aroused. In fear, that in the face of which Dasein is fearful is a specific determinable entity; in anxiety, that in the face of which Dasein is anxious is the emergent meaninglessness of its world. That about which Dasein is fearful is a particular potentiality of its being, while that about which Dasein is anxious is the totality of itself, grasped as a network of possibilities. Both anxiety and fear involve a form of fleeing. In the latter, it is a shrinking away from the fearsome, while in the former, it is a turning away from the uncertainty of Dasein's identity and an immersion in the entities of the world.

So much for the analyses and comparisons. But how does this help us to understand the fact that anxiety and fear are continually confused with each other? Obviously, both fear and anxiety are unpleasant affective states. In both there is some object or situation that threatens. In both there is a fleeing in the face of that which threatens. And, finally, in both there are senses of one's existence, either a particular potentiality or as a totality, which are at stake. From an observer's perspective, however, one can see no difference in these states. The affectively aroused, observed individual is seen as suffering discomfort; he seems to be concerned with his well-being, and he behaves as if he were fleeing from something that threatens him. The observer cannot distinguish anxiety from fear in his fellow man. To do this, he must inquire of the other's experience, and when such inquiry is absent or "forbidden" by certain methodological dictates, then anxiety and fear are confused.

Comments

In attempting to evaluate Heidegger's contribution to our understanding of anxiety, we must be careful to be clear about the questions that guided his analyses. As was stated at the very beginning of the exposition, Heidegger has addressed himself to the ontological dimension of human existence. He is not immediately concerned with man the bodily creature of this or that sex. He has not attempted a causal analysis of anxiety or any other state, at least not in the sense that most psychologists are apt to read about. Rather, his thinking is oriented to that or those processes, i.e., Dasein or dispositional states, etc., that must already exist in an ontological and not a temporal sense if there is to be such a creature as man and if such a creature is to be fearful or anxious. In at least one sense, Heidegger's analyses are analogous to those of Immanuel Kant. He does not ask *why* man becomes anxious or fearful. Instead, he already agrees that man does manifest these modes of being and thus he addresses himself to the question, "What must be the ontological nature of man and the world such that these states could occur?"

Keeping the above in mind, we may now try to specify concretely Heidegger's contribution. While the points to be enumerated are all extremely important, perhaps the most critical is Heidegger's insistence upon considering and analyzing the structure of the anxious individual's experience. Only from the perspective of the person living the particular affect can that affect be completely understood. If one adamantly remains rooted within the perspective of the observer, then anxiety becomes indistinguishable from fear.

Another aspect of the phenomenon that Heidegger's analyses bring to light is the fact that human beings are related not only to particular objects and events but also that they are continually related to the whole, to the world as a totality. Further, the world in which anxiety and fear occur is not primarily that of the astronomer or the physicist. It is, rather, the world of everyday life, the world of involvements, the world of humanly understood, meaningful relationships.

Heidegger's thought reveals quite clearly his understanding of the fact that an individual's identity is, at least potentially, forever open to threat. But this identity is not some static self-concept or image that gets carried around from situation to situation. It is, instead, a complex, organized structure, constituted by hierarchies of meaningful possibilities, as well as potentialities. What is more, although they are usually unquestioned and taken for granted, these possibilities are, for the most part, accessible to concernful awareness when they are threatened.

Finally, Heidegger's analyses suggest that fear is possible because man is a bodily, spatially oriented being. As such, he can respond to the injurious detrimental possibilities of some entities. He can discern their spatial relation to him as body. This is not the case with anxiety, which does not primarily involve things.

REFERENCES

Friedman, M. *The worlds of existentialism*. New York: Random House, 1964.

Heidegger, M. *Being and time* (trans. from *Sein und Zeit*, Erste Halfte, Jahrbuch fur Philosophie and Phenomenologische Forschung, vol. viii (1927), pp. 1–438 by John Macquarrie & Edward Robinson). New York: Harper & Row, 1963.

Kierkegaard, S. *The concept of dread* (original text written in 1844, trans. with introduction by Walter Lowrie). Princeton: Princeton University Press, 1944.

May, R. *The meaning of anxiety*. New York: Ronald, 1950.

Richardson, S. J. Wm., *Heidegger: through phenomenology to thought*. The Hague: Martinus Nijhoff, 1963.

7

The Approach of
Ernest Schachtel

Ernest G. Schachtel is a contemporary psychoanalyst who currently functions as a Training and Supervisory Analyst at the William Alanson White Institute of Psychiatry, Psychoanalysis and Psychology. Further, he is an Adjunct Professor of Psychology at the Postdoctoral Training Program of New York University. Aside from these responsibilities, as well as conducting an ongoing private practice of psychoanalysis and diagnostic testing, he still finds time to write scholarly, insightful treatises on various psychological phenomena. While his most recent work, *Experiential Foundations of Rorschach's Test* (1966), is exclusively devoted to testing theory and interpretation, *Metamorphosis* (1959) constitutes a major synthesis of his thinking about such processes as emotion, perception, attention, and memory.

According to Schachtel, the most significant task facing contemporary psychology is that of comprehending both change and continuity in human life. This enterprise, he argues, demands more than systematic explanation; it requires and presupposes careful descriptions of the phenomena to be explained as they unfold and show themselves. Furthermore, the final theoretical solution must be couched in terms of the developmental viewpoint. As the theorist pointedly states, "later stages [of life] still show traces of the earlier ones, and the condition of the newborn shows the seeds of, the Anlage for, the later developments" (1959, p. v).

While Schachtel recognizes and affirms the importance of Freud's contribution to modern psychological theory, he significantly departs from the founder's thought. He agrees that psychoanalytic formulations have accorded due weight to developmental factors, but he insists that "they do not suffice to account adequately for what we can actually observe in early development.

This is especially true of the concepts of the pleasure and reality principles and their relation to each other in the course of development" (1959, p. vi).

With regard to the phenomenological and Daseinsanalytic thinkers, Schachtel argues that although their work is important, it is necessarily incomplete. Such theoreticians as Boss, Binswanger, Straus, and von Gebsattel have rightly stressed the significance of experiential data, but they:

cannot raise the ontogenetic question of how certain modes of experiencing developed and became what they are. The understanding of adult man and his situation in the world requires both the careful, qualitative observations of his experiences and reactions, and the genetic exploration of the ways in which he came to develop them in his interaction with the environment (1959, p. vi).

In order to present Schachtel's position faithfully, we shall try to follow his line of reasoning rather than to approach his theory as an already-completed, self-contained product. As was suggested, he both acknowledges his debt to and yet departs from Freudian thought. Thus he introduces his fundamental concepts through an immediate comparison to those of Freud. He states, "Man lives throughout his life in a conflict which Freud at one time described as that between Eros, the principle of unification, and Thanatos, the death principle, and which I would describe as the conflict of emergence from embeddedness" (1959, p. 6). In spite of the apparent similarity of these two sets of polar principles—Eros and Thanatos on the one hand and emergence and embeddedness on the other—there is a basic divergence in their meanings. Eros, the principle of unification, refers to the tendency of all living things to establish and preserve even larger unities, to be fruitful, to multiply, and to fill up the earth. Thanatos, the death principle, refers to the tendency of all life to strive for and achieve a state of complete rest, inertia, even inorganicity. For Schachtel, the principle of emergence refers to the developing individual's continuing interest in and orientation toward an ever-expanding, stimulating world. The principle of embeddedness, on the other hand, refers to the developing individual's needs for safety, security, dependability, and familiarity in his dealings with others, with objects of the world, and even with himself. Thus, according to this theoretician, the basic conflicts that occur throughout life are not between id and ego; they are not between demands for an immediate discharge of tension and petitions for delay in deference to society; they are not between the pleasure and reality principles. Rather, the bases of the continuing manifestation of conflict in human life are the individual's needs to realize his skills, potentialities, and capacities while, at the same time, preserving his safety, familiarity, and "at homeness" with both himself and his environment.

In an effort to clarify and further differentiate his own position from that of the more traditional psychoanalytic thinkers, Schachtel criticizes both

Freud and the Ego-Psychologists, particularly Hartmann, for omitting or avoiding the stimulation-seeking side of the human being:

What Freud overlooked was that from birth on the infant and child also show an eagerness to turn toward an increasing variety of things in the environing reality and that sensory contact with them is enjoyed rather than experienced as a disturbing excitation. . . . Freud's negative pleasure principle blinded him to the significance of the phenomenon, so striking in the growing infant and child, of the pleasure and fulfillment found in the encounter with an expanding reality and in the development, exercise and realization of his growing capacities, skills, and powers (1959, p. 9).

Summing up his disagreement with Freud, Schachtel writes:

But man's need to relate to the world leads to encounters which are different from and go beyond those serving discharge of tension as described by Freud and Ego-Psychology. It leads to an encounter with world and fellow man in which they are not merely need-objects, but in which they are experienced in their own right and in which man, implicitly or explicitly, poses the questions "Who are you?", "What is the world?", "Who am I?" and "What is and what ought to be my place in and my relation to the world?" These questions arise because of man's openness toward the world and toward himself, which distinguishes him from even the highest mammals and the seeds of which are already visible in his infancy and childhood, although they often wither away during childhood and may be buried deeply and forgotten by the adult. Man's openness toward the world implies that the nature of pleasure cannot be reduced to the decrease and abolishment of excitation, nor the strivings of man to sexual or destructive ones. He experiences the world not merely as a need-object, and his conflicts cannot be reduced to that between instinct and reality (1959, pp. 12–13).

It is certainly thought-provoking to compare this view with that of the existentialists, Kierkegaard and Heidegger, on the one hand, and that of the modern learning theorists, Spence and Dollard and Miller, on the other.

Before specifically focusing upon Schachtel's theory of anxiety, we should briefly elaborate upon his conception of affects in general as this is the ground in which anxiety is to be situated. Here, again, the theorist takes as his point of departure the formulations of Freud. In this case, however, his criticism is that the founder of psychoanalysis, consistent with the thinking of his times, grasped emotions as primarily disorganizing and irrational, irrevocably opposed to perceptual and/or cognitive functioning. Concretely, Schachtel enumerates what he feels to be the three major touchstones of Freud's theory of affects. First, there is the assumption that all affects are "reproductions of emotions originally generated by past traumatic experiences, vital to the organism, which possibly even antedate the individual existence of the person" (1959, p. 20). Second, he attributes to Freud the tendency "to view affect and action upon the outer world as radically different from each other, as if they were op-posed to each other and mutually exclusive" (1959, p. 20). In other words, af-fects are said to involve only a change in the individual's bodily condition, but to have no meaning for events in the world. Finally, Schachtel claims that Freud "neglected the positive function of affect, namely, its tremendous role in communication and in effecting changes in the outer world by means of communication" (1959, p. 21).

In contrast to this orientation, Schachtel insists that affect and action are neither opposed to each other nor mutually exclusive. In fact, one does not occur except in the context of the other; every action is either prompted by or expressive of some affective state, while every affect refers to the state of the individual in his action-oriented relations with the world. Further, this theorist asserts that:

the function of affect can be fully grasped only if we do not confine our viewpoint to what goes on in the individual organism, but take as our object of study the life-scene in which the affect arises and in which it affects not only the body of the isolated organism, but also other organisms (animals, men) who perceive the expression of affect and react to it (1959, p. 21).

Thus, for Schachtel, the unit of study is not the isolated, worldless organism or psyche, but, rather, it is the person-in-situation.

With this comparison as his starting point, Schachtel goes on to consider the types of affectivity displayed by the infant. He finds that in some situa-tions, those in which the infant is apparently frustrated in his search for food, stimulation, warmth, and the like, the affect evidenced is, in fact, of the type described by psychoanalytic theory. That is to say, the infant's behavior and restlessness seems to be "a mere discharge of tension, without directedness" (1959, p. 24). On the other hand, there are alternative situations, nursing in particular, when:

we can see in quite a few of them an attitude which shows all the signs of eager concentration. Here the picture is entirely different from restless behavior. The torso and the limbs are held quite still and the whole energy is concentrated on the sucking activity. This activity is the eagerly pursued and gratifying goal of the infant. . . . I want to draw attention especially to the fact that we find in the very young infant an affect which does not impress us as unruly, diffuse, violent, but as a kind of goal-directed, positive tension feeling, and this at a time when, ac-cording to classical psychoanalytic theory, no "taming," counter-cathecting, or con-trolling of drive or affect has yet taken place. . . . It does point up the fact that we find . . . right from the beginning of life, two types of affect, one of which impresses us as the diffuse discharge of tension, familiar from Freud's theory, and the other as a positive, directed tension phenomenon which seems similar to the activity-affects of later life, and is encountered first in connection with a basic, bio-logical need (1959, pp. 24–25).

Thus, in contrast to psychoanalytic theory and yet encompassing it, Schachtel wants to describe, examine, and analyze two general types of affect, both of which are said to be present from birth. The first, which is the only type of affect that Freud speaks about, Schachtel designates as embeddedness-affect. It is primarily characterized by a diffuse, nongoal-directed discharge of tension, and it occurs whenever the individual has lost his sense of safety, familiarity, "at homeness" with both himself and his environment. Obviously the particular content of the embeddedness changes with the process of development. Thus, in infancy, the salient aspects of embeddedness are those that pertain to the symbiotic relationship of the infant with the mother. Later, in childhood, major aspects of embeddedness have to do with peer relations, total family situation, and so forth.

The second type of affect, the one that Schachtel claims the Freudians completely miss, he designates as activity-affect. This is basically characterized as "a directed, sustained, and activity-sustaining tension" (1959, p. 26). That is to say, activity-affects both support and accompany the individual's goal-directed pursuit of objects and states of affairs in the environment. Schachtel carefully describes the meaning and implications of activity-affects when he asserts:

the recognition of the existence of and predisposition to activity-affects speaks against the validity of a pure conflict theory of emotions. The function of the activity-affects is to establish an effective emotional link between the separate organism and the environment, so that the organism will be able to engage in those activities which will satisfy his needs, develop his capacities, and further his life. In contrast, the main biological function of the embeddedness-affects is, originally, to arouse the attention and activate the care of the mothering one, that is, to induce the environment to do something about the organism's needs (1959, p. 31).

According to Schachtel, the most striking example of the embeddedness-affects is anxiety, while the prime manifestations of the activity-affects are hope and joy. As our major concern is with anxiety, we shall now inquire as to this theorist's explicit description of and accounting for this phenomenon. The answer to our inquiry is given in the following excerpt.

[Anxiety] arises with any separation from the state of embeddedness or with the threat of such separation if the person is or feels helpless to cope with the situation of separation. . . . Such helplessness is experienced whenever in a particular "separation from embeddedness" situation, the activity-affect aiming at the establishment of relatedness on a higher level of development (of greater differentiation and independence) is not sufficiently strong or persistent. . . . The attempt to emerge from embeddedness sets off anxiety by which that side of the person which is afraid to leave the shelter of embeddedness warns him of the danger of helplessness in encountering the world. The areas in which the threat of separation is most readily experienced, the extent of these areas, and the kinds of events or situations which are most likely to constitute such a threat differ from one person to another, in accordance with their life histories and probably also with inborn predispositions toward anxiety. . . . Anxiety is ever present as a potentiality in all men. Indeed, the potentiality for anxiety is a much more powerful factor in the life of man than acute strong anxiety (1959, pp. 44–45).

Let us carefully dissect and digest these assertions before going on to this theorist's comparison of fear with anxiety. Obviously, Schachtel has presented us with an exceedingly rich, though condensed, account of the phenomenon in question. Therefore, in order that we may fully appreciate the statement's meaning and relevance, we will attempt to draw out its implications and ramifications.

In Schachtel's thinking, the original state of the organism is one of being in equilibrium with its environment. This is alleged to be the condition of the fetus in the womb. With the advent of birth, with the separation of the organism from its intrauterine existence, a context of separateness is created. Within this context, two ever-present, continually operative, and dialectically related tendencies emerge. They are the strivings for embeddedness, safety, and security on the one hand, and the strivings for emergence, growth, and differentiation on the other. That which is ultimately symbolized in the embeddedness tendencies is the condition of organism-environment equilibrium characteristic of intrauterine life. That which is symbolized in the emergence tendencies are independence, self-sufficiency, and freedom from the past. For Schachtel, much of human life and development—certainly all of its conflicts—reflects the existence of these two fundamentally opposed tendencies.

The affects that express, support, and sustain the emergence strivings are called the activity-affects. Depending upon their strength and persistence, the individual is able to enter into and pursue increasingly differentiated relations with the environment. Further, in the context of these affects' effectiveness, the organism's needs are satisfied, its capacities are developed, and its life is furthered. The affects that express disruptions in and demand a return to states of equilibrium, safety, and familiarity are designated as embeddedness-affects. They occur because the tensions of the activity-affects pushing toward increasingly independent modes of relatedness are insufficient to overcome the also-present demands for safety, security, and equilibrium.

Anxiety, as the most striking example of the embeddedness-affects, is an expression of the individual's anticipated or actual loss of embeddedness. The anxious individual either foresees or concretely experiences himself as no longer being at home in some situation. The most salient component of this experience is helplessness. The referents of this helplessness are twofold. First, there is the inability of the currently manifest activity-affect(s) to sustain the higher level of relatedness. Second, there is the individual's sense of impotence in the face of that which is too new to him, in the realization that he is truly no longer on familiar grounds.

It is not difficult to see why Schachtel claims that anxiety, or the potentiality for anxiety, is inherent in every movement toward increasing growth
and differentiation. For the older child, teenager, and adult, anxiety emerges
with the realization that some planned or contemplated activity has the potential to remove the individual from his safe, familiar grounds. It is this realization that constitutes, for Schachtel, the signal function of anxiety and that sets
in motion the maneuvers (defense mechanisms, security operations, etc.)
through which the individual hopes to reachieve a state of safer equilibrium.

Let us now consider this theorist's conception of the relation of fear to
anxiety. After accepting the usually posited distinction between the two, "that
while both are related to expectation, while both are about something, in anxiety the object of expectation is unknown, while in fear it is known" (1959, p.
47), Schachtel goes on to specify further the objects of the respective expectations. For him, "the unknown danger in anxiety is the new, unknown state of
being when leaving a particular constellation of embeddedness" (1959, p. 47).
Further, he implies that while fear may be the individual's response to some
object or entity that is perceived as injurious or detrimental, anxiety can also
occur when the individual attends to the implications for his state of being of
the encounter with that which is feared. Thus, Schachtel speaks of the "open-
endedness of fear toward anxiety," the fact that the encounter with the
feared object can also bring with it a separation from one's embeddedness and,
hence, anxiety.

Finally, in a rather brief but well-executed application of his concepts,
Schachtel demonstrates that he, too, can account for anxiety in infancy without resorting to hypothetical economic problems of excitation (Freud), or empathic induction (Sullivan), or contagion (Escalona). As he himself states:

we do not need to assume a special empathic transmission of anxiety or a transmission by contagion from the mother to the child. It seems to me simpler and more
likely if we assume that anxiety, tension, dislike on the part of the mother constitute a situation of separation between mother and child. True, the separation is
not a physical one but an emotional one. The mother can be turned fully toward
the infant only if she has an attitude of tender care. Anxiety and tension disrupt
such an attitude; dislike is the opposite of it. Hence, in anxiety and tension the
mother no longer is fully there . . . the infant probably experiences the global
discomfort of separation from the mother and the resulting separation anxiety
when one or the other of these emotions interferes with her full presence, i.e.,
with her being turned fully toward the child (1959, p. 51).

Comments

If one is not totally committed to the detached, physicalistically objecti-
fying, observer perspective (à la Eysenck), and if one can appreciate and allow
for the fact that human experience might have some significant role in the de-

termination of living, then a casual reading of Schachtel's work will leave one both enriched and bewildered. As should be clear even from the condensed presentation of his thought in the preceding pages, this theorist addresses himself to aspects of the human condition that are, in all probability, universal. The fundamental concepts of embeddedness and emergence, the idea that human development is a continual dialogue between demands for safety, security, and familiarity on the one hand, and strivings for independence and increasing differentiation on the other, strike the reader with an overwhelming sense of face validity. Further, the conceptualization of anxiety as an experience of helplessness, as a consequence of one's confrontation with the unfamiliar, as an expression of one's not being at home with some situation, also has the ring of truth. Finally, the assertion that human living must be understood within a developmental perspective, the claim that "later stages [of life] still show traces of the earlier ones, and the condition of the newborn shows the seeds of, the Anlage for, the later developments" (1959, p. v) is consistent with almost all major clinical theories. From whence, then, comes the bewilderment?

Sooner or later, the reader must ask: What is Schachtel's basic conception of the human being? From where is he viewing man that he can see him as an organism who has tensions, conflicts of embeddedness and emergence, and yet raises such questions as "Who am I and what is my place in the world?" Another way of asking the same question is to inquire how Schachtel can combine both the natural scientific perspective of Freud and the phenomenological perspective of Straus, Heidegger, and Binswanger? An answer to these questions emerges only after a painstakingly careful reflection upon this theorist's work.

It seems to us that Schachtel's fundamental conception of man, at least after birth, is that of natural science. That is to say, man, at all stages of development, is the isolated organism, the incarnate subject who is continually confronted with the task of establishing, through the activity-affects, relatedness to the world. The powers or forces that determine both the actuality and the form of this relatedness are spoken of as tensions. Even the organism-environment unit is understood to be a grand tension system. In this way it is possible to conceptualize intrauterine existence as a kind of homeostatic state. But Schachtel realizes that the observer's perspective is insufficient. As has already been suggested, he grasps the significance of the developing individual's experience. Thus he sensitively and empathically imputes meaningful experience to this isolated organism. Although he insists that development cannot be accounted for in terms of experiential phenomena—recall his criticisms of the phenomenologists, as noted at the beginning of this exposition—he equally maintains that development cannot be grasped without descriptions of experience.

In essence, then, Schachtel's conceptions constitute a rather creative and unusual use of both Freudian and phenomenological thought. He criticizes the founder of psychoanalysis for unduly restricting the meaning of certain basic experiences, e.g., Freud's negative pleasure principle. Still, he stays within the psychoanalytic mainstream, enlarging it where he feels this is necessary, e.g., with regard to pleasure, emotionality, and so forth. Further, he uses his own powers of observation and empathic sensitivity to grasp the meanings of certain experiences that he then attributes to the developing individual. Finally, he develops fundamental conceptions such as embeddedness and emergence that effectively enable him to synthesize both observer and inner experiential material.

REFERENCES

Schachtel, E. *Experiential foundations of Rorschach's test.* New York: Basic Books, 1966.
Schachtel, E. *Metamorphosis.* New York: Basic Books, 1959.

8
The Approach of
Kurt Goldstein

Kurt Goldstein was born in Upper Silesia on November 6, 1878. After specializing in neurology and psychiatry, he received his medical degree from the University of Breslau in 1903. Following an eight-year period of apprenticeship (residency) and research, he was appointed Professor of Neurology and Psychiatry at the Neurological Institute of the University of Frankfurt. Both during and after World War I, he investigated as well as treated brain-injured soldiers. While he was engaged in these activities, Goldstein established an institute for the study of the aftereffects of brain damage. It was at this time that he conducted the research that eventually constituted the foundations of his holistic, organismic point of view.

In 1933, while working in Amsterdam, he completed his most important book, *Der Aufbau des Organismus*, which was subsequently published under the translated title, *The Organism* (1940; 1963b). In this work, Goldstein concretely delineated his approach to understanding both normal and pathological human functioning.

After emigrating to the United States in 1935, he worked at the New York Psychiatric Institute, at Montefiore Hospital, and at the College of Physicians and Surgeons of Columbia University. For the most part, he presented his views on psychopathology and was eventually invited to give the William James Lectures at Harvard University. These talks were subsequently published under the title, *Human Nature in the Light of Psychopathology* (1940; 1963a). Currently, Dr. Goldstein is associated with Columbia University and the New School for Social Research. His most recent area of interest is language and he has published a book, *Language and Language Disturbances* (1948), on this topic as well.

While many reviewers have tended to associate Goldstein's thought with that of the Gestalt psychologists, he himself has explicitly denied this classification. Although he worked with Gelb (1920), for example, on the study of figure-ground relationships in visual perception, he has also been quite critical of certain Gestalt principles. Thus, rather than view his formulations as nothing but extensions or offshoots of Gestalt theory, we shall let the thinker speak for himself.

As has already been suggested, Kurt Goldstein has explicitly and emphatically heralded a holistic, organismic approach to the study of human living. In so doing, he has opposed himself to those perspectives that conceive of man in terms of externally related, inherently disconnected, parts—e.g., stimulus-response learning theories, certain physiological theories, and many versions of psychoanalytic thought. Instead, he approaches the human being as an organism that is always a becoming whole, an emerging gestalt. In one of his works, he puts it this way: "any phenomenon can be understood only when considered in relation to every other phenomenon; it can be evaluated only by recognizing its significance in the functioning of the organism as a whole" (1963a, p. vii).

Hence, there is a rejection of simple, one-to-one, causal thinking. In fact, there is a fundamental dissatisfaction with the general approach as well as with the methods of natural science. This is made quite clear in the following: "The attempt to understand life from the point of view of the natural science method alone is fruitless" (1963b, p. vii).

In his books as well as his research, Goldstein tries to demonstrate that a human science, a science of man as man, is more adequate. It would seem appropriate at this juncture to sketch at least the general guidelines of this theorist's alternative to the natural science approach. From what vantage point does he view man?

In a paper entitled "The Smiling of the Infant and the Problem of Understanding the Other" (1957), Goldstein calls his approach "biological-anthropological." This orientation stresses the importance of descriptive and experiential data. In *The Organism*, he states, "The holistic method cannot exclude experiences . . . they belong to man and must be evaluated in their relevance for man's existence" (1963b, p. vii). Further, "it is the first task of biology to *describe carefully all living beings* as they actually are" (1963b, p. 6; italics in original). Elsewhere, Goldstein argues that "the nervous system is an apparatus which always functions as a whole. It is always in a state of excitation, never at rest" (1963a, p. 11).

From these excerpts, the reader should begin to realize that Goldstein's holistic perspective vehemently rejects any naturalistic, atomistic, mechanistic, or simple tension-reduction homeostatic conception of man. Lately he has even articulated the necessity of studying the everyday life world as it is lived, not as it is theoretically conceived.

While in the concrete-abstract attitude, ordered life can be guaranteed by the application of reasoning; to understand human life in its fullness another sphere of behavior must be taken into consideration. When we are in this sphere, subject-object experiences remain more or less in the background and the feeling of unity comprising ourselves and the world in all respects and particularly in our relation to other human beings is dominant. This sphere I term the "sphere of immediacy." It is not a subjective experience. It is not an irrational assumption. It is governed, like our objective world, by laws which are different from so-called logical reasoning. It is not easy to describe. It has to be experienced in definite situations (1963b, pp. viii–ix).

Later, we will attempt to clarify the phrases "concrete-abstract attitude" and "ordered life," but for the present, it seems necessary to elaborate on the idea of a sphere of immediacy. In stressing the importance of the everyday life world as it is lived, Goldstein is advocating a respectful, detailed, description and analysis of human experience. He is asserting that this realm of living is not explicable in terms of logical, conceptual thought. It has its own rules, as it were, and these can be made explicit only through phenomenological analyses. However, although he is concerned with descriptions of experience, he clearly does not consider the phenomenological approach to be sufficient for the study of man. He writes:

Nevertheless, I believe it may be justified to investigate whether the phenomenological analysis represents the only adequate method of studying phenomena, whether the biological approach, as I have developed it, cannot contribute something to their [the phenomenological and the natural scientific] understanding or at least establish a bridge between the results of both procedures (1957, p. 188).

Thus Goldstein finds both the experiential and the natural scientific approaches to be necessary, yet incomplete in themselves. For him, each complements the other, each demands the other. Further, he believes that his biological-anthropological approach constitutes an effective synthesis of the former alternatives.

As he is profoundly guided by his holistic orientation, Goldstein refuses to view any phenomenon as isolated from an indigenous total context. Instead, his conception of man-world relations takes the form of a dialogue. The organism is always oriented toward the world, toward its environment, and each continually redefines and transforms the other. He writes:

Each organism has its own characteristic milieu. Only that, a certain segment of all that surrounds it, constitutes its world. We call this milieu the adequate milieu, that is, the milieu that is appropriate to the nature of the organism (1963a, p. 89).

If we put this in everyday language, we can say that every creature has, as it were, its own ball park. Further, although these domains overlap considerably, the objects, events, and relations that matter to each individual must be sought in *his* ball park. These are what Goldstein terms the "adequate stimuli" and he clarifies their meaning in the following manner:

We know that the organism does not react to all stimuli in the same way. There are many events to which a particular organism is not sensitive. I need not mention the fact that every organism . . . is insensitive to stimuli to which other organisms react. Each has its special organization as to sensory equipment, etc., and usually is responsive only to stimuli relevant to its "nature." Normally the organism responds only to those stimuli which are "adequate" . . . to its nature (1963a, p. 88).

According to Goldstein, the very existence of the organism depends upon the possibility of finding an appropriate environment, a milieu from which adequate stimuli emerge. In such a context, the organism can "equalize" itself, that is, it can establish and sustain an equilibrium—not a tension-reduction state—with both itself and its surroundings. This, in turn, makes possible ordered behavior, actions that adequately come to terms with the environment.

At the risk of being repetitious, we should like to stress the fact that when Goldstein speaks of equalization, ordered behavior, and an organism coming to terms with its environment, he is not describing a simple state of tension reduction. The goal of healthy living is not to discharge tensions or excitations as they arise. Rather, with his concepts, the theorist is addressing himself to the vicissitudes inherent in a dynamic process of becoming. The adequately functioning individual effectively uses the emerging stimuli of his environment, as well as his inner promptings, to realize or actualize himself as an unfolding project with particular orientations and potentialities. This process of self-realization or self-actualization Goldstein considers to be the primal and overarching concern of the organism. Again, it is not a question of intrapsychic processes or unencumbered drive discharges. It is, instead, a dialectical unfolding, organism-milieu transformation. It is a mutually co-defining process of give-and-take between the organism and its milieu. It is, in the theorist's own words, "the basic tendency of the organism to actualize itself in accordance with its nature" (1963a, p. 88). Whenever adequate coming to terms with the environment is impeded, the movement toward self-realization is thwarted and disordered behavior or a "catastrophic reaction" ensues. This last phrase, catastrophic reaction, is crucial to Goldstein's conception of anxiety and we shall elaborate upon its meaning later.

At this point, however, it seems appropriate to clarify the theorist's conception of order and disorder, especially as they pertain to the dialectical processes that occur between the organism and its milieu. The reader should immediately understand that these terms, order and disorder, when applied to states or behaviors, are evaluative relative to the organism in a particular task situation as well as to its trend toward self-actualization. In other words, order and disorder

can be defined only in relation to the structure of the organism and the task before it at a given moment. . . . [Order and disorder] are not simply different forms of functional organization; they can be defined only in terms of their relationship to the basic trend of the organism, that of self-actualization (1951, p. 37).

In the quotation just cited, Goldstein seems to be suggesting that the organism, in its project of self-actualization, is the only adequate context for evaluating ordered and disordered behavior. Behavior that is ordered is behavior that adequately comes to terms with the environment and is consistent with the organism's overarching strivings. Further, the meaning of any concrete task facing the organism, as well as the behaviors that such a task elicits, can be understood and evaluated only in the context of the organism's movement toward self-realization. An example may help to illuminate these assertions.

Consider the situation of a boy about to leave home to go to the ball field. He is already living in his anticipation of the game; he imagines the hits and catches he will make, the victorious struggle his team will wage. As he ties his sneakers and picks up his glove, his mother reminds him to make his bed and clean up his room. Obviously, from the boy's perspective, these demands of his environment are completely irrelevant to the project of playing ball. Still, they must be completed if he is to get out of the house. Hence, although he is tempted to perform them half-heartedly, he takes care to tuck in the sheets and place his toys in the corner of the room. When his mother comes to inspect her son's work, she is reasonably satisfied. To her way of thinking, her son has evidenced a developing sense of responsibility and competence. From the boy's perspective, the task of making the bed and straightening out the room was only tangentially relevant. Nonetheless, he was able to assess accurately the consequences of not meeting this demand and thus was able to sustain and further his project to become a great ballplayer. His behavior constituted an adequate coming to terms with his milieu.

Closely allied to Goldstein's conception of ordered behavior is his notion of "preferred behavior." He writes: "the organism has a tendency toward very decidedly preferred ways of behavior, be it in perception, motility, posture . . ." (1963b, p. 351). Further, preferred behaviors are always experienced as more comfortable, more secure, correct, etc. We mention this now because when we address ourselves specifically to anxious behavior, we shall find that, if anything, it is not experienced in this "preferred" manner.

Perhaps the most famous concepts espoused by Goldstein are those of the abstract and concrete attitudes. All adequate human behavior presupposes the concurrence and interdependence of these two types of orientations. Concrete behavior is always addressed to the here and now. It is, one might say, stimulus determined. On the other hand, the abstract attitude and the behavior that expresses it entails an orientation toward the possible. It involves an ability to see beyond the present as well as that which is present. It is manifested in planning, anticipating, and the grasping of relations. In his studies of brain-injured soldiers, Goldstein found that the abstract attitude was impaired to the extent that these people found it difficult to orient themselves in space and time, change direction willfully, analyze wholes into their component parts and then resynthesize them, plan their activities, and clearly separate that which is fantasy and that which is reality.

As was indicated earlier, Goldstein has recently found it necessary to supplement his conception of a concrete-abstract ordered life with the idea of a sphere of immediacy. On this point he has written: "While concrete-abstract behavior guarantees order and security, the sphere of immediacy makes unity possible between the world and ourselves, particularly in our relationship to other human beings" (1963a, p. xi).

The experience of being-at-one with the world as well as with our fellow man is, according to Goldstein, the foundation for all self-actualization. In other words, human existence is always co-existence and self-actualization is never, therefore, a solipsistic enterprise. The theorist is quite clear on this point when he asserts:

man can never realize himself unless the existence of the other is guaranteed. . . . [Ultimately] the *concern for the other's existence is an intrinsic property of man's nature.* . . . It is by the belonging of individuals to each other that *man becomes man and only in so far as he achieves this is he man* (1957, p. 191; italics in original).

This introduction to Goldstein's general perspective would be quite inadequate if we did not include some reference to his view of emotions, particularly fear. Not only would this help to situate the theorist's conception of anxiety, but, further, it would provide a preface to its discussion.

Again consistent with his holistic orientation, Goldstein refuses to accord an isolated, independent status to emotions. In his words, "Emotions are not comprehensible as separate phenomena but they belong to definite conditions of the totality of the organism" (1957, p. 180). Stated somewhat differently, there is no behavior without emotion. Indigenous to action is an emotional tonality, either figurally or as a silhouette. Emotions imbue experience with both color and vitality.

In a paper entitled, "On Emotions: Considerations from the Organismic Point of View," Goldstein takes issue with what he considers to be the prevalent conception of emotions. He emphatically denies that a one-to-one correspondence exists between a particular stimulus configuration and the specific emotion evoked. He rejects the position that emotions necessarily have a disruptive, disorganizing effect upon the activity of the organism. Fear, for example, "can inspire purposeful activity, thus helping in the maintenance of ordered behavior, allowing self-realization in a dangerous situation" (1951, p. 39). Fear sharpens the sensitivity of the organism and prepares it for action. Goldstein's experiential account of fear demonstrates that, in his view, this affect presupposes an intact attitude toward the abstract, toward the possible.

In the state of fear we have an object before us that we can meet, that we can attempt to remove, or from which we can flee. We are conscious of ourselves as well as of the object; we can deliberate as to how we shall behave toward it, and we can look at the cause of the fear, which actually lies before us. . . . In other words, what results in fear must be something which is found only in a specific relationship between organism and object (1963a, pp. 92–93).

Hence, according to Goldstein, fear is a possibility that exists only for the normal adult human being. As the abstract attitude is lacking in animals, merely developing in infants, and impaired in brain-damaged patients, such organisms are much more susceptible to anxiety. In fact, this capacity for taking an abstract approach constitutes the essential difference between fear and anxiety. It is also that factor by which Goldstein distinguishes anxiety from all other emotions. As he himself puts it, in anxiety "the emotion is so strong, . . . the organism is so highly altered in its function, that the abstract attitude can no longer be assumed by it" (1951, p. 43). As disorder is the principle feature of anxiety, and because the abstract attitude cannot be maintained, anxiety, strictly speaking, is "not an emotion, but an *inner experience of catastrophe*" (1951, p. 46; italics in original).

It is now time to focus specifically on Goldstein's conception of anxiety. In order to deal with this phenomenon as fully as possible, Goldstein alternately utilizes both the internal and external points of view. For example, he claims that whenever we observe someone in a state of anxiety,

we can disclose characteristic bodily changes as well, certain expressive movements of the face and the body, and certain states of physiological processes, motor phenomena, changes of pulse rate, and vasomotor phenomena, etc. And we certainly have no reason to exclude these changes from an investigation of the phenomenon of anxiety (1963b, p. 291).

On the other hand, from the internal point of view, from the perspective of the one who experiences the anxiety, "It is . . . the experience of the 'catastrophic situation,' of danger, of going to pieces, of 'losing one's existence'" (1951, p. 38). Experientially, then, anxiety has an uncanny feature that distinguishes it from fear. In contradistinction to the latter emotion, anxiety: (1) is not spatial, (2) is not connected causally with events in the external world, and (3) has no reference to an object—"Anxiety deals with nothingness. It is the inner experience of being faced with nothingness" (1963a, p. 92). Further, in anxiety:

we find meaningless frenzy, with rigid or distorted expression, accompanied by withdrawal from the world, a shutoff affectivity, in the light of which the world appears irrelevant, and any reference to the world, any useful perception and action, is suspended (1963b, p. 293).

From the observer's perspective, however, anxiety is not objectless or contentless. Rather, it involves a difficulty in adequate stimulus evaluation. Goldstein elaborates on this when he writes:

the organism which is seized by the catastrophic shock is . . . in the state of coping with a definite objective reality; the organism is faced with some "object." The state of anxiety becomes intelligible only if we consider the objective confrontation of the organism with a definite environment. Only then can we comprehend the basic phenomenon of anxiety: *the occurrence of disordered stimulus evaluation as it is conditioned through the conflict of the organism with a certain environment which is not adequate for it.* This objectively endangers the organism in the articulation of its nature (1963b, pp. 295–296; italics added).

In this condensed excerpt, Goldstein synthesizes the major elements of his conception. First, he insists that anxiety can emerge only in the context of an organism-environment relationship. That is to say, there is a definite, objective reality involved; it is not merely a question of intrapsychic dynamics. Second, the environment that confronts the organism is, in some critical way, experienced as inadequate to the organism's project of self-realization. As a result, the organism experiences a sense of real danger; its possibilities of self-actualization are threatened. Finally, in this state of experienced peril, the organism improperly evaluates certain aspects of its environment and is subsequently seized by a sense of catastrophe. It can no longer be itself in this situation; it is faced with the imminent possibility of nothingness or nonbeing.

The experiential differences that exist between fear and anxiety lead Goldstein to understand the former in terms of the latter. He writes: "What is it then that leads to fear? Nothing but the experience of the possibility of the onset of anxiety" (1963b, p. 296). Thus, unlike the learning theorists, for example, Goldstein does not equate anxiety with fear. Unlike the Freudians, he does not reduce anxiety to unrealistic fear. Rather, for this theorist, *anxiety is that for which fear fears.* To put it somewhat differently, fear is always fear of possible anxiety.

As we have already suggested, a major point to Goldstein's discussion of internal and external perspectives is that anxiety can be fully grasped only when understood in the context of a subject-world relationship. To describe it more comprehensively, we should recall some of the concepts mentioned earlier. In the catastrophic situation, the capacity for an ordered evaluation of environmental stimuli is impaired. Thus a functionally effective relationship with the object is precluded. Here, the implications of Goldstein's dialectical thinking come to the fore. As consciousness of one's self is always correlated with consciousness of objects, when the latter is impaired, the former must be also. Lacking the ability to react to and cope with an environmental situation, the organism finds ordered behavior impossible. Preferred action yields to behavior that may be characterized as "not fitting," "disagreeable," and "difficult." Without full functioning of the abstract attitude, the organism is less able to imagine alternative possibilities. It is less capable of changing its behavior meaningfully. Hence, it finds itself caught in the concrete, trapped in the present. Both poles of the subject-world dyad are disorganized. The dissolution of the world necessarily entails the concomitant crumbling of the self. Consequently, there exists a profound obstruction to self-actualization. Descriptively, it is inaccurate to say that the person "has" anxiety. More to the point would be the assertion that the person "is" or "embodies" anxiety; his potential range of behavior shrinks; he is less present to both himself and to the world.

While the above characterization emphasizes the negative, catastrophic, and disruptive aspects of anxiety, Goldstein also speaks of the transforming powers of this state. How is this possible? The theorist argues that man, in his quest for self-realization, is driven by an "inherent desire for new experiences, for conquests of the world, and for an expansion of the spheres of his activity in a practical and spiritual sense" (1963a, p. 111). Man has no instinctually predetermined niche in the world. He has no natural habitat such as the fish in the sea, the birds in the air and trees, or the worms in the ground. Instead, he continually defines, redefines, and constructs his environment. The adequate milieu that he needs for his existence, for life, turns out to be many possible habitats. Further, anxiety must emerge whenever the person comes to grips with his possible worlds, with the new challenges and inadequacies that each poses. The process of growth involves an ever-renewed coming to terms with multiple environments, each of which calls forth and tests the capabilities of the organism. Growth, by definition, includes the permanent possibility of anxiety. Culture is not a simple by-product of repression designed to avoid anxiety. The cultural world has assumed specific shapes suited for man's security requirements. It is an expression of man's creative urge to realize his powers. To this, Goldstein adds:

Only when the world is adequate to man's nature do we find what we call security. . . . This tendency toward actualization is primary, but it can achieve its ends only through a conflict with the opposing forces of the environment. This never happens without shock and anxiety. . . . [We] maintain that these shocks are essential to human nature . . . and life must, of necessity, take its course via uncertainty and shock (1963a, p. 112).

Anxiety, therefore, is the inevitable partner of development. Still, the normal person soon overcomes the shock; the enjoyed fruits of coming to terms with the environment and the satisfaction experienced when one has mastered a segment of the world more than outweigh the anxiety endured. According to Goldstein, the more creative the person, the greater the number of anxiety-provoking situations to be encountered. The capacity to meet and overcome anxiety is, for this theorist, the meaning of courage.

How does Goldstein reconcile his conception of anxiety as paralyzing and disruptive with his valuation of its transforming powers? He writes:
If it is true that these catastrophes are the expression of a clash of the individuality

of the organism with the "otherness" of the world, then the organism must proceed from catastrophe to catastrophe. But this is not its intrinsic Being, rather only the transition to its true realization. The clash . . . provides only a shake-up from which the re-patterning . . . the real pattern, the real performance, the revelation of the organism and the world emerges. Indeed there is no performance without a new region of the world becoming manifest (1963b, p. 512).

Anxiety, then, is a moment in the process through which both the organism and the world are continually transformed.

Comments

Because he has so thoroughly committed himself to the holistic, organismic perspective, Goldstein manages to avoid many of the pitfalls that have undermined other theories. For example, because he rejects both the mind-body and person-world dualities, he is not forced to reduce anxiety to some intrapsychic or intraorganismic process. It is not that he wants to dismiss either the experiential or the physiological. On the contrary, he affirms both types of events as constitutive of the anxiety state. But one cannot be subsumed under the other; the experiential is not merely a reflection of the physiological. Thus, the trap of epiphenomenalism is averted.

As he wants to account for behavior as well as experience, Goldstein utilizes data obtained from both the internal and the external points of view. Moreover, each is granted the status of being "real," and an attempt is made to synthesize their implications. Thus anxiety is allowed to be a phenomenon that is lived as well as observed.

As a consequence of his organismic orientation, Goldstein is able to break with homeostatic conceptions that grasp anxiety as a tension-reduction phenomenon. Further, because he understands human being as a becoming, he is not required to explain anxiety solely in terms of past learning, traumas, and the like. For Goldstein, the human organism is never complete, never perfected; and reality is not a given, preconstituted tableau. Both sides of the subject-world polarity must come to fruition. Man, as embodied subjectivity, transcends the objects of nature; he is not only a thing among things. Reality is also transcendent insofar as it is inexhaustible and never complete. The theorist writes: "Thus organism and world realize themselves simultaneously, and grow from the sphere of potentiality into that of actuality" (1963b, p. 513).

Given this ground work, it is not surprising, then, that Goldstein's thought is filled with ideas of emergence, reorganization, and transformation. The world and man are in continual dialogue. Each is constantly remaking the other; each is forever reappearing and yet unfolding as something new. The battleground upon which anxiety emerges, therefore, is not a closed circle, but an open, ever-expanding arena. The image one could use to describe Goldstein's conception of the place of anxiety in human life would not be that of a quantum of energy necessary to balance a bifurcated scale. Rather, it would be that of a gyrating vortex, not calculative, but transformative.

Anxiety, for Goldstein, is a temporal phenomenon, not a spatial one. Still, as we have already stated, the temporal referent is not just the past. Within his holistic orientation, Goldstein can comprehend past, present, and future as three abstract moments of a unitary structure. Man is open to all phases of this fluid structure.

It must be obvious by now that we are quite sympathetic to Goldstein's thought. Still, there are a number of critical reservations. First, we believe that his omission of an explicit interpersonal dimension in his conception constitutes a marked deficiency. Although he states that self-actualization is possible only in relation to the self-realization of the "other," he does not elaborate upon the implications of this for anxiety.

Secondly, while he affirms the experiential components of anxiety, he does not carry out explicit analysis of them. As a result, he speaks of a sense of catastrophe, of nonbeing, and of nothingness. All of these terms presuppose complex experiential organizations and structures that should be clarified and subjected to phenomenological analyses. It may be the case that Goldstein's implied equation of phenomenology with intuition blinds him to thoroughgoing experiential analyses.

Finally, we cannot help but wonder why Goldstein chose to speak of man as the organism. The implication is that of a biological reduction, that is, that the theorist wants to stress the continuity of man with other animals and that he may, to that extent, be less than fully open to human reality.

REFERENCES

Gelb, A., & Goldstein, K. *Psychologische analyson hirnpathologischer Falelle.* Leipzig: Barth, 1920.

Goldstein, K. *Language and language disturbances*. New York: Grune & Stratton, 1948.

Goldstein, K. On emotions. *Journal of Psychology*, 1951, *31*, 37–46.

Goldstein, K. The smiling of the infant and the problem of understanding the other. *Journal of Psychology*, 1957, *44*, 175–188.

Goldstein, K. *Human nature in the light of psychopathology*. New York: Schocken, 1963.

Goldstein, K. *The organism: a holistic approach to biology derived from pathological data in man*. Boston: Beacon, 1963b.

9
The Experience of Anxiety

In the preceding chapters we have presented a variety of theories, each of which purports either to explain the phenomenon of anxiety or to account for its possibility. Whether this is done in terms of the constructs and principles of natural science or in terms of an appeal to ontologically understood, transcendental preconditions, each theory presupposes a defining conception of anxiety. A few examples may serve to illustrate this assertion.

Freud grasped anxiety as a process in which the mental apparatus as a whole, or the ego in particular, is overwhelmed by or is threatened with being overwhelmed by quantities of unmastered excitation. Further, he specified the source(s) of this excitation, its ultimate meaning, and the original situation in which it was experienced as threatening. Sullivan and Schachtel also conceived of anxiety as being fundamentally a tensional phenomenon, but for them it emerges primarily in an interpersonal context and is pervaded with social meaning. The learning theorists define anxiety as a subtype of fear, the latter being understood as a learned drive—that is, a disruption in the organism's homeostasis, ultimately related to the occurrence of painful stimulation. Physiologically oriented theorists grasp anxiety as an effect, the cause of which is to be found in environmental stimuli. Further, this cause-effect relation is conceived in terms of the mediation of various patterns and levels of physiological arousal. Finally, Heidegger, in his analysis of the ontological dimensions of human living, understands anxiety as an affective disposition that expresses the individual's relatedness to a world that has lost its meaning. This philosopher accounts for the possibility of anxiety in terms of man's reluctance to come to grips with the inevitability of his death.

Thus we can understand that the process of explanation always presupposes a conception of that which is to be explained. To ask why a given phenomenon occurs, or to question the being of man in order to illuminate the possibility of the phenomenon, is to have already grasped in some manner the defining characteristics, the structure of what is being examined. Otherwise, one could literally not know what it was that one was trying to explain.

Still, it should be obvious from the above examples that little agreement exists as to the defining characteristics of anxiety. One theorist speaks of the ultimate reality of energy processes said to exist and flow between hypothetical psychical constructs; another addresses himself to tensions that somehow acquire social and personal significance; still others refer to physiological processes that are claimed to underlie cognitive perceptions of anxiety-provoking stimuli. In all, the multiplicity and heterogeneity of these explanatory formulations derive directly from the fact of divergent preconceptions of the phenomenon such theorists seek to explain. In other words, since they start with different definitions of anxiety, not to mention man in general, they cannot help but produce different theories of anxiety's occurrence.

In this chapter we shall attempt an explicit descriptive analysis of anxiety experience. Such an enterprise is not immediately concerned with ascertaining alleged causes or transcendental preconditions of this phenomenon. Nor is it bounded by the necessity of proving or justifying theoretical principles or presuppositions. Still less is it guided by any preconception of an ultimate stuff, or substance, or process that allegedly constitutes the really *real* human being. Instead, it is nothing more or less than what it presents itself as being: descriptions of anxiety experience that are reflectively analyzed so as to reveal their constitutive structures.

The scientifically oriented reader will, we are sure, ask the following questions: From where do we get our descriptions? To what extent are they typical, that is, are these descriptions intersubjectively valid? Further, why have we selected only two anxiety experiences to analyze? Certainly there are others, perhaps innumerable others, and each may have its own unique structure. Finally, how do we know that our analyses are, in fact, consensually valid? What if another person, acting in good faith, concludes that our analyses are incorrect?

These are, without doubt, legitimate questions and we feel obliged to answer them as best, as honestly, and as explicitly as we can. Only when the assumptions and procedures of our method are made clear can the contributions, if any, of our descriptions and reflective analyses be realized.

The sources of our descriptions are our own (as well as others') of everyday life experience. No extensive or systematic sampling of populations was attempted, nor was any believed to be required. Rather, it was assumed that anxiety experiences, though probably innumerable in their particularity, are monolithic in their fundamental structure. To state the matter even more explicitly, it was assumed that the anxious experiences of the child, the college student facing an examination, the woman about to give birth, the man about to get married, and even the senior citizen facing the possibility of death, are all rooted in and expressive of an essentially identical structure. Obviously, such an assumption is open to question and insofar as it is not borne out by our own as well as others' analyses, it will have to be modified.

While the reader may judge for himself the typicality of the experiences to be described, the descriptions themselves are admittedly not typical. We assert this because we realize that most people either omit (for reasons of privacy) or do not notice (for reasons of personal security) many aspects of their anxiety experiences. Again, the reader must judge for himself whether the descriptions presented are "doctored" or simply detailed.

The two experiences described were chosen because they seemed, at least initially, to be both typical and yet structurally different. In other words, we had no question that the two experiences were, in fact, intersubjectively valid. On the other hand, we were not sure that they were rooted in and expressive of essentially identical structures. Thus, our selection was one means of checking our assumption concerning the monolithic structure of anxiety experience.

As far as the final and perhaps most significant of our anticipated questions is concerned, that is, concerning the consensual validity of our analyses, we can only suggest that it is up to the reader to judge their veracity. To put the issue as succinctly and as explicitly as we can, if the reader or the scientist, acting in good faith and not bound by a priori theoretical commitments, concludes that our analyses are inadequate, then by all means a discussion should ensue and appropriate alterations should be made.

With the expression of these introductory remarks and explanations, we are ready to begin our descriptive analyses. Both of the experiences presented are described from the perspective of the one who experienced them. Thus we are taking what may be called the *internal* point of view. This is done because anxiety, insofar as it is an experience, has its greatest significance and meaning for the one who experiences it. We realize, nonetheless, that it is possible for an observer to grasp aspects of the anxious person's situation, even aspects that the anxious person himself does not notice. However, we will confine our descriptions to the internal point of view, recognizing the limitations that we have chosen to accept. During the reflective analysis, however, we will shift to the perspective of one who is not undergoing the anxiety experience. Rather, we will, at that point, be viewing the description from the vantage of one who is attempting to understand the constitutive interrelations of that experience.

The first description is one given by a student about to take a final examination. It proceeds as follows.

When I think about the exam I really feel sick . . . so much depends on it. I know I'm not prepared, at least not as much as I should be, but I keep hoping that I can sort of snow my way through it. He [the professor] said we would get to choose two of three essay questions. I've heard about his questions . . . they sort of cover the whole course, but they're still pretty general. Maybe I'll be able to mention a few of the right names and places. He can't expect us to put down everything in two hours. . . . I keep trying to remember some of the things he said in class, but my mind keeps wandering. God, my folks —What will they think if I don't pass and can't graduate? Will they have a fit! Boy! I can see their faces. Worse yet, I can hear their voices: "And with all the money we spent on your education." Mom's going to be hurt. She'll let me know I let her down. She'll be a martyr: "Well, Roger, didn't you realize how this reflects on us? Didn't you know how much we worked and saved so you could get an education? . . . You were probably too busy with other things. I don't know what I'm going to tell your aunt and uncle. They were planning to come to the graduation you know." Hell! What about me? What'll I do if I don't graduate? How about the plans I made? I had a good job lined up with that company. They really sounded like they wanted me, like I was going to be somebody. . . . And what about the car? I had it all planned out. I was going to pay seventy a month and still have enough left for fun. I've got to pass. Oh hell! What about Anne [girlfriend]? She's counting on my graduating. We had plans. What will she think? She knows I'm no brain, but . . . hell, I won't be anybody. I've got to find some way to remember those names. If I can just get him to think that I really know the material, but don't have time to put it all down. If I can just . . . if . . . too goddam many ifs. Poor dad. He'll really be hurt. All the plans we made—all the . . . I was going to be somebody. What did he say? "People will respect you. People respect a college graduate. You'll be something more than a storekeeper." What am I going to do? God, I can't think. You know, I might just luck out. I've done it before. He could ask just the right questions. What could he ask? Boy! I feel like I want to vomit. Do you think others are as scared as I am? They probably know it all or don't give a damn. I'll bet you most of them have parents who can set them up whether they have college degrees or not. God, it means so much to me. I've got to pass. I've just got to. Dammit, what are those names? What could he ask? I can't think . . . I can't. . . . Maybe if I had a beer I'd be able to relax a little. Is there anybody around who wants to get a beer? God, I don't want to go alone. Who wants to go to the show? What the hell am I thinking about? I've got to study. . . . I can't. What's going to happen to me? . . . The whole damn world is coming apart.

Before we continue, we would like to repeat and emphasize the goals that orient our reflective analysis. Our whole endeavor is guided by a desire to make explicit, to thematize the interrelated aspects of this experience *as it has been described.* Thus, as was previously stated, we are not concerned with its possible causes, nor with reducing it to already presupposed psychological principles or constructs. Further, although as clinicians we might be sorely tempted to indulge in evaluations of this individual's "rationalizations," "projections," etc., we shall avoid this parlor game. Instead, we shall take the person at his word and beginning there, we shall attempt to illuminate and highlight the structure of his experience. Let us return, then, to what he reveals for us. How does he experience this situation?

The exam of which he speaks is present to him as an object of thought. It is not perceived as a here-and-now event, as something that could be seen, heard, touched, etc. It is not given in sensory experience, nor is it something remembered. Rather, it is present in its virtuality, in its futurity, as that which will be encountered later. As an event to be undergone, it has the character of an ordeal, a hurdle, the thought of which is accompanied by feelings of sickness. Eventually, we shall have to clarify the relations of this thought and these feelings.

The exam is not simply experienced as such—that is, it is not conceptualized as an event in itself. It is not an isolated thought that presents itself as being unrelated to the individual's life, as essentially extrinsic to his general concerns. It is not something that occurs and is then forgotten. Instead, as the young man himself states, "so much depends on it." The meaning of this "so much" reveals itself to be a complex network of relationships (to parents, to girlfriend, to peers, etc.), projects (graduating, securing the job, paying for the car), and identities (being somebody). The meaning of his possible performance on the exam—it is this to which he is, in fact, oriented—points not only toward an anticipated future, but also it illuminates a past, a context of relations (with parents, girlfriend, peers) in which plans were made and promises enacted. There is a continuity, an unfolding, which is at stake here. In other words, the experienced meaning of the to-be-encountered exam is that of a hurdle or milestone. If it is passed, then a door is open to a world of "being somebody," a world that has already been envisioned and experienced. If it proves to be insurmountable, this lived-and-planned-for-world vanishes into meaningless oblivion; the past goes nowhere; the future is being nobody.

Given this character of a hurdle or milestone, the exam raises questions of preparedness, ability, and adequacy. With respect to these factors, the individual is profoundly uncertain. He must pass; he must realize the lived-for world, but he has no clear sense of himself as being competent to meet the exam adequately. The more he thinks about it, the more intrusive are the expressions of failure; the greater is his sense of alarm. Thus, in trying to sustain his orientation, he vacillates between hopeful, almost wishful anticipation, and surveys of the consequences of failure—destruction of his identity and world.

This vacillation between the alternatives of "being somebody" and "being nobody" constitutes one of the basic qualities of the experience. If we would speak in Gestalt terms, we would describe this as a profound lack of closure. In such a condition, the individual is unable to focus his attention upon the task at hand. He says, "My mind keeps wandering." The implications of a failure to surmount the hurdle are so great, so intrusive, they cannot be put aside. They constitute, in fact, the dissolution of his planned-for, lived-for world. Another way of saying this is that they radically undermine his sense of identity. Is there not the suggestion here that this person's identity is grounded in the unfolding of his life, in the various constellations of his relationships, in the projects and plans to which he has assigned himself? Is it not clear that his identity is not a concept or a thing, but rather a road upon which his personal history has been and is unfolding? His life, his world, his sense of self, are all grasped as a having-been-being-becoming that, in its unfolding, has its own internal unity and which, at all times, is constituted by an interlacing network of relationships and projects.

We can clearly see that the possibility of failing the exam, of not graduating, of not becoming somebody, illuminates and makes thematic the individual's relations with parents and girlfriend. Their hopes and expectations, their plans and affective ties to the individual, are brought to light in this experience. Further, personal goals and aspirations (the job, the car, etc.) emerge as must-be-attained signs of becoming somebody. Not only the terminus, but the whole road, as one which is being meaningfully traversed, is called into question by the uncertainty of overcoming this hurdle, the exam.

Finally, there is a terrible sense of aloneness. He wants to flee, to immerse himself in sociality, in unconcern, in the busy activities of impersonal everyday life. But he cannot tear himself away; his world, his life, his identity, all call him back as problematical, as being at stake, as threatening to dissolve into meaninglessness. His world is coming apart.

Let us try concretely to delineate and specify the structural components of this experience. First, we can see that, in this student's world, there is an event, the exam, and this constitutes the focus of his anxious experience. Thus we may assert that that in the face of which he is anxious is his possible performance on the exam. But, as has already been demonstrated, the possible performance, whether adequate or not, points toward and refers to the contexts of past, present, and anticipated relations, involvements, and projects. In other words, depending upon his coming performance, the door to an already lived-for-and-toward world may open wide or slam shut. Hence, in its fullest sense, that in the face of which he is anxious is his potential exile from and deprivation of a world.

As we have also seen, his identity, his sense of himself as a person going somewhere, as one who is becoming somebody, is tied to and actually expressed through a world that is in jeopardy. The struggle to sustain this world is his struggle to sustain himself. Each reflects the other. There is, then, another side to that in the face of which he is anxious. It is that about which he is anxious and it refers to the potential destruction of himself as someone who is becoming somebody. To state the matter alternatively, that in the face of which he is anxious is his lived-for world, while that about which he is anxious is his own viability, not as a biological organism or entity, but as an adequate, meaningful human being at home in his world.

This world, which may be slipping through his fingers and in the face of whose destruction he is anxious, is not simply one of many possible worlds for him. It is not the case that he says, "Well, if I can't have these relations and identities, if I can't become this, then I'll have those and become that." Rather, it is his only world, his only meaningful identity—at least as he experiences it. As such, he *must* attain it, he *must be* the one whose life embodies this identity expressed in this world.

What we are suggesting here is that the motivational component of this experience is *a must*. The individual's life, as it has been lived, demands successful performance on the exam; it demands that the world that has been lived-for-and-toward, the identity with which he is at home, be sustained. There is no question of mere preference, of an "I'd like this to happen, but my life doesn't depend on it." Nor is it a case of "I ought to pass and graduate because if I don't, I'll feel guilty and people might not like me." Instead, it is a *must*; there is no alternative, at least none that is thinkable.

While the must to be actualized involves a doing, a passing of an exam, a graduating from college, the meaning of this deed refers explicitly to the individual's *being*. In other words, it is a deed that both expresses and makes possible a certain way of living, a certain identity, a certain world. It is a doing in the service of being. The individual must pass the exam and graduate in order that he may continue to be who he already is.

Finally, although a successful passing of the exam and a graduation from college present themselves as musts, as demands of life that must be met and attained, there is a question of *ability*. In the individual's experience there is a haunting sense of uncertainty. Is he assured of success? No! Is he convinced of eventual failure? Again we must answer in the negative, No! He is *uncertain* and it is in this state of uncertainty that his world tantalizes and tortures him. He must do in order that he may continue to be, but he is uncertain of his ability.

From a temporal perspective, that is, from a view that orients itself toward the unfolding character of this person's life, we find ourselves capable of integrating these delineated structural components. We have already suggested that this individual's world and sense of self are implicitly grasped as a having-been-being-becoming, as a road that is constituted by milestones marking the achievement of various relationships and projects. We should now like to suggest that when one of these milestones, college graduation, becomes problematical, when there is profound uncertainty as to its achievement, the whole road is called into question. That toward which the individual was becoming, being a somebody, begins to loom as unattainable. That which has already been achieved and lived as supporting the road, now appears as going nowhere, as being pointless. But what is the alternative? Nothing! Being nobody! Thus the world that has been and is lived-for must be. There is no other. Nonetheless, the achievement of the milestone is uncertain and the whole road trembles in this uncertainty. In the face of possible collapse, and confronted with the potential pointlessness of his life, the individual stands alone with his world and is anxious.

The second description was given by a woman in the course of a psychotherapeutic interview.

You know, it's kind of upsetting talking to you. I mean, I'm never sure of where I stand . . . of what you think. That sort of makes me uncomfortable. You never seem to show much feeling on your face. It's not that you haven't an attractive face, but somehow, it doesn't seem to change very much. I mean . . . well, when I tell you certain things . . . you know, about myself . . . you don't seem to be very pleased, or angry . . . or anything. It makes me a little anxious. Aren't you supposed to show your feelings? It's very hard for me to talk to a man when he doesn't . . . somehow let me know what he's feeling. I mean, most of the men I know are very interested in me. I mean, I can tell when they talk to me that they're really concerned with what I think. I know what they're feeling. Most of the time it's written all over their faces. But you . . . you're different. I mean, are you like this with your wife? I don't know how she can take it. I mean . . . doesn't she want to know how you feel? . . . what you're thinking about her? I met the principal of Laurie's [her daughter] school yesterday. It's really something how young men are getting important jobs these days. He was really very nice and attractive too. . . . We had coffee together and sort of chatted. He really seemed interested in me. I mean, he asked me about my work with underprivileged children and everything . . . whether I liked what I was doing . . . you know, he was really interested in me—in what I felt. He even noticed my dress . . . told me I looked nice. He's a gentleman, not like some others I know. When I told him how much I was interested in children and how important I thought his work was, he really seemed pleased. I could tell he liked me. . . . You know, your face hasn't changed one bit, not a single bit. I mean, you just sit there and listen. I don't know what to do . . . I mean I don't know what to talk about. You're not helping me very much. I mean aren't you supposed to tell me what I should be doing—what's wrong with me and what I should do about it? You just sit there and listen. I don't know if I can go on . . . I mean, I need to know what you think. You know, when I talk to other men, I'm usually the listener. They talk to me. I know what they're feeling. I mean I can look at their faces and tell what's going on. I didn't realize this would be so different. I don't know if I can do it. Please tell me what you want me to talk about.

The clinically sophisticated reader has, no doubt, already noted the "pathology" of this woman's style of relating. If we were so inclined, we could spend pages discussing her attempts at seduction, her expressions of frustration and hostility, her self-centered, pseudointerest in underprivileged children, and the hypothetical causes of her generally hysterical orientation. However fascinating these excursions might prove, they are not appropriate to our current enterprise: a reflective analysis of her experience as described. Thus, as with the previous description, we shall confine ourselves to the meanings of this situation for her, that is, to her anxious experience of and participation in the relationship. What does she tell us about it?

Immediately, we are told that talking to or even being with this male therapist is upsetting to her. Further, the specific aspect of the relationship that proves to be upsetting shows itself to be her realization that she has, as yet, not been able to determine where she stands vis-à-vis this man. The complex meaning of "where she stands" is, in fact, the primary subject of her entire description. It is also, as the sophisticated clinician might guess, the major focus of her "pathology."

If we attempt to clarify the experienced and lived meaning of this "where she stands," we find that for this woman, it is given for the most part in the facial expressions of male others. She evidences both frustration and oblique resentment over her as-yet-unsuccessful efforts to elicit manifestations of feeling in the therapist's face. She chides him for his impassive, although attractive countenance. In her own words, "Well, when I tell you certain things . . . you know, about myself . . . you don't seem to be very pleased, or angry . . . or anything." Thus, the blame for this unpleasant state of affairs is cast, albeit somewhat indirectly, upon the therapist.

When we ask for a concrete specification of the kinds of feelings that this woman seeks to elicit, we find ourselves in the midst of ambiguity. On the one hand, there is always the implicit, though strikingly persistent, suggestion that she demands affirmation as a sexually interesting, attractive, even provocative person. She explicitly describes her usual relations with men, her ability to provoke and "read" expressions of interest and admiration from them, and her satisfaction with their allusions to her sexually feminine appearance. On the other hand, when she realizes that the therapist may grasp the sexual quality of her interest and remarks, she takes pains to deny and contradict them. Thus, she insists that her need to know where she stands vis-à-vis men is totally asexual. The slightest suggestion of her sexual interest must be qualified with an "I mean."

The fact that the continued existence of the relationship depends, at least for this woman, upon a successful eliciting of the therapist's feelings, the fact that she doesn't know if she can go on with it, speaks to the gravity of this requirement. It is not the case that she would simply like to know what this man thinks of her; it is not merely a question of curiosity or of deriving some personal sense of satisfaction from knowing that she is attractive. Rather, it is an absolute necessity, a *must*, which, if not fulfilled, makes the relationship untenable. What we are suggesting here is that this woman's world is one in which her relations with men are critical in a particular way. Her identity is continually at stake because her life is a never-to-be-completed project that endlessly seeks to determine whether she is sexually attractive to men. Qualifying this enterprise, however, is the requirement that she not reveal, to herself or others, the fact that she is concerned with being sexually attractive. At the moment, we are not concerned with the alleged causes or precipitating conditions of this qualification. We do realize, however, that in the face of the therapist's refusal to commit himself in answer to the constantly posed question (Am I sexually interesting to you?) this woman's world teeters. She questions her taken-for-granted ability to elicit some expression of feeling and when she is confronted with the fact that success might elude her, that she would exist in a world without knowing where she stood, she pleads for her identity. The only alternative is flight.

Can we now begin to specify the structural components of her experience? As with the previous example, we find an event in her world toward which she is anxiously oriented. In this case, however, it is her male therapist's face. More specifically, it is the possibility of his face's never expressing some identifiable sexual interest in her. But, the expression of male sexual interest is, as we have seen, that for which she lives. It is the food that nourishes and sustains her world, the world of the woman exclusively concerned with her sexual attractiveness. Thus we may assert that that in the face of which she is anxious is a male world that withholds its affirmation of her alluring female sexuality. Without such affirmation, she does not know where she stands; she does not know what to do—or who, for that matter, she is. Further, it is the burden of the male world to constitute her identity, to grant her sexually attractive being. It is her burden, on the other hand, to elicit expressions of these constituting acts. However, as we shall see, there is a rub to all this. Together with and fundamentally qualifying the demand that she makes upon men is the equally necessary requirement that she be treated as one who is not, in fact, making such a demand. She insists that others respond to her sexuality, yet they must not do so, or, at best (and this is still unsatisfactory), they must do so in such a way that it appears to come unsolicited. She can be and yet she cannot be who she is. If others do not relate to her as a sexually attractive woman, she does not know where she stands. If others do relate to her as a sexually attractive woman, she must insist that this has not been elicited, that she has not been concerned with this in the least. Further, she must reaffirm her asexual orientation by derogating such expressions of interest. Thus, while that in the face of which she is anxious is the loss or absence of sexual affirmation by a male world, that about which she is anxious are the implications of the very same affirmation she seeks. To be confirmed as a sexual woman is to be held responsible for that state; it is, at times, to be understood as reflecting one who openly solicits such confirmation. Hence, that about which she is anxious is the maintenance of her public identity as an asexual woman.

The clinician concerned with "psychopathology" might note the contrast between the two examples. In the first, that of the student anxious about his exam, there was a consonance between that in the face of which and that about which he was anxious. Each reflected the other. In this example, however, we find no such consonance. Rather, each is the negation of the other and yet both are musts. Might this not be the actual, lived meaning of conflict, usually said to underlie "psychopathology?" We shall address ourselves to this question in another work.

That in the face of which and that about which this woman is anxious has already been noted. Further, we have delineated the musts that they express. The reader should realize, however, that the affirmation which this woman seeks and must have is one that is not taken simply as a possession. Instead, it is a having in the service of being; it is an affirmation that tells her who she is.

If we now address ourselves to the temporal aspects of this experience, we find that, unlike the example of the student, there is no sense of becoming or unfolding. Rather, the having-been-being-becoming of this woman's life has been transformed into a sequence of repetitions. The affirmation that she seeks goes nowhere; nor does her sense of asexual identity. They are, as it were, ends in themselves, which must be continually reachieved. She is, one might say, stuck in a rut—"fixated." Does the structure of the experience itself shed light on this transformation? It would seem so. When the world that is sought and demanded cannot affirm the identity that is equally required, and vice versa, neither can be achieved. Life becomes bogged down at one of its milestones; the road as such is forgotten. Instead, there is a chronic vacillation between attainment and rejection of attainment. One can go no farther. Life is endless repetition.

Before we continue, let us stop for a moment and take stock of what has been suggested. Despite differences of content, situation, and even "pathological" overtone, both examples reveal a number of striking structural similarities. We may specify them as follows:

1. In each description we discovered a situational event that constituted the focus of the individual's anxious orientation. This event we provisionally described as that in the face of which the person was anxious. However, when we examined the person's own description of the event, particularly with regard to its meaning and implications, we found that it was not an isolated something that merely happened to occur. Rather, it was seen to be rooted in and expressive of the person's whole world. In other words, it was integral to the person's past, present, and anticipated relations and projects. Further, the event had the character of a milestone-to-be-achieved and, as such, it constituted that upon which the individual's world rested—at least, as he or she currently lived and experienced it. Insofar as the achievement of the event as milestone was questionable, the person's whole world became questionable. Thus, in its fullest sense, that in the face of which the person was anxious was the questionable character of his or her world.

2. In each example, there was also the question of the individual's identity. Further, as we saw, this identity was, in some maner, an expression of the person's world. In one case, it reflected the lived-for-and-toward realization of that world. In the situation of "pathology," it involved the negation of all or significant aspects of that world. Whichever the case, this question of identity, insofar as it became thematic, was referred to as that about which the person was anxious. Moreover, we found that whatever the identity that was at stake,

it could be grasped as a temporally constituted project, as a having-been-being-becoming, oriented toward some lived-for state of being. Thus identity was not a matter of self-concepts or intrapsychic dynamics; it was, instead, a question of lived biography, a style that the individual has, is, and projects as his, and with which he is more or less at home. If we now attempt to relate these questions of world and identity, we find that whether they reflect or contradict each other, they are inseparable. They constitute the object and subject poles, respectively, of a fundamentally unbreachable structure.

3. Both the particular world that the person lives-for-and-toward, as well as the identity that is expressed as either affirming or negating that world, reveal, in the condition of anxiety, the presence of musts. In other words, when an individual is anxious, it appears that the network of relations and projects that have been and continue to be constitutive of both his world and his identity emerge as demanding to be sustained. This demanding does not have the character of a want or even an ought. Rather, it is experienced as a question of necessity, an absolute requirement of life. There are no conceivable alternatives, or, to put the matter differently, the alternatives all involve not-being-myself. Further, although the questionable milestones-to-be-achieved may involve doing certain deeds or acquiring certain possessions, their significance lies in their implications for the person's being. That is to say, passing an exam and graduating from college or eliciting expressions of sexual affirmation and thereby feeling one's self to be an attractive woman are deeds and acquisitions in the service of continuing to live one's world and identity.

4. Finally, in both examples we encountered the problem of ability. For the student about to take his final exam, it was the question of his being able to convince the professor that he knew enough material to warrant a passing grade. For the woman in psychotherapy, it was the possibility of her being able to elicit expressions of sexual affirmation in her therapist's face. For both, the particular tasks-to-be-achieved were approached with a disarming sense of uncertainty. It was not the case that they were certain of either success or failure. If it had been the former, there could have been no anxiety. If it had been the latter, we would probably have been told of a state that might best be described as dread. That is to say, they would have been confronted with a task that had to be achieved, a task upon which rested both their worlds and identities, and they would have approached it with a sense of being about to lose both. Thus they would have been faced with a certain loss of all familiarity and an equally certain sense of becoming someone unknown, someone with whom they were not at all at home. What we are suggesting here is that the question of ability—specifically, the personal sense of uncertain ability or competence—is essential to the experience of anxiety. Just exactly what achievement is demanded may or may not be completely thematic. In our first example it was clear, while in our second, it was substantially befogged. Nonetheless, the realization that something must be accomplished or possessed

and the sense that one's competence may be inadequate to the task, is essential to the experience of anxiety.

Can we now synthesize these structural components of the subject's anxious experience? Would it not be accurate to say that the anxious experience is *The experience of being impelled to actualize that for which my ability has already been apprehended as uncertain?* Further that which I am impelled to actualize refers not only to a particular identity but also to a world—that is, to a context of relations and projects in which this identity is realizable. Thus, in the anxiety experience, both my identity and my world are questionable.

Throughout the preceding pages, we have frequently used the phrases "experience of anxiety" and "anxiety experience," as if they were interchangeable. It is time to question this equation. In what sense or under what conditions is the person's anxious experience of himself as an ongoing identity, or his anxious experience of the world as that wherein he is attempting to realize this identity, an experience of anxiety? To put the problem somewhat differently, is experiencing the questionable character of one's identity and one's world the same as experiencing anxiety? We think not, although the two seem to be integrally related.

If one is rigorously empirical, that is, if one adheres strictly to what is given in experience, then it will be found that anxiety, as such, is not an object of experience. Rather, what is given is I-am-anxious, you-are-anxious, or he-is-anxious. In other words, anxiety, as an object of experience, becomes thematic only in the form of someone-being-anxious. When it is myself, that is, when I experience myself-being-anxious, I encounter myself as already in this state. It is not the case that I find myself dispassionately experiencing some situation first and then "have" an affect. There is no purely intellectual experiencing that is then, somehow, followed by anxiety. Instead, it seems that *anxiously* is one way in which I can experience as well as act. It is a mode of behaving if the latter term is understood in its fullest sense. To make these assertions is to claim that people are, at a lived rather than reflected level, already there affectively with that which is experienced. There is no appeal here to an unconscious, at least not in the usual Freudian sense. Rather, one might say that we are describing a condition of unselfconsciousness. Thus the *already there* means that prior to any explicit thematization of one's affective state, one is experiencing some situation in an affective manner. Further, the particular affective manner of the experiencing contributes both to the forming and to the understanding of the situation.

Under certain circumstances, the affective manner in which the situation is experienced becomes salient. It is thematized in itself. In the case of anxiety, I can come to realize that I am anxiously experiencing this situation. When this happens, the unity of the experience can be broken. I can focus upon the anxious component or manner of the experiencing and ask, for example, "How come I feel this way?" With the asking of this question, the

event that emerged as the theme of my experience tends to be grasped as causing the manner in which it was experienced. The event that was experienced
and the manner in which it was experienced are separated. The former is now
seen as object, objective, out there, in itself; it is apprehended as the cause of
my "subjective" inner state. Further, the manner in which I experienced the
event has now turned into a thing, a possession that I have unhappily acquired, anxiety.

The question now arises—What does all this have to do with our structural analysis of the anxious experience? What does the experience of myself-
being-anxious have to do with my experience of being impelled to actualize
that for which my ability has already been apprehended as uncertain? Our
answer to this question seems to have a number of important implications, a
few of which we shall consider presently. We should like to assert that prior
to reflection, that is, at a lived, unselfconscious level, there is only anxious experiencing. That is to say, I experience myself as impelled to actualize certain
states of affairs. These to-be-realized accomplishments refer both to my world
and to my identity as confirmed by that world. Further, I tremble in the face
of these demands, for I have already grasped my ability to meet them as uncertain. If and when my anxious experience of this situation becomes salient
to the point that I now focus upon my anxious manner of experiencing, the
situation itself recedes and my-being-anxious emerges as thematic. If the my-
being-anxious is radically salient, the situation that was originally experienced
anxiously may be lost altogether. Clearly, we are making a distinction between
the lived and reflected levels of anxiety experience. To the former belongs the
structure that we have described earlier in the chapter. To the latter belongs
the experience of myself-being-anxious. This, we now have to elaborate.

In the reflective experience of myself-being-anxious, the objects, events,
and others of the world recede into a vaguely apprehended distance. My body
intrudes upon me as both "there" and "not right." I may notice that my
palms are sweating, my hands shaking. Attention may turn to my throat,
which is suddenly dry. I can follow my tongue as it searches my mouth for
moisture to swallow. Sometimes, I find that my teeth are clenched and that
the muscles of my jaws are aching because of their state of prolonged contrac-
tion. When I try to turn my head, I may notice that my neck is stiff. In standing, a tightness across my abdomen may cause me to bend slightly. At other
times, there are strange falling sensations in the area of my stomach. If an attempt is made to walk, my legs seem either wooden or rubbery; in fact, there
is a question as to whether they will support me at all.

If I am trying to speak to someone, despite the distance that now sep-
arates us, there seems to be an urgency that "causes" my speech to slur.
Words run into each other and occasionally, as I listen to myself speak, or as I
am thrown back upon my words by the other's uncomprehending face, I realize that I am not making the sense I intended. In looking at the other, I may

find him to be impassive, or concerned about me as if I were some strange phenomenon, or angry, but always distant. I can't seem to reach him. In searching about for avenues of more effective contact, I feel frustrated, frightened, and helpless. Nothing, neither my body nor my words seem to offer serviceability.

But, what if I am directed to the other? What is given when I experience the other-being-anxious? Further, why is it necessary to hyphenate this phrase?

I shall begin with the question of hyphenation, as my answer to this question provides an introduction to the experience of the other-being-anxious. Again, I would like to remind the reader of our abiding concern: to describe that which is given in experience exactly as it is given, to be as rigorously empirical as possible.

The technique of hyphenation was used because I wanted to emphasize the unitary character of the other-being-anxious as an object of experience. In other words, I am claiming that the other-being-anxious is a whole, a gestalt. It is not a simple sum of originally disconnected experiences involving a neutral other, a facial expression, an assortment of mannerisms, or the like. I do not initially experience uninvolved, unaffected others to whom I subsequently append involvements and affective conditions. Rather, insofar as someone is experienced, he is grasped immediately and unreflectively as being-in-some-way. This "way" may be clear (transparent) or not. If the former is the case, I feel that I understand how the other is and, if I so chose, I may direct myself to the possible reasons for his state. If the latter is the case and presuming that I am so inclined, I may attempt to deduce or "figure out" the particular meaning of the other's being-in-some-way. Whatever I do about the experience, the other's being-in-some-way is always an immediately given whole. Thus, in the experience of the other-being-anxious, this particular condition may be immediately perceived, or it may require reflection. If the latter, that is, if it was reflectively deduced, then that which was initially perceived was the other-being-distressed-in-some-way. Reflection on the assorted and concrete manifestations of this initially experienced distressful state permitted its specification. So much for the question of hyphenation.

Aside from overall unity or a gestalt quality, are there further aspects of the other-being-anxious that I can now describe? I should like to suggest that equally constitutive of this experience is a profound sense of distance. In other words, while the anxious person experiences himself as cut off from a world, the observer of the other-being-anxious experiences an unsolicited, imposed, and unbridgeable distance between himself and the other. Let us try to specify the particular qualities of this distance.

Obviously, I am not speaking here of the spatial relations that can exist between things. Hence, the distance to which I have referred is in no sense a matter of feet and inches. I could be standing or sitting immediately next to this anxious other, but we would not be any closer than if we were separated by a room. In fact, there would be no sense of "we" in such a situation. In my experience, there would be only he-being-anxious and myself-trying-to-understand.

Nor am I speaking of the distance that exists between individuals who don't like each other. In such a situation, the separation is chosen, at least by one of the members. It involves an active moving away from the other, usually because of something I feel I understand about him. But, in the experience of the other-being-anxious, the separation is not chosen; rather, it is imposed. Further, I do not necessarily dislike the other. In fact, the contrary is equally possible.

Finally, the distance that exists between strangers seems more to the point—but here, too, the analogy breaks down. While strangers, at least initially, confront each other as more or less mysterious, they experience closeness and sharing as possible options. They can decide to establish and explore their common, present situation, the "here" and "now" that they share. Such is not the case in the relation of the observer and the other-being-anxious. How, then, can we positively specify this experienced distance?

In my experience of the other-being-anxious, there is a sense in which he seems to be preoccupied. No matter how strenuously I attempt to share his situation, there is always an impasse. I experience him as being intensely concerned with and distressed about something that is not immediately evident to me. It is not like the situation of a man in the street with a car bearing down upon him. There, as observer, I both apprehend and comprehend the other's distress. A circumspection of the environment is fruitful and after such, I can empathically share the other's situation. But, with the other-being-anxious, even a meticulous examination of our physical milieu is of no avail. The other and I are not present to the same situation, no matter what a third person might experience and believe. The other-being-anxious and I, the observer, do not share a common here and now. In not being present to a common domain of concern, we cannot be fully present to each other. Where does this leave me, as observer?

Given the uselessness of environmental inspection, my attention focuses upon the bodily features and gestures of the other. Here, I hope to find some clue as to his invisible situation, to that with which he is distressfully concerned. But all that is given to me is his bodily-being-anxious: his grimacing and generally uncomfortable facial expressions; the shaking and sweating of his hands; the hesitating, faltering quality of his movements; the urgency of his speech, and so forth. As long as I do not ask him to reveal his situation to me—and, in some cases, even if he does—he is for me a distant, animated body involved in an invisible world.

Conclusions

In the first paragraph of this chapter, as well as in comments and remarks made in the previous chapters, we have pointed to the fact that each theory of anxiety discussed in this book has already presupposed a defining conception of the phenomenon in question. That is to say, every theory has already decided what anxiety is. Given this, the theories have set for themselves the task of explaining anxiety's occurrence and/or accounting for its possibility. Concretely, this means that anxiety has, in advance, been conceptualized as an experience, or a learned drive, or a learned response with drive properties, or a state of physiological arousal, or a particular pattern of cortical or endocrinological functioning, or a certain type of human tension, or an expression of man's flight from either pain or death, or a consequence of a person's efforts to sustain his individuality, or some combination of these. Further, we have also noted that each presupposed definition of this phenomenon has, in fact, followed from the theorist's own prior commitment to a conception of the ultimate "stuff" of human reality. Thus, albeit sometimes rather subtly, metaphysical assumptions have invariably grounded scientific formulations. One of the inevitable consequences of this state of affairs is that there are as many conceptions of anxiety as there are theories of man.

As each theory is, after all, an attempt to collate and systematize the structural components of someone's experience, even if it be only that of the theorist himself, we have, in the present chapter, chosen to explore and analyze the constitutive elements of this experience. In other words, we have recognized that anxiety—or, more properly speaking, anxious experiencing and/ or being-anxious pertains to someone's experience. In the case of the theorist, it may be the actions, either overt or physiological, of the Other. In the case of the subject, it may be the state of affairs of his world, or, his own condition as reflectively grasped. In either case, every theory, whether formally stated or merely implicit in an answer to the question "How come?", is an attempt to make sense of someone's experience. Thus we have devoted the present chapter to the goal of clarifying these experiences, particularly those of the subject.

It seems appropriate at this point to summarize the findings of our reflective analyses. Of greatest importance, perhaps, is our distinction between anxious experiencing and someone-being-anxious as an object of experience. The former, as we have seen, refers to the lived, unselfconscious type of structure that includes both the person and his world. In this realm of behavior, which appears to be analogous to, if not identical with, Goldstein's sphere of immediacy, there is no radical separation of the subject and the world. Rather, in anxious experiencing, both are intimately intertwined. There is an identity that is lived and that requires perpetuation; also, there is a world of relations and projects that demand realization. Further, each, in some manner, reflects the other, and both, in anxious experiencing, are questionable. Thus we have been able to delineate a motivational component (a must), an action component (either a having or a doing in the service of being), an ability component (an apprehended uncertainty with regard to those aspects of the world and one's identity that are to be actualized), a world component (that in the face of which one is anxious), and an identity component (that about which one is anxious) of anxious experiencing.

When the object of experience is someone-being-anxious—this is reflectively given if it is myself, but immediately given if it is the Other—we have found that there tends to be a separation of subject and world. The focus of attention shrinks to the subject who is now grasped as being relatively isolated in his affective state. Moreover, this affective state presents itself as the effect of some causally understood, objective, external event in the world. Further, in this experience of someone-being-anxious, the body as a whole or certain of its parts emerge as objects. One notices that the hands are sweating, the legs are shaking, the throat is dry, etc. Taken together, these bodily conditions are apprehended as expressions of the general state, being-anxious. As we have already suggested in the chapters dealing with the learning-theory and physiological approaches to anxiety, the activities of the overt and covert body, experienced by the scientifically oriented other, are understood as the basic meaning of being-anxious. We will have more to say about this in the next chapter.

Finally, we have noted that anxiety is not the effect of certain experiences; one does not have purely intellectual experience that is subsequently followed by an affect. Rather, anxiety is first manifested as anxious behavior: as a manner in which certain objects, events, states of affairs, etc., are experienced. Only later, in reflection, is it made into a thing, a possession that I or the other happens to have.

I O
Integration: One

We have already asserted that each of the theories presented in this book is, in fact, an expression of someone's experience. That is to say, each theory constitutes a formal conceptualization of experiences that refer to anxiety phenomena. These experiences may have been those of the theorist himself, or, they may have been those of another. Further, some of them were grounded in perception while others were objects of conception. Wherever their source and whatever the mode in which they were given, such experiences comprised the domain from which each theoretician selected his theory-building material. In other words, *each theory represents the particular theorist's own effort at rigorously formulating perceptual and/or conceptual experiences pertaining to anxiety phenomena*. But, as we have begun to realize, the word "anxiety" is an abstraction. As such, it refers to, as well as encompasses, both a mode of experiencing, i.e., anxious experiencing, and objects of experiencing, i.e., myself or another's being anxious. Thus each of the already-discussed theories expresses an effort at conceptualizing these referents. Moreover, in his theorizing, the theorist may have been oriented toward problems of explanation; he may have been more concerned with a causal analysis of anxiety than with an accurate description of its structure. Or, he may have been primarily interested in transcendental questions, e.g., What is it in human life or living that makes anxiety a possibility? Finally, as we have already demonstrated, each theory rests upon and is grounded in particular metaphysical assumptions as to the ultimate nature of human reality. In some cases, this means that human phenomena must be reduced to the language of physics. In others, it demands that all experience be understood as subjective, as prone to error, and that only the scientist's experience be granted validity. In still others, it requires that experiences be translated into the language of physiology. Certain theorists demand that an event be intersubjectively reliable before it is considered real. Others are not comfortable with an experience or a formulation of that experience unless it is already consistent with "established" theories. Whatever the criteria, the metaphysical assumptions are always and inevitably operative.

How are we to assemble these theories in some form of fruitful dialogue? We are faced with the following difficulties: each theory starts with a different definitional conception of anxiety; each poses a somewhat different question to the experiences with which it deals; and each makes its own particular metaphysical commitments. Are we now forced, like so many of our colleagues, to choose one conception and negate the others? Must we be eclectic in the sense of appropriating certain aspects of each theory, but never possessing an integrated, comprehensive whole? Is psychology condemned to continual bickering, with each faction constantly accusing the others of being "unscientific" or "insignificant"? We think not.

If the descriptive-reflective analyses presented in the previous chapter are correct, then we should have a means of organizing and situating each of the various theories with respect to a common domain. In other words, we are claiming that, unlike the others, we have not defined anxiety in advance. Our analyses of anxiety experience were not bound by the usual restrictive metaphysical commitments enumerated above. We accepted all experiences of this phenomenon as equally valid, equally real in their own right. Therefore, we should be in a position to integrate different theories born of differing experiential perspectives. To state the matter alternatively, if each theory is an attempt to formulate certain experiences referring to anxiety phenomena systematically, and if our analyses have, in fact, revealed the structural dimensions of these experiences, then we should be able to relate each theory to these dimensions. This we now propose to do. Further, in the process we may find ourselves capable of understanding to which dimensions a given theory speaks, why it speaks only to these, and how it addresses itself to them.

Before we re-examine and re-evaluate each of the theories, it seems appropriate to summarize carefully the structural dimensions revealed in our previous analyses. As we have stated, the term "anxiety" appears to be an abstraction. Its referents are, on the one hand, a particular mode of experiencing that can be described as anxious and, on the other hand, particular objects of experiencing that can be characterized as myself- or another-being-anxious. Let us concretely delineate the constitutive components of each of these referents.

The mode of experiencing that we described as anxious is lived, unreflected, and unselfconscious. It illuminates a structure whose poles are a world that is lived-for-and-toward, and an existing identity that demands affirmation and perpetuation. The world pole, as was revealed in our analyses, is not a simple aggregation of objects and entities. Rather, it is a temporally constituted network of relationships and involvements to which the individual has committed himself and in which he comprehends and realizes his identity. The latter, that is, the identity pole, is a temporally unfolding project, a having-been-being-becoming, that is oriented toward the establishment of a particular form of human living. As such, this project is constituted by milestones, each of which derives its full meaning from the unfolding process taken as a totality. Thus, while the overall unity of the identity-world structure is expressed in the project, the concrete manifestations of its coherence are given in the implications of its milestones. That is to say, each milestone participates in, as well as reflects, the fundamental project that is in the process of being realized. Another way of stating this would be to say that the project is the particular orientation of the identity-world structure.

This project or orientation is lived rather than reflected. It is, we might say, taken for granted, at least usually. The milestones, however, are thematic. They are focal points of experience and emerge as hurdles that must be surmounted if the project is to be sustained. Hence, faced with each hurdle, the question of ability arises and the individual, himself, apprehends and lives his evaluation of his own possibility.

In anxious experiencing, the orderly, unquestioned unfolding of both the world and identity poles becomes problematic. A milestone has emerged in the form of a possibly insurmountable hurdle. It must be realized and yet the individual apprehends his ability to do so as uncertain. In such a situation, the whole project becomes thematized as that which may be lost, or as that which may be going nowhere. The world-identity structure threatens to dissolve. Descriptively, we have termed the experienced dissolution of the world pole as that in the face of which the individual is anxious. He is anxious in the face of the potential or possible unrealizability of his relationships and involvements. Concurrent with this, there is the threatened loss of the existing and lived-for identity pole. This experience we have described as that about which the individual is anxious. Further, there is an experienced form of motivation that refers to the perpetuation and realization of both poles. In both cases, it is a "must." Whether this "must" pertains to a doing or to a having makes little difference. We claim this because we already realize that both the doing and the having are used in the service of being. That which is done or that which is acquired is understood as expressive of that which I am.

We may now summarize our analysis of anxious experiencing. It is a structure that involves the following interrelated components:

1. An Identity.   This is an unfolding project, constituted by milestones, which is oriented toward the establishment of a particular form of human living. Its threatened loss is that about which the individual is anxious.

2. A World.   This is a lived-for-and-toward network of relations and involvements expressed to differing extents in each of the milestones. When one of the latter emerges as possibly insurmountable, the world threatens to dissolve and this potential dissolution is that in the face of which the individual is anxious.

3. Motivation.   A "must" or "musts" that refer to the perpetuation and realization of the individual's world, as well as his identity.

4. An Action.   A having or doing that constitutes the acheivement of the particular milestone in question. This having or doing is apprehended as expressive of the individual's being.

5. Ability.   The individual's lived evaluation of his uncertain competence with regard to the achievement of the milestone.

As we have already noted, the term "anxiety" refers to two distinct types of experiential phenomena: anxious experiencing and the experience of myself- or the other-being-anxious. The first we have just summarized; the second we are about to schematize. However, as our immediate concern is with the problems of integration, and as the theories to be integrated are all formulations that deal with the other's being-anxious, we shall confine ourselves to this experiential object. What, then, is revealed in the experience of the other-being-anxious?

In an earlier chapter, we characterized the other-being-anxious as a unitary object of experience. It is, we claimed, given as a gestalt, a whole, not the simple addition of independent elements. Further, two interrelated components were thematized as essential to this whole. On the one hand, there was the character of distance. That is to say, the other-being-anxious is experienced as remote, as preoccupied. He and I, though physically juxtaposed in the eyes of an observer, are concernfully "miles apart." We do not share the same locale; we dwell in different situations. As a result, the second essential component, the manifest bodily distress of the other, is environmentally inexplicable to me. No matter how meticulously I measure the objects and entities that apparently surround us, I do not find the reasons for his distress. If I refuse to elicit *his* experience of *his* situation, if I insist upon comprehending his bodily condition in terms of my experience, I am left with an enigma that I can solve only by appealing to some invisible internal state. Thus, in the experience of the other-being-anxious, I am confronted with a distant, apparently worldless, distressed body.

Freud

Having summarized the structural characteristics of anxiety experience, we are ready to "dialogue" with the different theories. In our presentation of the orthodox Freudian approach (see Chapter 1), we saw that the founder of psychoanalysis delineated not one but three distinct forms of anxiety: reality anxiety, moral anxiety, and neurotic anxiety. When we asked about that which entitled each of these to be characterized as anxiety, we found that all three involved an essential reference to the ego as potentially or actually helpless in the face of being overwhelmed. When, on the other hand, we inquired as to the bases for distinguishing between these three forms of anxiety, we found that each emerged from its own unique relational context. That is to say, each form of anxiety was seen to be grounded in the ego's transactions with a particular "world." Thus, in the case of reality anxiety, this context is the ego's concern with the external world; in the case of moral anxiety, it is the ego's dealings with the world of parental values and principles; and, in the case of neurotic anxiety, it is the ego's struggle with the world of instinctual, unchosen, and frequently alien needs and cravings.

Specific to each of these contextual relations there are particular goals that the ego is attempting to realize. In its struggle with the instincts, for example, the ego is seeking to facilitate some gratification while, at the same time, striving to maintain its own structure and identity. When this ceases to be possible, free-floating or so-called neurotic anxiety occurs. Hence, the particular form of the ego's anxiety experience can be explained in terms of the relational context in which it occurs and the goals that are at stake therein. Let us discuss these anxiety experiences one at a time. In so doing, we shall attempt to demonstrate that each can be understood as a mode of anxious experiencing. In other words, each form of anxiety delineated by Freud can, in fact, be grasped in terms of the structural characteristics of anxiety experience.

Reality anxiety is grounded in the ego's relations with the so-called external world. These relations revolve around the problem of safe, yet instinctually gratifying, object procurement. In other words, it is the ego's task to facilitate instinctual gratification without, at the same time exposing the organism to peril. When the ego judges that the pursuit of this gratification may also lead to organismic injury, it experiences fear. Thus, according to Freud, fear is synonymous with the ego's anxiety in the face of a threatening external world. If we now state this in terms of our structural analyses, we can claim the following: That in the face of which the ego is fearfully anxious is a condition of the external world that threatens to injure the organism if it seeks certain types of instinctual gratification at this time and in this way. Further, that about which the ego is fearfully anxious is the continued integrity and functioning of the organism as a whole. If we now ask about the experienced motive-action sequence involved in this form of anxious experiencing, we find "I *must have* this object, but I *must not* risk injury." When the ego is uncertain of its ability to implement these demands, it is fearfully anxious.

Moral anxiety emerges in the context of the ego's relations with the superego. This is a different world, involving different transactions. Here, the ego's acts—its efforts at facilitating instinctual gratification—and even its inclinations are judged by the yardstick of idealized parental values and principles. With respect to the world of the superego, the ego seeks to actualize and sustain its own sense of goodness. Nonetheless, it is also concerned with placating the instinctual demands. Hence, when its facilitating behavior does not conform to the requirements of the superego, it experiences anxiety in the form of shame or guilt. To use the language of our structural analyses, that in the face of which the ego is guiltily anxious is the condemning world of the individual's parents. That about which the ego is guiltily anxious is its now questionable sense of being interpersonally acceptable and loveworthy. The experienced motive-action sequence involved in this form of anxious experiencing is, "If I am to be good, I *must not* do this." However, when it is confronted with the burgeoning and insistent character of certain instinctual demands, the ego is uncertain of its ability to meet superego requirements. Thus it is guiltily anxious.

Finally, neurotic anxiety is founded upon the ego's dual relation to the world of the instincts. That is to say, while on the one hand the ego strives to facilitate either direct or indirect instinctual satisfaction, it also and at the same time seeks to sustain its own already-existing identity, structure, and orientation. When these are endangered, when a radically alien instinctual demand threatens to overwhelm the existing ego structure and thereby obtain expression, then the latter experiences free-floating, neurotic anxiety. In the language of our structural analyses, that in the face of which the ego is neurotically anxious is the alien and potentially overwhelming character of certain organismic strivings. That about which the ego is neurotically anxious is the potential dissolution of its existing identity. The complex experienced motive-action sequence involved in this form of anxious experiencing is, "I *must have* or *do* this, but I *must not* experience myself as the one who has or does this." Given the mutually exclusive character of this problem, the ego, until it has effectively modified one of the demands, is uncertain of its ability to implement either, let alone both. In such a state, it experiences neurotic anxiety.

Thus Freud's three forms of anxiety can be understood in terms of the structure of anxious experiencing. Each can be analyzed with respect to its world and identity poles, as well as its motivational, actional, and experienced ability components. But does that mean that fear, guilt, and shame are really modes of anxious experience? Is self-consciously experienced helplessness, whether in the face of potential or actual threat, the ultimate defining characteristic of anxiety? Further, are the differences that exist among fear, guilt, shame, and "pathological" anxiety completely reducible to variations in the source of the experienced threat? We think not and in the next chapter we shall devote ourselves specifically to the relations that exist among these phenomena.

In what sense, then, can we affirm Freud's theory of anxiety? While we seriously question his formulations regarding reality and moral anxiety—that is, fear, guilt, and shame—we believe that his conception of neurotic anxiety points, in spite of its obscuring theoretical language, to a real phenomenon. That is to say, if one cuts through the psychoanalytic jargon as well as the Cartesian and natural scientific assumptions that pervade Freudian theory, one finds that the description of neurotic anxiety given by the founder of psychoanalysis is essentially identical to our own portrayal of the structure of "pathological" anxious experiencing. Whereas Freud spoke in terms of a conflict between id and ego demands, we have described the incompatibility of simultaneous "musts." Whereas the id-versus-ego conflict is depicted as intrapsychic, the incompatibility of simultaneous "musts" describes an individual who is oriented toward the realization of a particular world but is determined to sustain an identity that is not responsible for this world. Ultimately, both descriptions refer to the irreconcilability of certain forms of having and/or doing with certain modes of being. Further, while Freud claimed that the consequences of this state of affairs included excessive ambivalence, mechanical repetitiousness, gaps in consciousness, and a life that is relatively deprived of satisfaction, we found that "pathological" anxious experiencing involves, of necessity, an inability to fully realize either "must," a cessation of normal human becoming, a vacillation between various attempts to actualize each "must," and an inability to self-consciously experience the "must" that is oriented toward the realization of a particular world.

But what of the experience of the other-being-anxious? Do any of Freud's formulations emerge from this type of experiential context? More specifically, does the theory of anxiety as proposed by the founder of psychoanalysis ever attempt to describe, either theoretically or otherwise, the analyst's experience of the other-being-anxious?

As we tried to suggest in Chapter 1, the whole psychoanalytic edifice can be understood as a structure built upon various observer experiences of the other-being-in-some-way. Essentially, psychoanalytic theory tries to do two things with these experiences: (1) it seeks, within the limits of certain theoretical a prioris, to grasp empathically that which the other must be experiencing for him to be experienced as he is, and (2) it strives to explain its own experience of the other-being-in-some-way by postulating events or processes "in" the other.

In the preceding pages we have already discussed Freud's effort at empathically grasping the other's anxious experience. Now we should like to ask: Did the founder of psychoanalysis impute processes "in" the other so as both to describe and to account for his own experience of the other-being-anxious? Our answer to this question is a decisive "Yes."

The so-called mechanisms of defense, e.g., repression, projection, denial, and others, are not merely techniques or maneuvers that the ego utilizes in coping with anxiety-arousing excitation. They are not just possible consequences of an anxiety signal. Rather, it seems to us that *each mechanism of defense is, in fact, a mode of being-anxious.* The names of these defensive maneuvers are convenient theoretical labels for various psychoanalytically oriented experiences of the other-being-anxious. We may illustrate this assertion with a concrete example.

Imagine the following interchange between an analyst and his patient.

The latter has just finished an angrily given description of the punishments that his father inflicted upon him. He is still breathing heavily and clenching his teeth and he shifts his position on the couch. At this point, the analyst interjects, "It seems that you are still very angry at your father for the way he treated you." Immediately, the patient bolts up to a sitting position and exclaims: "That's not true. . . . I am not angry at my father. . . . I was never angry at him. . . . What kind of son do you think I am? If he punished me severely, then it was because I deserved it." Taken aback by the vehemence of the patient's outburst, the analyst wonders to himself, "Why does this man have to *deny* his feelings of anger for his father? What is he afraid he might do if he let himself feel his anger?"

The analyst's use of the term "deny" requires explanation. Its meaning in this context is not the same as that which is intended in everyday usage. Hence, if we draw out and articulate a fuller sense of the analyst's inquiry— Why does this man have to deny his feelings?—we find something like the following: "What is the structure of this patient's ego such that its existing coherence is threatened when angry impulses, directed at the father, demand integration and expression?"

In other words, the analyst realizes that the patient is struggling to maintain a particular identity. Further, it is evident that this identity is threatened when it is called upon to appropriate and acknowledge self-consciously feelings of anger for the father. Thus, as a means of preventing this threat, and as a technique for preserving its already existing coherence, the ego disavows (that is, *denies*) the feelings of anger. It has permitted their expression, but it will neither own them nor take responsibility for them. However, in maintaining its distance from these feelings, the ego exposes itself to the danger of being overwhelmed by them, i.e., to being-anxious. Further, as long as it continues to deny them, it will be exposed to them as alien and threatening. Denying the feelings of anger is one way of being-anxious with respect to them.

Sullivan

From our earlier discussion (see Chapter 2), the reader may recall that Harry Stack Sullivan conceived of human life as the process through which a gifted animal strives and is encouraged to become an interpersonally acceptable human being. In this context, anxiety was understood as a phenomenon of paramount importance. It was portrayed as an experienced tension arising from as well as expressing disjunctions in the individual's significant interpersonal relations. Specifically, it was said to occur insofar as significant others, whether real or fantasied, expressed or were expected to express condemnation of one's manner of being human. That is to say, the other's condemnation— Sullivan termed it the other's "forbidding gesture"—tended to undermine the individual's striving to become an interpersonally acceptable human being. It undercut his lived, taken-for-granted belief in his ability to be somebody in his society.

Even from this brief and summarizing characterization, it should be obvious that Sullivan tried to grasp empathically aspects of that which we have termed anxious experiencing. However, because he was fundamentally committed to the perspective of an observer and to a causal analysis, he conceptualized these aspects as conditions that supposedly gave rise to the individual's experience of anxiety. In other words, these aspects were not understood as constitutive components of the anxious experience, but were, instead, characterized as necessary conditions antecedent to the experience of anxiety.

At this point, we should like to show that the so-called "causal conditions" illuminated in Sullivanian thought are, in fact, particular specifications of the structural components of anxious experiencing. Thus the forbidding gesture of the significant other is not some external event that is productively related to one's experience of anxiety. Rather, it is that in the face of which one is already anxiously experiencing. As such, it literally threatens to deprive the individual of his world—the world of being an interpersonally acceptable human being. Further, the questioning of one's adequacy and worth as a person is not some consequent effect of having been previously anxious. Instead, it is integral to the anxious experience and is that about which the individual is, in fact, anxious.

With regard to the experienced motive-action sequence that we have held to be inherent in the anxious experience, Sullivan's position is quite clear. For him, the developing individual is always concerned with one fundamental and continuing problem: the adequately human achievement of need satisfaction. Thus the experienced motive-action sequence inherent in the anxious experiencing of the Sullivanian person may be stated as follows: "I must have or do this, but in so having or doing, I must not incur your disapproval of my being." Finally, it is in the anticipation or actuality of the forbidding gesture that the individual questions his ability to implement these demands.

Like Freud, Sullivan also addressed himself to the experience of the other-being-anxious. However, while the founder of psychoanalysis formulated that which he experienced in terms of id, ego, superego, and defensive processes, the neo-Freudian Sullivan characterized the objects of his psychiatric experience in terms of the self-system, the rest of the personality, and the security operations. Both theorists attempted to describe as well as to explain their experience of the other-being-anxious with systems involving imputed, hypothetical entities and processes. Let us take a closer look at Sullivan's manner of relating the so-called security operations to his experience of the other-being-anxious.

As we saw in Chapter 2, the self-system comes into existence to protect the individual from unpalatable and disruptive experiences of anxiety. Its

major means of accomplishing this end is through the control of focal awareness. That is to say, the self-system has the power to organize the contents of
experience in such a way as to eliminate or otherwise preclude from thematic
awareness those meanings that radically undermine the individual's sense of
personal and interpersonal worth. The principal tools involved in this enterprise are the security operations. They are the maneuvers that the self-system
uses in its efforts to control the contents of focal awareness. In other words,
the *raison d'être* of each security operation is its ability to defend the person's
feelings of adequacy and worth, i.e., his personal and interpersonal security.
How do they accomplish this? Again, as we noted in Chapter 2, those meanings that threaten to destroy the person's security are either differentially not
noted or unquestioned (selective inattention), immediately shifted to nonfo-
cal awareness (substitution), or altogether prohibited from focal awareness
(dissociation). Whichever technique is used, one thing is clear: the self-system must, in some way, recognize that which is about to emerge thematically
in awareness. Otherwise, it would not know what to defend itself against.
Thus the operations utilized by the self-system are actually means of preventing the anxiety (feelings of unworthiness, inadequacy, and the like) from getting worse. To state the matter even more precisely, the security operations are
the self-system's modes of being-anxious in order to keep itself from becoming
more anxious.

Jacobson

A rather formidable problem arises when we attempt to relate the thought
of Edith Jacobson to our own analyses of anxiety experience. Her conceptions are always couched in terms of the economic and structural perspectives of psychoanalysis, while our formulations are, for the most part, stated in
the language of everyday life. How are we to bring the two together?

We have already argued that each theory is, in fact, a particular formalization of the theorist's own experience and that this formalization has been
guided by certain a priori metaphysical commitments as to the ultimate nature of reality. If we are correct in this, then an understanding of the theorist's
metaphysical commitments should enable us to retranslate Jacobson's theoretical language and hence recapture the original everyday life experiences with
which she began. This we now propose to do. Needless to say, the discussion
that follows is limited by the accuracy of our retranslation. Therefore, we
invite the reader to scrutinize our reasoning and criticize our conclusions
freely.

One conception that seems to be fundamental to all of Jacobson's theorizing is that of the medium or optimal level of organismic excitation. If the
reader will reflect for a moment, he will realize that this conception is actually

a variant of the principle of homeostasis and that some version of this principle is, in fact, basic to all natural scientific psychologies. For the present, we are not concerned with the particular levels that the various theories posit as optimal. What does concern us is the fact that use of this conception, by Jacobson as well as other theorists, demands that human functioning be conceptualized in terms of energy levels and distributions. Thus, in our attempt to understand the meaning of the medium or optimal level of organismic excitation, we must ask ourselves: What possible experience of the other is this theorist trying to describe? Certainly, medium or optimal levels of organismic excitation are not objects of everyday life experience. We do not perceive each other as manifesting different levels of organismic excitation. On the other hand, we do experience each other as being involved in particular relationships and projects. Further, whereas one is understood as being involved in some project only casually, another is grasped as being involved in the same project as if it were his sole *raison d'être*. In other words, there are both qualitative and quantitative aspects to our experience of the other and his involvements. Moreover, with regard to each of these, we experience the other as being more or less at-home.

Once one has "caught on," it seems fairly clear that Jacobson is trying to characterize her experience of the other's ever-changing relation to his involvements. However, her prior metaphysical commitments necessitate exclusive use of certain modes of characterization. Thus she must reduce both the qualitative and the quantitative aspects of the other's involvements to variations in the quality and quantity of internal excitation. When she attempts to describe the type of involvement with which the other is engaged, she must speak of the various energy sources of his state of excitation. In other words, the types of involvement must be described in terms that explain them as functions of internal stimulation. When she wants to portray the extent of the other's involvement, Jacobson is confined to statements depicting the level of the other's excitation. Finally, when she wants to characterize the at-homeness of the other with his involvements, she can do so only by positing and then describing an optimal level of organismic excitation.

If the phrase "a medium or optimal level of organismic excitation" is merely a theoretical way of saying that the other is at home with himself in his situation, then statements concerning significant departures from this optimal level should constitute theoretical descriptions of states of not-at-homeness, i.e., states of discomfort. For example, if the theorist speaks of the individual's sex drive or sexual instincts as raising his level of organismic excitation significantly above its optimal state, then this is the same as saying that the theorist experiences the individual as being uncomfortable, as being aroused about his unsatisfying sexual relations, or as being actively concerned with reestablishing contact with both the world and his inner promptings.

When human beings or animals are characterized as structured energy systems, their behavior can be described in terms of the types and amounts of energies dissipated, as well as the manner in which this dissipation occurs. Thus, when Jacobson wants to refer to a particular mode of human behavior, or when she wants to describe a particular option available to an individual in some situation, she speaks of the particular discharge pathways his ego has at its disposal. In other words, if types and degrees of human concern are characterized as types and degrees of energy excitation, then behaviors expressing these concerns can be described as pathways for the discharge of energy excitation. Further, should the theorist wish to differentiate between preferred and unpreferred modes of expressing concern, she can do so only by awkard references to preferred or unpreferred discharge pathways. One gets the feeling of an homunculus, sitting astride a steam engine, trying to make up his mind as to which exhaust valve he wants to open.

As we tried to suggest in Chapter 3, the pleasure principle refers to the organism's tendency to return to a state of optimal excitation through the use of preferred discharge pathways. If we now apply our rules of retranslation, we find that this is a theoretical way of referring to the fact that human beings seek to sustain a sense of at-homeness by expressing their concerns in a manner that is consistent with who they are trying to be. Simply put, we have preferred modes of being ourselves; of being angry, of being sexual, etc. Nonetheless, on many occasions people do not experience the possibility of being able to express themselves in the manner that they prefer. While they are concerned with some state of affairs and while they are eager to express this in their own particular way, thereby reachieving a sense of at-homeness, they find this option unavailable.

Following Freud, Jacobson argues that in situations of the type just described, the individual is still seeking a state of optimal excitation, that is, a sense of being-at-home. In an effort to accomplish this, nonpreferred discharge pathways may be utilized. That is to say, the individual may be forced to express his concerns in a manner that is not consistent with who he is trying to be; the demand to express concern is more important than the manner in which it is expressed.

What we have just described is the priority of the reality principle over the pleasure principle. But what does that really mean? In Jacobson's theory, it suggests that human beings are characterized as being primarily concerned with adapting to the world, with reachieving at-homeness with respective surroundings. Doing this in a manner that is self-consistent, sustaining the total integrity of the ego—though important—is secondary. Thus the reality principle refers to the fact that I may do things that are "not me" when my being-at-home-in-the-world is in a state of jeopardy.

If we keep in mind the retranslations suggested above, we may attempt to relate Jacobson's thought to our own analyses of anxiety experience. In Chapter 3, we stressed the fact that for this theorist, anxiety is a signal experience involving discharge phenomena. That is to say, anxiety is an experience originating in and used by the ego; it is based upon the anticipation of impending danger and is associated with behaviors related to the reachievement of an optimal level of organismic excitation.

Couched in the language of everyday life, the above-stated definition suggests that in certain situations an individual is able to realize reflectively that his manner of being related to those situations is anxiously tinged. In other words, the individual gradually becomes aware of the fact that his involvement is an anxious one. Further, he is able to anticipate that a continuation of this involvement in this manner is going to be associated with increasing anxiousness. Because being anxious is, by definition, unpalatable, the individual uses his reflectively realized information—I am getting anxious—as a signal to shift or otherwise alter the nature of his involvement.

According to Jacobson, there are three types of situations in which the ego uses its anticipation of impending danger as an anxiety signal: (1) when the ego anticipates a drastic and unmanageable increase in the level of its organismic excitation, usually because of the intrusion of an alien instinctual wish; (2) when the ego anticipates a significant decrease in the level of its organismic excitation, usually as a result of the overdefended character of intrapsychic and external world relations; and (3) when the ego experiences itself as being unable to utilize particular preferred discharge pathways in its efforts to reachieve an optimal level of organismic excitation.

If we now apply our suggested rules of retranslation, we may characterize these three anxiety-related situations in the following manner: (1) when the individual self-consciously experiences himself as impelled by some inner demand to act in a way that is radically inconsistent with who he understands himself to be, i.e., his lived and experienced identity; (2) when the individual self-consciously experiences himself as losing his sense of reality as well as his relations to it, i.e., his world; and (3) when the individual finds himself inexplicably unable to express his concerns in his way—i.e., when, for some unknown reason, he cannot be himself.

The theoretically oriented reader will, perhaps, have already discerned the central theme common to each of these situations: the individual is unable to sustain and/or reachieve his sense of at-homeness with himself in his situation. Thus, when Jacobson claims that anxiety is a signal experience of the ego associated with behaviors relating to the reachievement of an optimal level of organismic excitation, she is referring to the fact that in particular situations, people reflectively realize that they are not at home with themselves, that the manner in which they are involved in that situation is an anxious one, and that if they don't alter this manner of being involved, things will get even more anxious.

When it is expressed in the language of our structural analyses, the experience of signal anxiety, at least as Jacobson conceptualizes it, reveals the following: that in the face of which the ego is anxious is any external (i.e., alien-to-the-ego) event that threatens to undermine the ego's efforts at facilitating the maintenance of an optimal level of organismic excitation; that about which the ego is anxious is its own identity or coherence, particularly as it is expressed through preferred behaviors; the motive-action sequence involved in this form of anxious experiencing is expressed as, "I must be able to adapt, that is, sustain my own identity while, at the same time, facilitating an optimal level of organismic excitation." With regard to this complex demand upon its ability, the ego is uncertain. Thus it is anxious and it must utilize this condition to mobilize its resources.

Physiological Approaches

As we noted in the comments at the conclusion of Chapter 4, proponents of the physiological approach are not really interested in either the content or the structure of the other's anxious experience. While they accept his verbal report, or his Manifest Anxiety Test score, or his apparent bodily state as indices of his anxious condition, they immediately proceed, in the context of prior metaphysical commitments, to explain this condition on grounds that are independent of the other's experience. Thus, in terms of our previous clarification of the term "anxiety"—i.e., that it is an abstraction and that as such it refers to two types of phenomena: anxious experiencing and the experience of myself- or the other-being-anxious—we can say that those who have adopted the physiological approach have not been concerned with the process of anxious experiencing. Instead, physiological theory and research has directed itself to those anatomical, endocrinological, and, in some cases, imputed cognitive factors that are held to be essential to the possibility of the other's being-anxious. That is to say, theoreticians and researchers of the physiological perspective have attempted to account for their own and/or another scientist's perceptual and/or conceptual experience of the other-being-anxious. The principal technique used in this enterprise has been the investigation of the hidden interior of the other, now understood as a complex, container mechanism. Specifically, it has meant that the physiological correlates of the other's reported or otherwise manifested anxiety must be clarified. Further, this type of investigation has frequently been guided by the assumption that reported anxiety experiences are nothing but shadowy reflections of the real anxiety processes occurring in the body. In other cases, however, it has meant an attempt to stipulate the interrelations of physiological processes and experiential processes, anxiety having already been grasped as an experiential process caused by so-called underlying physiological processes.

We are now tempted to assert that the proponents of the physiological perspective have devoted themselves to the experience of the other-being-anxious. However, without the corrective influence of certain significant qualifications, this assertion would be quite misleading.

In the first place, researchers and theoreticians of this orientation have generally been committed to the natural scientific perspective. This means that, for them, human experience, especially that of the naive subject, is to be distrusted. Insofar as it is not reducible to sense data, to the language of physics, or to the other side of the psychophysical equation, it is to be regarded as subjective and illusory. Thus, given this a priori metaphysical commitment, physiological psychologists have disparaged the validity of the other's experience, the experience of everyday life, and have, therefore, been both unable and unwilling to distinguish between fear and anxiety. Hence, our first qualification is with regard to the allegedly constitutive physiological processes, e.g., changes in hormonal functioning. Are they essential to anxiety, to fear, or to both?

Secondly, whether they refer to the other-being-anxious or the other-being-fearful, the physiological syndromes or constellations delineated by the researchers are already transformed descriptions. They do not reawaken or remind one of the everyday life experience that one may have of the other-being-anxious. There is no description of a psychologically distant, distressed individual who is apparently concerned with some state of affairs that is not physically present. There is no reference to the observer or to the relationship of the observer to the one observed. Instead, the other-being-anxious is presented as an objective fact, as a thing in himself, as fundamentally independent of anyone's experience. The signs of his being anxious are also portrayed as unsolicited, brute data. His verbal report is no longer a communication of one individual to another; his Manifest Anxiety Test score is no longer understood in terms of a dynamic relationship in which one person reveals himself to another called the examiner. Both types of data are taken and used in the same manner as is the subject's blood pressure. Thus all data refer to a skin-encapsulated, worldless subject who is conceived of as the one who emits responses to hypothetical, invisible stimuli. In other words, the data that both demonstrate and constitute the other's anxiousness are such that, to all intents and purposes, they minimize the necessity of even referring to an observer, let alone an experienced relationship. This is the essential meaning of natural science objectivity. It is also a radical transformation of the experience of the other-being-anxious.

How, then, are we to relate the physiological conceptions of anxiety to our own analyses of anxious experiencing? If we keep in mind the qualifications we have stated, we may say that the physiological conceptions begin with the everyday experience of the other-being-anxious. This is what these workers want to explain. However, rather than describe this experience as it actually occurs, they seek its causes in the hidden, microscopic processes of the other's body. Further, these processes are mechanistically conceived and causally related. The body's fundamental dialogue with the world is reduced to a passive responsiveness. Its tendency to function as an integrated whole is, in many cases, lost. Even with those who espouse the theory of general arousal, the body is deprived of its initiative, its subjectivity. Physiological reactions to so-called external stimuli still require the interpretation of a more "ethereal" cognitive realm. Meaning and the mental are slipped in through the back door as a necessary afterthought; the body is just a machine.

Learning Theorists

As two reasonably typical examples of the perspective of natural science, the learning-theory and the physiological approaches to the phenomenon of anxiety share several fundamental orientations. For example, because explanatory attitudes are given priority over ones devoted to understanding, both approaches are primarily concerned with accounting for the scientist's experience of the other-being-anxious. As the validity of the subject's experience is, at best, questionable, neither approach is intrinsically interested in the phenomenon of anxious experiencing. Finally, because no serious attempt is made to understand the subject's experience, neither approach clearly distinguishes between fear and anxiety.

Still, there are some basic differences between these two disciplines. While both seek to explain the scientist's experience of the other-being-anxious, the physiologists do this in terms of the causally conceived, anatomical and endocrinological processes in the subject's body. The learning theorists, on the other hand, look to the life historical conditions of the subject as seen from the perspective of the observer. In particular, they are oriented toward the manner in which his innately given fear response was conditioned to certain configurations of previously neutral stimuli. Further, while neither approach clearly distinguishes between fear and anxiety, each collapses the two somewhat differently. Thus, for example, the physiologists baldly state that for experimental purposes, fear and anxiety are synonymous. The learning theorists, however, speak of anxiety as conditioned fear. Dollard and Miller even speak of anxiety as fear, the source of which has been obscured by inhibition.

Aside from the general differences that exist between the physiologists and the learning theorists, there are some rather important divergences among the learning theorists themselves. For example, Eysenck, in his approach to anxiety, lays greatest stress upon hereditary and constitutional factors. Not only do these factors determine one's tendency to be anxious but they also influence the extent to which one will learn to fear—that is, learn to be anxious about certain previously neutral stimuli. Dollard and Miller, on the other hand, give little or no weight to hereditary and constitutional factors. Instead, they place greatest emphasis upon the individual's reinforcement history. Further, they even appeal, albeit somewhat obliquely, to the individual's awareness of certain stimuli as precipitating factors in his anxiety. Thus, in our attempt to relate the learning theoretical conceptions to our own analyses, we have found it fruitful to discuss their relation to the physiologists as well as to each other.

As his approach is closest to that of the physiologists, we should like to focus on Eysenck first. From Chapter 5, the reader may recall that this theorist defines anxiety as conditioned fear. That is to say, anxiety is being-anxious and this, in turn means that a subject manifests fear responses to stimuli that were contiguously associated with pain-producing stimuli. If one asks why some people are more anxious than others, that is, why some people learn to manifest fear responses more frequently than others, Eysenck answers that hereditary factors determine the individual's sensitivity and reactivity to fear-provoking stimuli. Thus these people tend to respond more strongly and are more easily conditioned. It should be evident by now that in this theory we are dealing with the scientist's experience of the other-being-anxious and that Eysenck explains this experience in terms of the impact of the individual's heredity upon both his autonomic nervous system and his response repertoire. The similarity of this approach to that of the physiologists is striking and the comments that we made with regard to them apply equally to Eysenck.

In trying to relate the formulations of Dollard and Miller to our own analyses, we are confronted with a certain ambiguity. On the one hand, it seems fairly clear that these thinkers have built their theory upon the scientist's experience of the other-being-anxious. In accordance with the overall strategy of natural science, they have generally described the other's situation and behavior from the objective perspective of the observer-scientist. They have avoided all references to the other's experience if these could not, at least in principle, be translated into a physicalistic language.

On the other hand, it is equally clear that Dollard and Miller have appealed to the personal, private, and allegedly subjective experience of the other as a means of distinguishing anxiety from fear. Let us recall the gist of their thought. First, we are told that anxiety is conditioned fear. Still, the theorists are quick to point out that not all conditioned fear is anxiety. It is only when the buildup of conditioned inhibition makes it impossible for the individual to experience and explicitly verbally label the particular stimulus configuration that is arousing his conditioned fear that we can call the conditioned fear anxiety. But doesn't this mean that the nonscientist individual's experience is crucial? Doesn't this imply that the scientific definition of anxiety depends upon experiential possibilities that are independent of the scientist? It would seem so, and therein lies the ambiguity. How are we to reconcile Dollard and Miller's appeal to the experience of the other with our initial characterization of them as being essentially concerned with explaining the scientist's experience of the other-being-anxious? Must we now assume that these theorists are really interested in the phenomenon of anxious experiencing too—that is, in the structure of the other's experience?

The answer to this question must be a categorical "No!" Instead, we may find it possible to understand this appeal to the other's experience if we recall the general purpose of the Dollard and Miller book. As we suggested in Chapter 5, these theorists wrote *Personality and Psychotherapy* in an effort to provide a learning-theory translation of Freudian psychoanalysis. It was hoped that this would satisfy the Freudians without alienating the experimentally oriented academicians. Consistent with this endeavor, Dollard and Miller were required to make some distinction between fear and anxiety, as neurosis was conceived to be a function of the latter and not the former. Further, it was necessary to find some means of referring to such phenomena as consciousness, unconsciousness, and repression. At least in principle, these theorists accomplished all of this. They distinguished between fear and anxiety by making the latter a special form of the former. They distinguished between conscious and unconscious processes by requiring conscious processes to be manifested in verbal behavior. Thus, if the individual could label certain stimuli or behaviors, they were conscious; if he could not or did not, they were assumed to be unconscious. The beauty of this particular translation was that, while it acknowledged the fact of the other's experience, it ultimately anchored that fact in the objective experience of the observer-scientist. That is to say, if the latter did not hear the verbal labeling behavior of the other, he had no need to speak of the other's experience.

Are we now able to resolve the apparent ambiguity? It would seem so. Dollard and Miller began with the everyday experience of the other-being-anxious. This was immediately transformed into the observer-scientist's experience of the other-being-anxious. That is to say, the data that both demonstrated and explained the other's manifest anxiousness were located exclusively in the other. The relation to the observer was, in essence, severed. It was no longer necessary to refer to that observer as an individual, as all observers were now interchangeable. In order to be faithful to the psychoanalytic theory of psychopathology, it was necessary to distinguish between fear and anxiety as well as between consciousness and unconsciousness. This the theorists were able to do by tying the other's experience to his verbal behavior, which, in turn, could be grounded in the objective experience of the observer-scientist. Thus Dollard and Miller's appeal to the other's experience is not a manifestation of their interest in anxious experiencing. It is, rather, an objectively anchored technique whereby they can effectively distinguish between the other-being-anxious and the other-being-fearful. Further, it assists them in their effort at explaining the observer-scientist's experience of the other-being-anxious.

The Existentialists

In striking contrast to the physiologists and the learning theorists, the existentialists have been exclusively concerned with the other's experience. Further, they have generally understood this experience as being valid in its own right, as not requiring anchorage in either the observer-scientist or in the physics side of the psychophysical equation. Thus their approach to the phenomenon of anxiety has tended to avoid references to hypothetical internal bodily states, to allegedly objective observer perspectives, and to the explanatory power of some life historical event of the past. Instead, they have tried to describe the other's experience of his situation and himself when he is anxious. Moreover, from these descriptions they have usually asked about the meaning of anxiety for human life, e.g., What does it mean about man that he can be and is anxious? Finally, to the best of our knowledge, the existentialists have never attempted to explain anxiety in the sense of enumerating its causes.

In Chapter 6, we presented Kierkegaard's theory of anxiety as well as his thoughts about its meaning for human life. As we noted at that time, anxiety, for this thinker, is an experiential state constituted by the individual's realization of several co-present facts: that he has, in his life, a limited number of options or possibilities and that he must choose among them; that he has no ultimate moral or ethical justification for the choice that he eventually makes; that he cannot, at the time that he must make the choice, foresee all the consequences of that choice; and that others will hold him accountable for whichever choice he makes, regardless of the previously described limitations. According to Kierkegaard, this is the situation that confronts man again and again; this is the situation to which he responds anxiously.

If we now attempt to relate Kierkegaard's thought to our own analysis of anxious experiencing, we find that the following statements seem to capture his theory. That in the face of which man is anxious is his finite freedom, his being caught in the necessity of choosing from among limited alternatives without prior knowledge of the consequences and with the realization that others will hold him responsible for the choice that he makes. That about which man is anxious is the meaning of his life. That is to say, given the fact that he must make his choice and that he has no ultimate ethical or moral justification for the choice that he makes, man is anxious about the worth and significance of his life. The experienced motive-action sequence constitutive of this anxious experience is: "I must make a choice that guarantees meaningfulness for my life." Still, without knowledge of all the consequences, without an ultimate, objective justification upon which to hang the choice, and without the absolute freedom to contemplate all possible alternatives, man is profoundly uncertain of his ability to make such a choice.

Like Kierkegaard, Heidegger's approach to anxiety is confined to an analysis of anxious experiencing. More precisely, one might say that Heidegger has attempted to analyze the ontological bases of man's anxious experience. However, unlike the father of existentialism, this German ontologist does not attempt to ground anxiety or anxious experience in man's confrontation with his finite freedom. Rather, but still consistent with the Kierkegaardian perspective, Heidegger seems to grasp anxious experiencing as an expression of man's constant concern with the meaning of his life and the meaningfulness of his world.

Obviously, our own analysis of anxious experiencing strongly supports and heavily leans upon the Heideggerian view. We have even appropriated some of his language, e.g., that in the face of which one is anxious and that about which one is anxious. However, in spite of the brilliance of his analysis, we believe that Heidegger has taken for granted and underplayed the importance of the motive, action, and ability components of anxious experiencing. While he has stressed that which is anxiously experienced, i.e., the world and one's unfolding self in that world, he has neglected the factors that constitute the inner horizon of the anxious stance. We have, we believe, ameliorated this shortcoming.

Another criticism that we might make of Heidegger, as well as of Kierkegaard, is to suggest that these theorists have ignored the experience of the other-being-anxious. The reasons for this are not completely clear to us. However, it is evident that both thinkers were primarily concerned with the perspective of the individual actor. They tended not to grapple with the interpersonal aspects of the phenomenon. Thus, while we are grateful to Kierkegaard and Hiedegger for their descriptions of the anxious world as it appears to the anxious individual, we believe that the observer can also tell us something of value. He can describe the physiognomy and behavior of the anxious individual; he can describe this individual's being-for-another.

Schachtel

In the spirit of his mentors, Freud and Sullivan, Ernest Schachtel has sensitively and empathically imputed experience to an organism that he always grasped from the perspective of an observer. In other words, while Schachtel started from the experience of the other, he realized the necessity of affirming as well as comprehending the other's experiential possibilities; he realized the fundamentally mediational role of human experiencing. Still, it is one thing to realize the significance of human experiencing and it is something else to communicate this. If one is to be acceptable to the propitiators of natural science, the experience of the other as well as his state of being must, at least to some extent, be grounded in the language of physics. Thus the people referred to in

Schachtel's writings are spoken of as organisms and the influences that are manifest in their lives are characterized as tensions, discharge patterns, and the like.

As we shall see, it is not difficult to relate Schachtel's thought to our own analysis of anxious experiencing; it is necessary only to omit or retranslate the occasional pseudophysics. Hence, for this theorist, that in the face of which one is anxious is the new, the unfamiliar, and the untested; that in the face of which one is anxious is any situation in which going forward, relating at a more mature level, and/or achieving greater independence means being at least temporarily deprived of a sense of at-homeness, of a feeling of familiarity, of being secure. That about which one is anxious is the realization of personal helplessness, the sense of being inadequate to the situation, the awareness that one has lost one's bearings. The experienced motive-action sequence characteristic of this type of anxious experiencing is: "I must establish a greater sense of independence and a higher level of relatedness, but I must not, at the same time, lose my sense of familiarity, safety, and security." Because of the inherently conflictual character of these musts, the individual is radically uncertain of his ability to implement them.

Although Schachtel does not deal explicitly with the experience of the other-being-anxious, he does refer to the manner in which people cope with their anxious experiences. In this context he essentially accepts Freud's defense mechanisms and Sullivan's security operations. Thus the comments that were made earlier with regard to those theoreticians would be applicable to Schachtel.

Goldstein

As we tried to suggest in Chapter 8, Kurt Goldstein approaches the study of man from a biologically grounded, holistic, organismic perspective. This means that he has rejected the traditional mind-body, subject-world dualisms. Man the organism is grasped as having both physiological and experiential components; both are real and, with the exception of pathological states, both are always integrated. For Goldstein, to speak of the purely experiential or the purely physiological is to speak in unrealistic, fanciful abstractions.

With regard to the usual dichotomy of subject and world, Goldstein claims that each of these terms refers to poles of an unbreachable structural whole. Both subject and world, both organism and milieu, realize their respective potentialities in relation to each other. Neither is preformed or predetermined, at least not in any exhaustive sense. Both participate in a process of mutual becoming, concurrent unfolding. Obviously, an essential corollary of this viewpoint is that one must speak of different milieus for different organisms. It is meaningless to speak of two individuals, let alone two different species, as having identical environments. Further, as we noted in our earlier exposition, one must ask about the adequacy of each organism's milieu. How does the organism come to terms with that milieu, adequate or not? How orderly or disorderly is its behavior? Above all, what is the overarching, context-creating project of the organism? What are the particular potentialities, the specific styles, which it is trying to articulate and realize? These are the basic assumptions and questions of Goldstein's approach.

In his attempt to grasp the phenomenon of anxiety, Goldstein recognizes the internal as well as the external perspective. If we use the language of our own analyses, we may say that this theorist tries to describe both anxious experiencing and the experience of the other-being-anxious. Let us briefly summarize his formulations with regard to each of these phenomena.

According to Goldstein, anxiety, from the internal perspective, involves the experience of the catastrophic situation. One has a sense of going to pieces, of losing one's existence. It is not the case that the person experiences some external object or event that then gets itself understood as the source or the cause of the distress. Rather, in the experience of anxiety from the internal perspective, the whole world has already ceased to make sense. Further, because one's sense of self is inextricably intertwined with the meaningfulness of the world, one finds oneself confronted with the possibility of nonbeing, of one's existence being meaningless. The project of self-realization that one has lived and advanced is decisively called into question. It is experienced as crumbling.

Clearly, Goldstein's characterization of anxiety from the internal perspective is completely consistent with our own portrayal of anxious experiencing. That in the face of which the individual is anxious is the inadequate, senseless world, the one that is no longer relevant to the organism's project of self-realization. That about which one is anxious is the imminent possibility of nonbeing, of living a senseless life. The experienced motive-action sequence characteristic of this form of experience is: "I must have the opportunity to realize that which I am already becoming, but the world does not offer it to me." Faced with his inadequate milieu, the individual is fundamentally uncertain of his possibilities of becoming himself.

With regard to the external point of view (the perspective of the observer who views the anxious individual), Goldstein moves between descriptive and explanatory postures. After describing that which can be observed, he undertakes an explanation of both the internal and the external points of view. Let us follow his argument.

Goldstein claims that when we observe the other-being-anxious, we witness certain characteristic bodily changes. Some of these, such as facial expressions and movements of the appendages, are immediately and directly visible. Others—such as, for example, the various internal physiological processes—are not directly observable. They may be inferred from the individual's manifest bodily condition, or they may be detected with the use of special instruments. Further, there are striking alterations in the other's general behavior. Goldstein describes these changes as being meaningless frenzy, with rigid or distorted expression. Finally, the other-being-anxious lends himself to being characterized as withdrawn or cut off from the shared consensual world.

So far so good; we have no quarrel with the theorist as yet. In fact, we wish to pay further tribute to his excellent descriptions. However, at this point, and from the perspective of an observer, Goldstein now attempts an explanation of both the other's anxious experiencing and his own experience of the other-being-anxious. In so doing, he partially negates or undermines the validity of the other's experience; the other's sense of the whole world's collapsing into meaninglessness becomes, in Goldstein's explanation, a kind of subjective phenomenon. As being more objective and more realistic, he substitutes his own observer perspective and claims that the other's anxiety, in both its inner experience and in the eyes of the observer, is ultimately the result of incorrect evaluation of environmental stimuli. But, one may ask, why has this misevaluation occurred and how does it result in anxiety? Goldstein argues that the organism and the environment have come into conflict. The latter has been inadequate to the organism's project of self-realization and to this threat the organism has responded with disorderly behavior, i.e., misevaluations of environmental stimuli. Eventually, the organism experiences itself as fundamentally endangered; to misevaluate the environment is to place oneself in jeopardy. It is the experience of being fundamentally endangered that, for Goldstein, constitutes the inner experience of anxiety, the experience of the catastrophic situation.

At least initially, there is a certain appeal to this line of reasoning. It is parsimonious, apparently logical, and it is couched in the language of the objective, scientific observer. However, upon reflection, a number of questions emerge. In what sense can Goldstein, as an observer, claim that the anxious individuals observed by him misevaluate environmental stimuli? As we saw in our analysis of the experience of the other-being-anxious, unless the observer interrogates the observed, he cannot share the latter's situation. Have Goldstein's anxious individuals told him that they misevaluated environmental stimuli? If so, he has not revealed this to us. What seems more likely is that Goldstein has imputed these misevaluations to his observed individuals. That is to say, in an effort to make sense of their behavior, in order to explain his experience of them, he has attributed processes to them that they do not experience. In so doing, he fundamentally undermines the validity of their experience and accords to his own a privileged position.

Another question that arises has to do with the meaning of the term "endangered." In what sense does the alleged misevaluation of environmental stimuli endanger the observed individuals? Goldstein has already claimed that the environment has been experienced as inadequate to the individuals' project of self-realization. Supposedly, it is this initial experience that conditions or leads to the misevaluation process. Once the project of self-realization is endangered, what else or in what other sense can the individual be threatened? Is it a question of some specific external object? If so, what is the difference between anxiety and fear? Unfortunately, these questions remain unanswered. Thus, we find ourselves extremely sympathetic to Goldstein's descriptions, but quite dubious as to his explanations.

It is time to take stock. We began the present chapter with several insights we believe to be important. On the one hand, we saw that the term "anxiety," at least as it is currently used by psychologists, actually refers to two types of experiential phenomena: anxious experiencing and the experience of the other-being-anxious. On the other hand, we realized that each of the theories presented in this book is, in fact, a particular formalization of the theorist's own experience, whether this be perceptual or conceptual. Thus, despite the striking differences that exist among the theories, we claimed that we could compare them with respect to their common origins. All that was needed was a retranslation of the various theoretical terms back to their everyday life experiential bases. This would provide a common language for all the theories and would facilitate the processes of comparison and integration.

By and large, we believe that we have succeeded in retranslating and integrating the various theories. In so doing, we have examined some of the consequences of adopting certain a priori metaphysical assumptions. Specifically, we have no doubt communicated our rejection of natural scientific philosophy as a basis for psychology, especially a psychology of human life. For the reader interested in an alternative, we would suggest the recent work of Giorgi (1970).

Finally, we hope that we have demonstrated that each theory, insofar as it began with an untranslated everyday life experience of anxiety, has captured a truth or even a cluster of truths concerning this phenomenon. However, to the extent that its a priori metaphysical commitments limited the undistorted expression of that experience, the truth(s) of the theory has been obscured.

REFERENCE

Giorgi, A. *Psychology as a human science.* New York: Harper & Row, 1970.

11
Integration: Two

We have tried to demonstrate that each of the previously discussed theories systematically attempts to express as well as to account for two everyday life phenomena. That is to say, each formulation constitutes a particular formalization of anxious experiencing and/or the experience of the other-being-anxious. Despite these common origins, however, we note that most of the theories evidenced rather striking divergencies. Further, as was clearly seen, these differences could be grasped as functions of the variable and a priori guiding metaphysical commitments of the respective theoreticians.

In this, the book's last chapter, we want to explore a number of relationships. First, we should like to focus upon certain bodily aspects of anxious experiencing, i.e., my experience of my body when I am anxious. In the course of this exploration, we shall, of necessity, touch upon some issues related to the so-called mind-body problem. However, while it might be illuminating to examine a number of alternative approaches to this dilemma, our major goal is simply to reunify that which was already a unity before any analysis. Later, we will attempt to thematize certain aspects of being-fearful. Then it will be possible to compare this affective state with being-anxious.

Most of the characteristics of anxious experiencing have already been discussed in the past two chapters. However, while we have carefully analyzed the identity and world poles of this structure, and while we have pointed to the experienced motive-action-ability sequences that unite these poles in any given situation, we have conspicuously avoided a thorough treatment of *the bodily phenomena experienced by the subject*. It is as if we have tacitly accepted the approaches of the physiologically oriented thinkers, particularly that of Stanley Schachter. Only in our discussion of the experience of myself-being-anxious did we fleetingly mention some of these subject-experienced bodily events. It is time to rectify this omission and, if possible reintegrate the bodily with the experiential.

In Chapter 9, we suggested that when I experience myself-being-anxious, my body has already intruded itself as "there" and "not right." If we now re-enumerate some of the experienced manifestations of this "not-right" intrusiveness, we find that the following phenomena occur, though not always together: perspiring palms, shaking hands, dry mouth and throat, stiff neck and shoulders, pounding heart, tightness across the chest (making breathing difficult), pain or some form of tension across the abdomen, "butterflies" and/or falling sensations in the area of the stomach, a weakness in the knees that makes walking seem problematical, and a general, overall sense of bodily impotence. How shall we grasp the relations of these phenomena to anxiety and anxious experiencing?

One way in which we can make our answer to this question as explicit as possible is to contrast it with that of another theorist. In other words, if another theorist has grappled with the very same question, i.e., the relations of affective experiencing to the experience of one's own body, then through an analysis and discussion of his answer, we should be able to clarify our own. Thus, we will re-present and carefully analyze Stanley Schachter's rather creative approach to affective experiencing. As we have already suggested, he at least tried to formulate explicitly the relations of the subject's affective experience to his experienced bodily state.

In Chapter 4, we described the fact that for Schachter, specific emotions exist solely at the experiential level; physiological or bodily arousal is emotionally nonspecific. Thus there are no particular patterns of bodily arousal that are correlative to specific affective states. Still, the experienced affect is contingent upon the experienced bodily arousal. In fact, according to this theorist, the particular affect that is experienced is nothing more than the personal interpretation that the individual has given to his experienced bodily state. That is to say, in a given situation a person may discover that his body is aroused, e.g., his hands are shaking, his palms are perspiring, his heart is pounding, the muscles of his chest feel constricted, his knees feel weak, etc. When this happens and when the individual has no immediate explanation for what is happening to him, he will attempt to evaluate, interpret, and label his specific condition as well as its possible causes. But, according to Schachter, the particular manifestations of his arousal, e.g., his pounding heart and his perspiring palms, tell him nothing about his condition's specific quality or its possible causes. If the individual wishes to understand how he is, what is happening to him, and what he is responding to, he will have to go to the external environment, to the particular situation in which he has found himself. Only from his perceptions of and cognitions about this situation will he be able to interpret the meaning as well as the possible causes of his aroused bodily state.

If we now apply these formulations to the phenomena of anxiety, we find that while Schachter might agree to the experienced manifestations of the "not-right" intrusiveness of my body, he would insist that they are not specific to anxiety and that they probably occur in all strong affective states. That is to say, he would claim that my pounding heart and my perspiring palms are affectively nonspecific and that, therefore, they require interpretation. Is this true? Does this, in fact, correspond to what we experience? Is not the Schachter type of perceptual-cognitive interpretation of bodily states necessary only when we have been exposed to some radically unusual and new condition, such as when we have ingested a powerful drug? Is it not a fact that for the most part we already understand and enjoy an intimate familiarity with the meaning of our bodily condition? We do not interpret a previously neutral and inexplicable pounding heart or perspiring palm as meaning "I am anxious because the situation I am in is one that should make me anxious." Rather, in coming upon myself as *already anxious in this bodily way*, I can thematize or make explicit that which is already implicitly understood: my affective condition.

Let us try to clarify these alternatives further. Schachter's formulations are always grounded in and emerge from a Cartesian metaphysical perspective. That is, for him the experiential and the bodily are irrevocably separate and distinct. If meaning occurs at all, it develops at the experiential level. The body, on the other hand, is impersonal, mechanistic, and quantitative; it cannot respond qualitatively nor, for that matter, can it manifest any form of subjectivity. Thus all bodily arousal must be interpreted by the "mind," the experiential-perceptual-cognitive realm of functioning. Further, it is only in the light of these interpretations that meaning—in this case, a particular affect—comes into existence.

In contrast to Schachter's views, we have not accepted the dualistic Cartesian metaphysics as a basis for our analysis. Thus we have been able to interrogate our own as well as others' experience without having decided in advance that all meaning must develop and reside in some distinct mental domain and that anything bodily must be exclusively quantitative and mechanistic. As a result, we have found that not only do we come upon our own bodies as aroused —this is Schachter's contention—but also that we already understand, though not self-consciously, the qualitative character of this arousal. Specifically, I already grasp my pounding heart, my perspiring palms, and my wobbling knees, etc., as expressions of my anxious condition as I live in that condition. *They do not require cognitive interpretation.* Further, and here we would tend to agree with Schachter, when I make this condition explicit to myself, when I thematize it as an object of my experience rather than sense it as horizon, then I know it in a way that allows me to speak of it as my possession, as anxiety that I have. At this point, my being-anxious is no longer a relatively unreflected state that I live; it is also a condition that I have, one with respect to which I can take a stand, and one that I can even discuss with an other. In fact, at this point, I move back and forth between focusing upon my body and the anxiety that I have, and thematizing the world that I anxiously experience.

In Chapter 9, we noted that under certain circumstances the anxious manner in which a situation is experienced becomes salient. That is to say, anxious experiencing gives way to the experience of myself-being-anxious. That which was given in anxious experiencing recedes and the manner in which it was given emerges as thematic. I should like to suggest that it is through my experience of my body in its already anxious condition that I come to make explicit the anxious character of my experiencing. In other words, it is by making explicit to myself the meaning of my pounding heart, my perspiring palms, and the like that I come to know in a possessing way my anxious mode of experiencing. However, in appropriating this mode of experiencing as mine, in thematizing the fact of my anxiousness, that which has been anxiously experienced tends to get blurred and my originally discovered condition tends to change. Thus my experience of my body being-anxious both belongs to and yet makes possible the transformation of prereflective, lived anxious experiencing into the explicit reflective experience of myself-being-anxious.

At this point the reader may ask: What do we mean when we say that I can make explicit to myself the meaning of my pounding heart, my perspiring palms, etc.? Hasn't Schachter claimed that the bodily events experienced by the individual tell him nothing about the quality of his state? Further, isn't there a wide variety of bodily expressions that different people actualize and thematize as manifestations of their anxiousness? Do we really wish to claim that there is one meaning common to all of them? Our answer to this last question is a clear "Yes!" All of the bodily phenomena that we have enumerated signify one and the same condition: my uncertain impotence and imminent collapse in the face of my crumbling world. Thus we can affirm with Schachter that different people manifest different bodily "signs" of anxiety; some express this condition through palpitations, others perspire, others tremble, etc. However, all of these bodily events have the same common experiential significance to the individuals undergoing them and only if the theoretician grasps the holistic character of human bodily functioning will he be able to realize that which the everyday individual already understands.

Before we go on to explore as well as to contrast some of the relations of being-anxious to being-fearful, let us briefly recapitulate our views on the genesis of anxiety. If we view this unfolding process from its most fully developed manifestations—that is, from the explicit, self-conscious experience of being-anxious in an anxiously unrealizable world—then we can delineate the following. Originally, at a lived, unreflected level that is unselfconscious, I am busy affirming and actualizing both my world and my identity. Although each is constituted by a series of ongoing and unfolding relationships, possibilities, and involvements, both are, for the most part, unquestioned. As long as my ability to realize them is already apprehended as being reasonably adequate, I live in and between these poles and rarely, if ever, grasp them as such. My life is my project of affirmation and actualization. However, it can happen that a milestone, integral to this affirming and actualizing project, emerges as obstacle, as challenging my ability, as uncertain of realization. Insofar as this milestone shows itself to be critical to my life as I project it, and to the degree that this milestone looms as superior and unyielding to my already-apprehended ability, then to that extent my whole project emerges as problematical, as potentially unrealizable. Further, living completely in the context of this now uncertain life, hovering over and moving back and forth between an identity and a world that now appear to be questionable, I begin bodily to resonate to and vibrate with my uncertain project. Faced with the potential unrealizability of my lived-for-and-toward world and my to-be-realized identity, I bodily express my already-apprehended uncertain ability to make these structures be. But now, the manner in which my body is already anxious, already resonating to and vibrating with the threatened, potentially unrealizable project, thematically intrudes itself upon my awareness. The relations, possibilities, and involvements that constitute my lived-for-and-toward world and my to-be-realized identity now recede to the horizon of my experience, and in their place my attention rivets itself upon a body that mirrors my potentially unrealizable life. The explicit awareness of my being-anxious fills my vision. For the moment, there is nothing else but this. Then, assuming the situation is not cataclysmic—in which case I would be "frozen"—I return to the milestone fortified with an explicit knowledge of my anxiousness; I re-experience my uncertain relation to achievement. In fact, until some concrete stand is taken, some specific course of action is adopted, I vacillate back and forth, first thematizing the fact of myself-being-anxious and then making explicit the anxiously experienced, uncertain milestone of my life.

Being-Anxious and Being-Fearful

Aside from the formal analyses that have already been discussed, there were two alternative ways in which we attempted to clarify further our understanding of being-anxious. One of these involved asking the question: How does this affective state differ from others? The other was to begin with the vaguely apprehended realization of a difference, such as between being-anxious and being-fearful, and to pursue this difference as systematically as possible. The formulations that follow emerged as answers to and by-products of these types of questions and reflections. While we make no pretense as to their exhaustiveness, we do present them seriously and hope that someday they will be integrated into a general theory of human affectivity.

Throughout our efforts at integrating the various aspects of being-anxious, we have tried to emphasize the structural character of this affective state. That is to say, we have stressed the fact that being-anxious is something that can only happen to a being who is the project to actualize simultaneously a to-be-realized identity and a lived-for-and-toward world. In other words, being-anxious is a possibility for an unfolding identity-world project that has been guided beforehand by that which is to-be-actualized. As such, it involves having a future as one's own, envisioning and living for that future, accepting the task of making that future an actuality, and experiencing the uncertainty of one's ability to realize that task successfully.

As a result of our questioning and reflection, we can also affirm the structural character of being-fearful. Here, too, we find mutually co-defining identity and world poles of a temporally oriented human project. However, in this affective state, that which is threatened and at stake is not the loss of some envisioned future. It is neither my to-be-realized identity nor my lived-for-and-toward world. Rather, in being-fearful, a particular actuality of the present, a specific possession, a state of being, a personal attribute, or an interpersonal relationship that has already been realized is explicitly revealed as mine, as cherished, and as about to be lost. For the most part, my possession of this particular activity, e.g., my car, my home, my job, my rank, my appearance, my health, my wife, my son, etc., has been unquestioned and taken for granted. The struggles that may have been involved in its achievement are over and done with. Now, it is simply a part of my life. But, something happens and the tenuous, transient, possibly-to-be-terminated character of this possessive relationship emerges as thematic. Thus that which is threatened in being-fearful is a significant aspect of the present as it is lived. The future, insofar as it is apprehended at all, is experienced as nothing more than a deficient present.

Whereas the task and ability aspects of being-anxious involved the uncertain actualization of a lived-for-and-toward world and a to-be-realized identity, the task and ability aspects of being-fearful involve an uncertain defense of and holding onto that which I already am and have. Being-fearful, therefore, is a defensive attempt to preserve the integrity of that which already is, to continue its having-been and being, and to protect this existing state of affairs from a potentially depriving future.

These task differences are clearly reflected in the respective bodily expressions of being-anxious and being-fearful. As we have already suggested, in the case of the former my body reveals its impotence when confronted with a task for which my ability has already been apprehended as uncertain. In being-fearful, on the other hand, there is no impotence, there is no threatened collapse. Instead, my body expresses a defensive posture, a vigilant waiting for the unchosen intruder who comes to diminish that which is already full. The increased acuity of the senses, the heightened tonus of the muscles, and the general readiness of the body are all well-documented characteristics of being-fearful.

Following Heidegger, we shall refer to that which threatens the unaltered continuation of some cherished, already existing actuality as the fearsome. In being that in the face of which we are fearful, it has made itself known as a definite object or event, e.g., a flat tire, a fire in the basement, a serious cold, being laid off, a gray hair, getting fat. Whatever it is, it comes to us in a particular way and thus its manner of threatening that which is cherished, that about which we are fearful, is immediately recognizable and describable. In being-fearful, we are able to point to, speak about, and on some occasions even turn away from that which threatens.

Finally, we should like to mention a rather curious and unexpected relationship that seems to exist between being-anxious and being-fearful. If we have been correct in asserting that a fundamental precondition for being-anxious is that my identity-world project is yet to be actualized, that my being is still a becoming, then it would also follow that when I experience myself as having "arrived," as having realized my lived-for-and-toward world and my to-be-realized identity, being-anxious should no longer be possible. Living would have reached its pinnacle and the future could only be experienced as either a continuation of the present or as a diminution thereof. In other words, when one experiences one's self as having "made it," there is no place to go but "down" and the appropriate affect in the face of this possibility is being-fearful.

However, the relations between being-anxious and being-fearful are not symmetrical. That is to say, it is not the case that when one is busy realizing an identity-world project, being-fearful is not possible and there is only being-anxious. Being-fearful can and does occur while being-anxious is still a viable possibility, while one is still actualizing his project. How can this be? While there are many changes in my life that I welcome as milestones of my unfolding project, there are also others that I would rather not change. Whether these "belongings" be possessions, personal attributes, states of being, or interpersonal relationships, they are not milestones to be surmounted; they are integral aspects of my continuing identity. When any of them is threatened with imminent, unchosen change or loss, then I am fearful.

Index

Ability, uncertainty of, 130 ff., 140, 149
Activity-affects, 101, 102–105
Adaption: ego processes and, 41
and the signal function of anxiety, 47
Adaptive perspective, 6, 10, 40
Adolescence, as development stages, 26, 27
Affective involvement, Dasein: experience colored by, 93
fear and anxiety compared, 94–96
Affects: activity, 101, 102, 103
communication and, 101
embeddedness and, 102–105
Freudian view of, 100–101
goal-directed, 101, 102
holism and, 112 ff.
infancy and, 101, 102
tensions and, 45–46, 48
Anonymity, Dasein: preoccupation with, 93–94
Anxiety neurosis, 14, 62
Anxious experiencing: bodily aspects, 133, 161–165

components of, 139–140
See also under specific theories of anxiety
Apprehension, recognition of, 15
Attention, selective, 29, 30–32
Automaticity, primary anxiety, 9–10
Autonomic nervous system, 74–75, 153

Behaviorism, 61, 72 ff.
Being process, 90 ff.
comprehension of entities, 92
Dasein, 92 ff.
and "disposition," 93
and the existentials, 93–94
fear and anxiety, 94–97
ontology and, 91 ff.
theology and, 91
Binswanger, Ludwig, 90, 92, 99
Biological-anthropological approach, 108 ff.
Biologism, 19
Birth: prototype of anxiety, 6, 8–9
as trauma, Rank, 9
Bodily aspects of anxiety, 132–134, 161–165, 166

Body image and ego formation, 11
Boss, Medard, 90, 92, 99

Catastrophe, anxiety as inner experience of, 113–116, 158
Catatonic schizophrenia and birth, 9
Central nervous system: and emotional arousal, 54–57
and excitation-inhibition balance, 76–78, 153
Childhood: and conflict creation according to Dollard and Miller, 68
as a developmental stage according to Sullivan, 25
and dissociation from the self-system, 33
and embeddedness according to Schachtel, 102
and original anxiety according to Kierkegaard, 86
and sublimation according to Sullivan, 29–30
Choice, freedom of, 84, 85 ff., 155

Christianity, Kierkegaard and the meaning of, 83, 85
Communal existence: principle of, 24, 25
Communication: affects and, 101
of anxiety, 28, 104
Competition: the juvenile and, 26, 27
Compromise: the ego and, 3, 4, 37
the juvenile and, 26
Concrete-abstract attitudes, 109, 111–112
fear and anxiety, 113 ff.
Conditioning, 74–75, 153
and the excitation-inhibition balance, 77
Conflict: in childhood according to Dollard and Miller, 68
of emergence and embeddedness, 99
fear and, 67–69, 70–71
forms of, 68
between id and ego, 99
neurosis and, according to Dollard and Miller, 67 ff.
between the pleasure and reality principles, 99, 148–149
tension discharge and delay, 99
Consciousness: psychology of, according to Freud, 3
unconscious, and meaning of, 5
Constitution, 72
anxiety-proneness and, 74, 75, 153
learning processes and, 75 ff.
personality dynamics and, 78–79
Cue, 67
labeling and perception, 69–70

Darwinism and Freud, 2–3, 6, 19–20, 36–37
Dasein, 92 ff.
comprehension of entities, 92
and "disposition," 93

and the existentials, 93–94
fear and anxiety, 94–97
Daseinsanalysis, 92
Death principle (Thanatos), 99
Defense mechanisms, 21, 38–39, 40
as modes of being-anxious, 143–144
Denial, 143–144
Descartes, Rene: separation of man and world (res cogitans and res extensa), 19, 23–24, 51, 60–61, 93, 163
Development: ego, 3–4, 11–12
as a process of becoming, 89
Sullivanian stages of, 25–26
Developmental approach: and anxious experiencing, 156–157
Freudian psychoanalysis and, 98 ff.
Schachtel, 98–106
and self-actualization, 110–111
Sullivan, 23
Disposition, Dasein, 93
Dissociation, 29, 32–33
Distance, anxiety experience and experiencing of, 132–134
Dollard, J., 64–72, 153–154
Dreams, 3, 21
Drive(s): conditioning and, 74–75
primary and innate, 65
reduction and reinforcement, 64 ff.
secondary or learned, 65 ff., 119
Dynamic perspective of Freud, 5, 10
Dynamisms of the self-system, 29–33
Dysthymia, 79

Early adolescence according to Sullivan, 26, 27

Economic perspective of Freud, 5, 146 ff.
and primary anxiety, 10
and repression, 39
Ego, 2, 17, 21
adaptive character of, 40, 41
affects and tensions, 45–46
anxiety and, 12, 17, 46, 47
autonomy, 40, 41, 43
and defense mechanisms, 38–39, 40
development, 3–4, 11–12
energies, 41
as equioriginal with the id, 38, 41
homeostasis, 44
id, see Id
instincts, 38–39
and moral anxiety, 13–14, 140–143
and neurotic anxiety, 14, 140–141, 142–143
nonself objects and need-satisfaction, 12
peace-keeping function, 3–4, 37
as a perceptual system, 12, 39–40
reality and, 11, 39 ff.
reality anxiety, 13–14, 140–141
status of, 37 ff.
structuralized delay in, 15–16
superego, see Superego
Ego-ideal, 13
Ego psychology, 36–49
anxious experiencing and, 146–150
Freudian psychology and, 36 ff.
See also Ego
Embeddedness, 99
-affects, 102–105
anxiety and, 102–105
in childhood, 102
and the signal function of anxiety, 104
Emergence, 99
activity-affects and, 103
stimulation-seeking, 100
Empathy, 28, 104

Empiricism, 61, 62
Endocrinological factors, 54, 57
Environment: activity-affects and, 102, 103, 105
adequate, and ordered behavior, 109 ff.
anxiety and, 114 ff.
communal existence, 24, 25
conflict with, and disordered stimulus evaluation, 114, 159–160
from the economic perspective, 5
Freudian conception of, 19–20
and functional activity, 24
and human development, 24 ff.
neo-Freudian conception of, 20, 24 ff.
personality dynamics and, 78
self-realization and, 110–111
Epiphenomenalism, 52
Erikson, Erik, 37, 40
Eros, unification principle, 99
Excitation: homeostasis, see Homeostasis
individual differences, postulate of, 78–79
-inhibition balance, 76–78, 133
preferred state, 44 ff., 146 ff.
Existentialism, 82–97
anxious experiencing and, 155–156
Being process, 90 ff.
choice, freedom and anxiety, 84, 85 ff.
Dasein, see Dasein
Experience: affective involvement, 93
of anxiety and anxiety experience, 131 ff.
biological-anthropological approach to, 108 ff.
ontology and the unity of, 92

phenomenological analysis of anxiety, 109
Experimental psychology, 61 ff.
Extraversion, 72
characteristics, typical, 74
conditioning, ease of, and, 77
excitation-inhibition balance, 77–78
excitatory potentials, 78–79
learning process and, 75 ff.
Eysenck, H. J., 72–81

"Fallen-ness," Dasein, 93–94
Fear: as an adaptive response, 33–34
being-fearful and being-anxious, 165–167
compared to anxiety, 33–34, 88, 94–96, 97, 104, 113–114
conditioning, 74–75, 77
conflict and, 67–69, 70–71
confusion with anxiety, 95–96
as a cue or a drive, 67
Dasein and, 94–96, 119
of definite object, 88, 94–96, 97, 104, 113–114
desire and, 87
guilt and, 67
identification with anxiety, 64, 65–66
innate tendencies toward, 13
of one's instincts, 15
as a learned drive, 64 ff., 119
neo-Freudian concept of, 33–34
neurotic, 67 ff.
ordered behavior and, 113 ff.
repression and, 67, 69, 71
shame and, 67
symptom formation and, 67, 70, 71
Federn, Paul, 37

Forbidding gestures, 27 ff., 144–145
Freedom: choice, anxiety and necessity, 83, 84
Free-floating anxiety, 14, 142–143
Freud, Anna, 37
Freudian psychoanalysis, 1–18
anxious experiencing and, 140–144
developmental approach and, 98 ff.
ego psychology and, 36 ff.
Eysenck's rejection of, 72
the genetic perspective, 6, 10, 72
neo-Freudianism and, 20 ff.
stimulus-response learning theory and, 62 ff.

General arousal theory, 55–57
Gestalt psychology, 108
Goldstein, Kurt, 107–118, 157–160
Gratification and anxiety, 46
Growth and anxiety: the existentialist view, 87–88
holistic view, 115–116
Guilt, 142
fear in, 67
superego and, 13–14

Habit and habit strength, 63
Hartmann, Heinz, 37, 40–41, 42, 100
Hegelianism, 83, 85
Heidegger, Martin, 85, 90–97, 156, 167
Heredity, 72
and anxiety-proneness, 74, 75, 153
learning processes and, 75 ff.
personality dynamics and, 78–79
Holism, 107–118
adequate milieu, 109–111

Holism (*Continued*)
 anxious experiencing,
  157–160
 and emotions, 112 ff.
 fear and anxiety, 113 ff.
 man as emerging, 108
 ordered behavior, 109,
  110–112
 preferred behavior, 111
Homeostasis, 20
 as intrauterine exis-
  tence, 103, 105
 optimum level of exci-
  tation and, 16, 146–
  147
 priority over pleasure,
  44
 tension and, 42–43, 63
Homo natura, 3
 existentialist rejection
  of, 83
Horney, Karen, 40
Hume, David, 61
Hysterical neurosis, excitation-inhibition bal-
  ance and, 76, 78–79

Id, 2, 17, 21, 43
 control by ego, 12–13
 ego development and,
  11, 38, 40, 41, 43
 neurotic anxiety and,
  14
 superego and control
  of, 13
Idealism, existentialist rejection of, 85, 93
Identity, and anxious ex-
  periencing, 129–130,
  131, 139, 149, 167
Immediacy, sphere of,
  109, 112
Infancy: affectivity of,
  101, 102
 communication of anx-
  iety during, 28, 104
 as a developmental
  stage, 25
 and ego development,
  11
 embeddedness in, 102
 and the self-system, 28,
  32–33
 and separation anxiety,
  104
Infantile anxiety, 7, 46

Instincts: fear of, 15
 gratification of, 37–39
Instinctual energy: equi-
  originality of ego and
  id, 41
 transformation of un-
  differentiated, 42–43
Interactionism, 52, 53,
  55–56
Interpersonal relations:
 development and,
  25 ff.
 disjunction of, 26 ff.
 forbidding gestures and,
  27 ff., 144–145
 self-realization and,
  112, 117
Intrauterine existence, homeostasis, 103, 105
Introspectionism, 61
Introversion, 72
 characteristics, typical,
  74
 conditioning, ease of,
  and, 77
 excitation-inhibition
  balance, 77–79

Jacobson, Edith, 36–49,
  146–150
James-Lange theory, 53–
  54
Juvenile era: as develop-
  mental stage, 26, 27
 and selective inatten-
  tion, 30–32

Kant, Immanuel, 96
Kardiner, Abraham, 40
Kierkegaard, Sören, 83,
  85–90, 153, 156
Kris, Ernest, 37, 40

Late adolescence, as de-
  velopmental stage, 26
Learning processes, fear
  and, 13, 64
 heredity and, 75 ff.
 introversion-extraversion
  and, 75 ff.
 stimulus-response the-
  ory, 63–64
Learning-theory approach,
  62–81
 anxious experiencing
  and, 152–154
 conditioning, 74–75, 77

Instincts: fear of, 15
fear identified with anx-
  iety, 64
Libido: affects, and re-
  pression of, 46
 birth disturbance of, 9
 ego energy and, 41
 primordiality of, 21
 repressed, and nonreal-
  istic anxiety, 7–8
Limbic system, 54
Lived and reflected anx-
  iety experience,
  131 ff.
Locke, primary and sec-
  ondary qualities, 60–
  61
Lowenstein, Robert, 40

Man and world: Carte-
  sian separation of, 19,
  23–24, 51, 60–61,
  93, 163
 Dasein as common
  ground of, 93
 existential co-definition
  of, 83, 84, 93
 holistic mutual redefi-
  nition and transfor-
  mation of, 109 ff.
 See also Environ-
  ment
Meaning: co-constitution,
  existential, 84
 Dasein as frame of ref-
  erence, 92
 unconscious and, 5
Meaninglessness and anx-
  iety, 17
 and Dasein, 95, 119
 and fear, 67 ff.
 in free-floating anxiety,
  14, 142–143
 in a panic state, 14
 in phobia, 14
Mechanism, 19, 48, 60–
  61, 163
 holistic rejection of,
  108–109
Merleau-Ponty, Maurice,
  90
Metaphysics and method-
  ology, 50 ff., 60 ff.
Mild anxiety, 27
Miller, N. E., 64–72,
  153–154
Moral anxiety, 13–14,
  140–142

Motivation, neo-Freudian, 21
Musts (motivation), presence of, and anxious experiencing, 130, 140, 143

Natural science: Freudian perspectives and, 2–4, 19–20, 36–37
holistic rejection of method of, 108
psychology accepted as, 61–62
Necessity, freedom and, 83, 85
Neo-Freudian perspective, 20 ff.
anxious experiencing and, 144–146
Neurosis: conflict and, 67 ff.
frustration and, 37–38
Neurotic anxiety, 14
anxiety proneness, 74
anxious experiencing, 142–144
Neuroticism as dysthymia, 79
genetic basis of, 74, 75 ff.
personality and, 73 ff.

Ontology, Being process and, 91 ff.
Ordered behavior: adequate milieu and, 110–111
catastrophic reaction and, 110, 111 ff.
concrete-abstract attitudes and, 109, 111–112
fear and, 113
preferred behavior and, 111
sphere of immediacy and, 109, 112
Organization principle of, 24

Paleocortex, 54
Panic state, 14
Parallelism of mental and physical processes, 51–52, 54

Passivity, and primary anxiety, 9
Perceptual system, ego relationship to, 12, 39–40
Personality: dynamics, 21, 78–79
introversion-extraversion, 73–74, 75 ff.
neuroticism, 73 ff.
organism, stimulus and response, 73
Pessimism and free-floating anxiety, 14
Phobic anxiety, 7, 14
Phylogenetic perspective of Freud, 6, 10
Physiological approaches, 50–58
anxious experiencing and, 150–154
central nervous system and, 54–57
endocrinology of, 54, 57
epiphenomenalism and, 52
general arousal theory, 55–57
interactionism and, 52, 53, 55–56
reticular activating system (RAS), 54–55
Pleasure: inability to achieve and anxiety signal, 47
and pleasure principle, 44
preferred behavior and, 44–45, 148
Pleasure principle: priority of reality principle, 148–149
in relation to pleasure, 44
stimulation-seeking and, 100
tension level and, 20, 43–44, 148
Positivism, 19
Postinfantile anxiety, 46
Preadolescence as a developmental stage, 26
Preferred behavior, 44–45, 111, 148,
Primary anxiety, 8–10

shift to subsequent anxiety, 10–11
Psychosexual development, meaning of, 4

Realism, existentialist rejection of, 93
Realistic anxiety, 7
Reality: ego development and, 11, 39 ff.
existential conception, of, 84
holistic conception of, 108–109, 116–117
loss of contact with, and anxiety signal, 47
Reality anxiety, 13–14, 140–141
Reality principle, priority over pleasure principle, 148–149
Reciprocal emotion, theorem of, 25
Reinforcement, 64 ff.
Repression: affects and, 46
as the inhibition of cue perception and labeling, 69–70
fear and, 67, 69, 71
Freudian concept of, 8, 39
Res cogitans and res extensa (separation of mind and body), 19, 23–24, 51, 60–61, 93, 163
Responsibility, choice and anxiety, 86 ff.
Reticular activating system (RAS), 54–55

Sartre, Jean-Paul, 82, 83, 85, 90
Schachtel, Ernest, 98–106, 156–157
Schachter, Stanley, 56–57, 161–163
Schizophrenia, 9, 32
Secondary or subjective qualities, 60–61
Security operations of self-system, 29–33
Selective inattention, 29, 30–32
Self as Dasein, 92 ff.

Self-actualization: adequate milieu and, 110–111
anxiety and, 115–116
Self-awareness, choice and anxiety, 85–88
Selfhood, anxiety and attainment of, 87 ff.
Self-system, 28–33, 145–146
dynamisms of, 29–33
as organizations of experience, 32–33
Separation anxiety, infantile, 104
Separation fears, birth and, 9
Shame, 142
fear and, 67
superego and, 13–14
Signal function of anxiety, 46–47, 149–150
embeddedness and, 104
Social accommodation juvenile, 26
Social phenomenon, anxiety as, 34, 119
Socialization, introversion-extraversion dimension and, 75
Sphere of immediacy, 109, 112
Stimulus: cue value, 67
disordered evaluation and conflict with environment, 114, 159
generalization, 71
organism and response, 73
-response theory of learning, 63–64
Stimulation-seeking, 100
Straus, Erwin, 99
Structural perspective of psychoanalysis, 5–6, 10, 146 ff.
Structuralized delay, 15–16
Sublimation, 29–30
Subsequent anxiety, 8
maturation and, 10–11
Substitution, 29, 32
Sudden anxiety, 27
Sullivan, Harry Stack, 19–35, 40; 144–146
Superego, 21, 40, 43
autonomy and, 43
ego-ideal, 13
mastery of id and, 13
Symptom formation: fear and, 67, 70–71
learned, 70–71
unlearned symptoms, 70

Taylor Manifest Anxiety Scale, 50
Tenderness, theorem of, 25
Tension: affects and, 45–46
discharges and pleasure, 43–44
homeostasis, 43–44, 63, 103, 105
self-system and, 28 ff.
systemic, and affects, 45
Thanatos or death principle, 99
Theology: Being as creator of beings, 91
contemporary spiritual crisis and, 83
Therapist, role of, 25–26
Trauma: birth, 9
conditioning and, 74
excitation, mastery of, and, 9

Unconscious, meaning of, and, 5
neo-Freudian conception of, 21
Unification principle (Eros), 99

Verbalization process, 154
ego and, 17
repression of, 69–71
von Gebsattel, E., 99

World, uncertainty of, and anxious experiencing, 130 ff., 139, 149